Business Creativity

BUSINESS CREATIVITY

Breaking the invisible barriers

Arthur Gogatz

and

Reuben Mondejar

School of Management ICN NANCY palgrave macmillan

First published 2005 by
PALGRAVE MACMILLAN
Houndmills, Basingstoke, Hampshire RG21 6XS and
175 Fifth Avenue, New York, N.Y. 10010
Companies and representatives throughout the world

PALGRAVE MACMILLAN is the global academic imprint of the Palgrave Macmillan division of St. Martin's Press, LLC and of Palgrave Macmillan Ltd. Macmillan® is a registered trademark in the United States, United Kingdom and other countries. Palgrave is a registered trademark in the European Union and other countries.

ISBN 1–4039–4509–8

This book is printed on paper suitable for recycling and made from fully managed and sustained forest sources.

A catalogue record for this book is available from the British Library.

Library of Congress Cataloging-in-Publication Data

Gogatz, Arthur.
    Business creativity : breaking the invisible barriers / Arthur Gogatz and Reuben Mondejar.
        p. cm.
    Includes bibliographical references and index.
    ISBN 1–4039–4509–8
    1. Creative ability in business. I. Mondejar, Reuben. II. Title.

HD53.G64 2004
658.4'094—dc22

                                                                2004056538

10 9 8 7 6 5 4 3 2 1
14 13 12 11 10 09 08 07 06 05

Printed and bound in Great Britain by
Creative Print & Design (Wales), Ebbw Vale

CONTENTS

Contents

Contents

ACKNOWLEDGEMENTS

The authors would like to thank Richard Farson for permission to reproduce copyright material in this publication, from his book, *Management of the Absurd*.

Every effort has been made to trace all the copyright holders but if any have been inadvertently overlooked the publishers will be pleased to make the necessary arrangements at the first opportunity.

INTRODUCTION

This book takes a bold new look at creativity enhancement. It targets twelve invisible barriers that prevent you from accessing the natural creativity you had as a child and shows you how to surmount them. This is something which anyone can do. The process will focus on getting you to drop some of your defense mechanisms which prevent you from seeing new ideas, solutions and perspectives.

Creativity is something we all possess, yet something which very few of us are able to use on a regular basis. Many people still cling to the myth that creativity can't be taught. We don't believe that. We believe that creativity is something anyone can learn.

Within these pages you'll find a guide that will permit you to rediscover the intensely creative spirit you had when you were a child. The process will push you to take a hard look at yourself, your plans, hopes, dreams and also your fears. It may well even enable you to realize previously suppressed goals and objectives.

You may find some of the things in this book outrageous, even shocking. They're designed to be. They're meant to get you to think about a lot of things you take for granted and confront what you normally avoid. This book contains chapters that deal with taboos, obscenity, violence and censorship. There's a reason for this. To be creative you must look everywhere and at everything, you must be willing to at least consider everything, be able to cope with everything, and that means confronting what most people try to avoid.

Books on creativity enhancement aren't new. Unfortunately the cosmetic changes that most business creativity books offer don't help their readers to become more creative. People today aren't more creative than they were before all those books were written. We believe it's because previous books didn't go far enough. A book on creativity has to come right at you, nothing subtle, nothing held back, and that was our starting point when we began writing. With creativity, it's not enough to slip outside the box occasionally, you have to be able to climb atop the box and then stand there alone, and that requires overcoming certain invisible barriers, obstacles which are represented by our thought patterns, habits and fears.

Why aren't we all more naturally and consistently creative? The answer is fear, inhibitions, negative personal judgment, concern for self-image, the need to impress, anxiety over living up to the expectations of others, and the pressure to conform. These act as invisible nets, transparent but formidable barriers, which keep us from accessing our creativity. They're nets we acquire early in life, and they're nets which most of us take to our graves.

We believe that this book will help you to cast off those invisible nets, ropes, which bind you only because you let them. The book is intended to give you the insight and motivation required to throw off those nets. If you succeed it will let you use your creativity in all aspects of your life, personal as well as professional, because it is impossible to be creative in only one of the two areas.

The process is both simple and both difficult. Shall we begin?

PART I

Understanding What Needs to be Done

"Don't need creativity"

*To raise new questions, new possibilities, to regard old questions
from new angles, requires creative imagination.*
ALBERT EINSTEIN, GERMAN-BORN US PHYSICIST, MATHEMATICIAN

I'm not very creative. It's just not something I'm good at.

I think I can be creative when I have to.

Most people will agree with one of these two statements. Both thoughts
inhibit creativity because both impel you to do nothing. The first person
believes, "I'm not naturally creative. Therefore it's a waste of time to try to
become something I'm not." The second person says, "I'm creative
enough. While I don't need to use my creativity most of the time, I think I
can turn it on when I have to. I don't see any need for improvement."
Invisible barrier number one destroys your creativity because it gives you
reasons to do nothing.

Creativity is a subject that conjures up a potpourri of images, misconceptions and myths. For most people it's a shadowy, elusive, phantomlike
will-o'-the-wisp. Most of us never ever come to understand what it is or
how it functions. We hold ourselves back from becoming highly creative
by believing the myths that creativity is something people are born with
and it can't be learned.

Creativity is also difficult to measure. There are no reliable, universal
tests. Who can say to what degree people are creative? Estimates vary
wildly. The only thing that can be said with any certainty is that most
people are not as creative as they would like to be or could be.

In fact, creativity is something we all possess yet something which few
of us are able to use consistently. Just because you think you aren't naturally creative doesn't mean you can't be. You can, if you really want to.
You don't need that magical thing called "talent." All you need is desire, a
desire to regain the creativity you had when you were a child.

The following terms are often used to describe highly creative people.
You will notice that they also pertain to children.

curious	impatient	idealistic	rebellious
egotistical	easily bored	blunt, rude	adventurous
sensitive	exhibitionistic	voyeuristic	self-motivated

It is said that while 90% of children are highly creative, only 2% of adults are

Most adults lose their creativity before they're old enough to drive a car or vote. The good news is that it's not gone forever. You can get it back if you really want to.

Creativity and children

The world around us is changing rapidly, so rapidly that we sometimes feel we're in some kind of strange wonderland. Children often feel this way and so curiously do highly creative adults.

Alice in Wonderland and its sequel *Through the Looking Glass*, by Lewis Carroll, are more than just fables for children. They are books which deal with creativity. In both, Carroll points out that it's the socialization and learning processes of adolescence which take us away from the creative wonderlands of childhood. As we grow we learn social rules, rules that teach us to build elaborate, invisible defense shields to protect ourselves from slights and blows to our egos and all sorts of threatening situations, both real and imagined. We learn not to blurt out everything we think, learn to temper our curiosities and a lot of our desires, learn that nudity is not as natural as it first appeared and learn to master the adult skills of tact, diplomacy and prudence. Growing up means learning to do things in the culturally accepted way and much of that process dampens our natural creativity. In order to be creative adults, we must understand and manage, rather than be managed by, what we learned during our formative years. That's the difficult part.

Even if you've lost touch with your creativity, it's still in you. It never goes away. It just needs to be rekindled. The basis of creativity is being able to see perspectives, paths, solutions, opportunities and ideas that others either can't or don't want to see, and to do so the average person needs to drop their defense shields which prevent them from reaching out. The process of regaining ones creativity is a process of shedding the "invisible nets" which were acquired in adolescence. These nets or shields prevent you from finding and embracing other perspectives. Creative people are unconstrained by the net of social rules, regulations, procedures and definitions that surround the subject or problem they are working on. They are thus capable of going beyond these limitations whenever they need to be creative, while other people are not.

It has often been argued that adults are stopped from using their creativity because there is no key with which to unlock the door that has been locked by traditional, rigid education. We disagree. There are keys. We all have them. The sad part is that most of us never use them. It's fear which stops us from opening our personal doors. It's frightening to open any door if we don't know where it will lead. It's much easier to keep the door closed. In the beginning of *Alice in Wonderland,* there is a symbolic reference to doors.

> Alice found herself in a long, low hall. There were doors all round but they were locked. Suddenly she came upon a little table. There was nothing on it but a tiny, golden key. Alas! Either the locks were too large, or the key too small, but it would not open any of them.

Like *Alice in Wonderland*, you too have a key. Like her, you too possess the means of unlocking the doors to your creativity. In order to open her doors, Alice had to change, physically as well as mentally. She had to adapt to a strange and constantly changing world. You too will probably have to undergo changes, if you are to begin consistently to see other and perhaps unusual perspectives.

Traditional educational systems, which rely heavily on order, drill, memorization and repetition, have little room or tolerance for innovativeness. Freedom is the heart and soul of creativity. What smothers it is nothing more than order, drill, memorization and repetition.

> The world just slams the creativity out of us after the age of ten. Our teachers and parents tell us that what comes from our imagination isn't true, it's just imaginary. Adults prefer facts, because facts are limited. Like truth, imagination is unlimited and that's why so many people are afraid of it.
>
> *Madeleine L'Engle, American author*

Think of the mind as if it were a parachute. A parachute only works when it's open and that's also true for the mind.

Young children spend a good part of their time collecting information by asking, what, when, where and why? Sadly, the years between ages five and twelve are the only creative period for most people. This is when they try out new ideas and ways of looking at the world. After that, they are pressured to adopt the established way of looking at things and do things as society says they should be done. Parents expect their young children to be creative, but not their teenagers. Imitation and acceptance are what matter from puberty onwards, and imitation and acceptance continue to dominate our adult lives.

Some children have personalities which lead them to resist these social pressures, others are born into families and environments which help them to resist, while others are fortunate to go to schools which are less rigid, and thereby encourage bold, inventive thinking.

The road back

No matter how old you are, however, you can learn to be more creative than you are now.

> Since the process by which you came to lock up your creativity was a learned rather than natural one, the unlocking process too can be learned

If the unlocking process can be learned, then why isn't creativity widely taught? This is an important question and brings us back to our first barrier. The prevailing view of creativity is that it's some mysterious, magical quality which only a few of us have. The ones who have it don't need to be taught and trying to teach the others is a waste of time. We don't agree with that. The theories of creativity can and should be taught to adults as well as children.

Creativity isn't something we try to teach. In fact, it's rarely ever explained, even in art schools. The vast majority of these schools either assume that their students are naturally creative and hence don't need to be taught, or think that teaching people to draw, paint, sculpt, take photographs or play music also teaches them how to be creative. It doesn't. Most people are therefore likely to be more familiar with the popular misconceptions about creativity than the actual theories.

There are numerous links between creativity and sex, as we'll see later, but there are also parallels between how the two are treated. Until recently, sex education was not something we tried to teach in schools. In fact, the current trend toward having some form of sex education is due primarily to stopping the spread of sexually transmitted diseases like AIDS, rather than from any realization that sex is a subject which needs to be taught.

Art Gogatz studied fine arts at one of New York's most progressive schools, yet the theories of creativity were not part of the curriculum. He recalls:

We just did it. We learned by doing, by practicing. We were taught the mechanics of drawing, painting, film, photography and sculpture, but not the theories of creativity. None of us really understood why we were creative, and that was a handicap. My European friends who studied fine arts had similar experiences. Creative writing classes teach writing, but they don't teach you to understand what creativity is all about. My wife studied psychology, in the States and then in France, but there was nothing in her curriculum either.

Many people still insist that they don't have to be taught, reasoning that, if creativity is something they possess, they must instinctively know how to use it. If that were true, everyone would be fully creative. Becoming creative requires the same dedication as playing a sport or speaking a foreign language. It will not just come to you. You have to work at it. Sure, some people have more natural ability than others, just as in sport, but anyone can learn.

It must be noted that there is a difference between creativity and sport. In sport, if you're motivated, and have some athletic ability, you'll probably be able to play reasonably well. It's difficult, however, to be partially creative. People tend to be highly creative or slightly creative. It's the middle ground that causes problems. There is, in fact, virtually no middle ground. With creativity it's pretty much all or nothing.

For some of you the road back to creativity may turn out to be a winding, twisting, dirt road trek through the mountains, for others a four-lane expressway. It depends on your upbringing, your environment, the people around you, and how badly you want to return.

> Creativity needs development and practice. If you don't use your creativity, you won't be able to turn it on whenever you want

This is an important point and one a lot of people don't fully accept. Watch someone hit a tennis ball, or swing a golf club for a few minutes and you'll be able to tell how he or she plays. Listening to a person speak tells you how well he or she can function in a foreign language. With creativity it is more difficult. There are no simple, accurate measures. This, combined with the fact that we don't need to be creative for most of what we do, is why many people who are slightly creative view themselves as being much more.

Joyce M. is a teacher at an exclusive private school in Florida. She regularly invents projects and exercises for her seventh grade science classes. Because of this, she proudly proclaims, "I am creative". Joyce, however, is not creative when it comes to other things. If you are highly creative, it will appear in everything you do. It has to. People who are creative at work are also creative at home and vice versa.

> **If you are creative, it will appear in everything you do**

That one statement is a very simple but amazingly revealing test of creativity. Highly creative people understand and agree with the statement, while other people do not. Many businesspeople do not, in fact, most businesspeople do not. This is an important point and one which businesspeople need to understand. Someone who is not creative at home cannot be expected to turn on his or her creativity when he or she gets to work. If you are truly creative, it will fill every aspect of your life.

Art Gogatz says:

> Whenever I tell a businessperson that there is no such thing as marginal creativity, that highly creative people live and breathe their creativity all day long, they protest, if I did that I'd be exhausted! No, I answer, you won't be exhausted, you'll be energized.

Everyone wants to be creative. Non-creative people actually get very defensive and touchy if you tell them they're not that creative, especially intelligent, highly educated people. Creativity, however, is not a reflection of one's intelligence or education but of personality, and that's a difficult thing for intelligent, highly educated people to accept.

We all consider ourselves individuals, yet psychologists maintain that true individuals are indeed quite rare. Still, many people fancy themselves individuals just as they fancy themselves creative.

In a recent article in one of America's fashion magazines, an editor described how she set out to improve her life by adopting a series of ten measures advocated by a well-known doctor. One of these measures was to try to increase creativity and flexibility. While she freely confessed the need to work on certain areas, she asserted that creativity was one of her strengths. "I work at a magazine, so I have an opportunity to be creative every ten minutes," she wrote, then went on to describe how inflexible she was. It's very difficult to be creative if you're intransigent. Inflexibility kills creativity, kills it cold. The other point that must be made is that working for a magazine won't make you a creative person anymore than working for an advertising agency will. If you're creative, you will bring creativity to your job. No particular job will make you creative; you'll do that yourself.

> Art is not a handicraft; it is the transmission of feeling the artist has experienced.
> *Leo Tolstoy, Russian novelist*

Creativity also is not a handicraft or a sporadic, once in a month condition, it too is the transmission of what the creative person has experienced.

The fact that someone likes occasionally to create new (for them) dishes in the kitchen or undertake craft projects in the garage does not in itself make that person highly creative.

What is creativity?

Look up the word "creativity" in a dictionary and you may find *artistic or intellectual inventiveness*. That's a good definition, but a lot of people don't fully understand it, so let's go a little further and look up the verb "to invent." The dictionary says it's *to think out or produce a new device or process*. Let's try "innovativeness." The definition is *to introduce new methods, to change the way of doing or perceiving things*.

A large part of the creative process is the ability to rearrange what we see. To think creatively we must be able to look differently at what we normally take for granted. A creative person sees something differently from everyone else at a certain moment in time. It's as simple, and difficult, as that. It's the ability consistently to generate novel responses to all sorts of issues, problems, situations and challenges.

> Discovery consists of seeing what everybody has seen and thinking what nobody has thought.   *Albert Szent-Gyorgyi, Hungarian-born American biochemist*

In order to think what nobody has thought, you must be able to see what others see, and also what they don't see. It is this ability to see what people don't see, or don't want to see, that defines the creative person.

> In order to compose, all you need to do is remember a tune that nobody else has thought of.   *Robert Schumann, German composer*

Creativity is recognizing the uniqueness in the unimpressive. Fundamental to creativity is the ability to look differently at what we normally take for granted.

> **Creativity is the ability to see what other people don't see or don't want to see**

Another dictionary definition of creativity reads: *A human activity that produces original ideas or knowledge, frequently by testing combinations of data to produce unique results.*

Creativity often involves recombining or making connections between things that may appear to be unconnected. Logic pushes us away from those connections. In order to be creative, one often needs to look beyond what it logical and consider as well the unrealistic, the fantastic and even the ridiculously absurd. Children find that easy, but the overwhelming majority of adults don't.

> To become truly immortal, a work of art must escape all human limits: logic and common sense will only interfere. But once these barriers are broken, it will enter the realms of childhood vision and dreams.   *Giorgio DeChirico, Italian artist*

All creative acts break barriers

All creative acts escape human limits, logic and common sense. All creative acts break barriers. All creative acts stem from a kind of vision and our dreams.

Creativity is simple in theory, but not in practice. It is difficult to see perspectives other than our own, difficult to break out of our established patterns, difficult to connect things in our lives that seem to have no reason to be placed together. The creative person, like the artist, needs courage because in order to see things that other people don't see you may have to momentarily step away from the crowd and accepted thinking. It sounds easy, but it's not. People unfortunately tend to have one way of dealing with everyone else. People unfortunately tend to have one way of dealing with the world.

Any particular way of looking at something is only one from among many other possible ways

If you can see only what everybody around you can see, you are not only a product of your culture but you are also a victim of it. Anyone can be taught to look for other perspectives. In order to do so, you must constantly remind yourself that those perspectives exist. You must always ask, is this the only perspective? Is this the only way of looking at this? You must constantly remind yourself until you do it automatically.

It should be noted that it's not enough merely to remind yourself that other perspectives exist. You also can't be afraid to go where those perspectives might take you, and in order truly to see other subjects and points of view, you must be ready to embrace them as the equal of your own.

Artistic and intellectual inventiveness

Our first definition of creativity was *artistic or intellectual inventiveness* and it's a good definition. There are essentially two kinds of creativity, one being artistic and the other intellectual. The child uses both, while the highly creative adult tends to believe that he or she is a specialist in one or the other.

It is the function of both the fine and performing arts to renew and energize the way we perceive things. It is a fact that what we are familiar with we cease to really see. A writer may shake up a familiar scene, perhaps merely by changing a single thing and, as if by magic, we are able to see a new meaning in it. The same can be said for the artist, designer, painter, sculptor, musician, filmmaker, photographer, dancer, actor, inventor or comic. They isolate, combine, rearrange and or reverse what everyone else takes for granted.

> Art does not reproduce what is visible. It makes things visible.
>
> *Paul Klee, Swiss artist*

Intellectual creativity, or the generation of new ideas, is far more difficult to predict than artistic creativity because all adults can and do have creative ideas. Most of these ideas are not planned and come to us from out of the blue. Unfortunately we then tend to treat them as accidents. Rarely are we able to use or integrate them into our lives.

Artistic creativity involves many interacting factors, including craftsmanship, expression, sensitivity and emotional resonance. It is constantly argued that this is quite apart from the ability to generate new ideas. It is further argued that many artists are not especially good at generating new ideas. This is true. Not all artists are good at intellectual creativity. Not all artists are highly creative. They may be able to draw, paint or write, but it doesn't mean they can see the world from multi-perspectives. Mastery of the mechanics of a fine or applied art by itself does not ensure creativity.

All artists need to understand the theories of creativity and develop their capacities for idea generation. All non-artists need to get away from the notion that art is semi-mystical and that it's more a gift than a skill. Artistic and intellectual creativity should not be treated or taught independently, for they go hand in hand. To separate them, which is what is normally done, only diminishes their effectiveness.

Real creativity is a blend of the artistic and the intellectual

---

We tend to think of art as something for the few, but it is something everyone can and should do. Everyone can be an artist, not professionally of course, but at least to the extent that they use their art as a means to practice their creativity.

A lot of people think that the word "artist" refers to only those people who draw or paint, when in fact the word refers to anyone who practices any fine or performing art and that includes drawing, painting, sculpture, design, photography, film, music, dance, theatre and writing. When we use the term "artist" in this book, we will be referring not to someone who can draw or paint, but to any person who practices, and we must stress the word "practices", rather than performs or works in, one of the fine or performing arts.

Fighting against yourself

The vast majority of people involved in the arts have little understanding of what makes them creative. They create by feel, without fully understanding the whys and hows of what they're doing. Because of this, they often fight against themselves and are not as creative as they could be.

> People would be more creative if they understood the theories of creativity

Highly creative people tend to get bored easily. You have to understand that and accept it or you'll end up telling yourself: "I shouldn't get bored so easily," or "I'm superficial," or "I'm bored because I bore myself." If you believe this, which is what a lot of people around you, friends, relatives, maybe even your husband or wife, will be telling you, you'll be fighting against your own creativity.

Creative people say what they think. You have to understand that and accept it or you'll end up feeling guilty that you're hurting someone's feelings, when in fact you're just communicating on a different level than most everyone around you. You'll be fighting your creativity.

Creative people need change, while everyone else wants security. If you fail to understand that need, and the needs of those around you, which may well pull you in the opposite direction, you'll be fighting your creativity. A large part of becoming creative again is learning to work with instead of against yourself.

How to break through invisible barrier one

This barrier is actually one of the easiest to break through. All you need do is accept three principles. The first is that creativity does not depend on talent, intelligence or education. The notion that it's something for the select few is the old way of looking at creativity. You can become highly creative once again if you really want to and if you resolve to start working at it.

The second thing that you must accept is that no matter who you are, or what your background is, you can be vastly more creative than you now are. That means you must drop the notion that you're creative enough. To improve, you must come to agree that there's always room for improvement, even if you come from the fine or performing arts.

The third thing that must be embraced is the idea that creativity is all consuming, and that it will appear in everything you do. You cannot merely dip your toes into the creative waters from time to time, instead you've got to plunge in, the same way you did when you were a kid.

If you can accept all three of these ideas, you are well on your way to breaking through your first major barrier.

Important: Don't think that you have to completely break through each barrier before moving on the next. Most of these barriers have been with you for years, and dispelling them will take time and effort. Working to banish one will also help to get rid of others because most of these barriers are connected. The aim of this book is to help you get rid of as many of these invisible barriers as you can. How many you finally do succeed in breaking through won't be known for a while, so don't worry if you find some of your old habits difficult to shake.

ACTIVITIES

We would now like you to complete three exercises, which we'll go over later in the book. The reason we want you to do them now is so that you'll be able to look back at your comments later and see the evolution of your thinking.

1. Write down three things you would love to do but are too embarrassed to do. Be as honest as you can possibly be. The only stipulation is that they should be legal things. If you want to list more or fewer than three things, that's okay. Think of three only as a guide.
2. Write down three things you would never ever do under any circumstances. Again they should be things which are not against the law, and again you may list any number you wish.
3. Tomorrow, keep track of everything you do, absolutely everything, and write them down. They don't have to be in order, but make sure you list everything. If you can't do it tomorrow, then do it at your first opportunity.

"I should be practical, reasonable, and rational"

The development of inventiveness may not be the specific goal of play, but it is nevertheless its predominant feature and its most valuable bonus.

DESMOND MORRIS, BRITISH ZOOLOGIST, ANTHROPOLOGIST

"Want to play?" This is an everyday question between children, but a strange one between adults. Adults don't play. Oh, they may think they do when they say they play tennis or golf or chess or cards, but they really don't, at least not in the imagination-driven way children do. For the child, life is an adventure, where anything is possible, everything is conceivable. The adult, on the other hand, will usually refuse to waste time on anything that doesn't give results toward a specific goal. Kids do something else that adults don't; they practice their creativity all the time. It's called play.

From *Alice in Wonderland*:

> "Who are you?" said the caterpillar.
> "I hardly know," Alice replied. "At least I know who I was when I got up this morning, but I think I must have been changed several times since then."

How many times have you changed since you got up this morning? Sorry, that's a childish question. Alice, after all, was in wonderland, while we have to live in the real world. Creative people don't live in wonderland, they too live in the real world. The difference is that, like Alice, they are capable of entering their wonderlands whenever they choose to, while non-creative people have denied themselves access.

Invisible barrier number two is the notion that we must strive to be practical, reasonable, rational adults, that we can no longer afford to be silly or nonsensical. If we believe this, there are many things that we will stop ourselves from doing. The child uses his or her imagination every day, while the adult has to turn on the television or open a book to enter an imaginary world.

A person who is highly creative wants to create, in fact, needs to create. The medium of expression doesn't matter and, to a large degree, the results take secondary importance to the process. Highly creative people have surmounted the immobilizing fears that stop everyone else. They don't care what anyone thinks about what they write, design, photograph or play. They don't want to let a day go by without creating something. It's more than what they love to do. It's what they have to do.

> I don't want people who want to dance. I want people who have to dance.
> George Balanchine, Russian choreographer

We all have things we say we want to do:

- I want to lose weight.
- I want to start exercising.
- I do so want to see Paris.
- I've always wanted to play the piano.
- I wish I could find the time to put all my thoughts into a book.

There's a big difference between wanting to do something and actually doing it. Most of us actually accomplish a small fraction of what we want to do. Not having enough time is the excuse we most frequently use. In truth it's not a question of time, or money, but of motivation and desire. We limit ourselves by not even trying. Most of us are afraid to try because we're afraid to fail, afraid of what others will think of us, afraid that we'll look foolish in the process, afraid to assert ourselves, afraid to begin.

Art is something all children but relatively few adults practice. Why do we abandon things like art and music after we grow up? The answer is fear. We are afraid that our drawings, poems or songs aren't good enough, and that we'd be wasting our time by doing them.

> Every child is an artist. The problem is how to remain an artist once he grows up.
> Pablo Picasso, Spanish artist

Somewhere, sometime, someone told you didn't have enough talent, (with the notion that it's a God-given quality), that it didn't pay for you to get involved in art because you'd never be good enough at it. You looked at your tentative drawings or poems and agreed, so you stopped. That was a shame. In fact, it was a tragedy, a tragedy that continues to be played out around in the world countless times each and every day.

Quitting art because someone else thought you wouldn't be very good at it is like quitting a sport because you think you'll never become a top professional. How are you going to be good at anything if you don't do it, if you don't try, if you don't stick with it?

One of the problems with art is that it produces something tangible and immediate. An adult will do a drawing and immediately judge it. A child doesn't, because the result is not as important as the process. Adults save everything they produce. They sign all their drawings. They frame them. They even give them titles. Children don't. A five-year-old will do a drawing and walk away from it. That's because it was the process of drawing that mattered, not the drawing itself. Not every drawing, not every poem, not every photograph can be good, just as not every shot in golf or tennis can be good, yet if you're an adult, try painting or writing for a full year and throw away everything you produce. It will be difficult, if not impossible. Now think back to a sport you play. When you began, did you film all your shots and movements and show the film to everyone? Did you abandon the sport just because someone said you didn't play well enough?

Regrettably a lot of people do. That's an adult notion. Children just want to play the sport. Adults are more concerned about playing well than they are about playing. There are two important differences here between adults and children. First, an adult doesn't want to look bad playing a sport. The child just wants playing time. Second, the adult thinks that if he or she plays badly, he or she is wasting his or her time. That's not the thinking of an eight-year-old. The child doesn't care that much about the result, or about time. It's all about the process. For the child, there's no investment, no waste of time, and no frustration over the results. There's enjoyment, pure and simple. A child comes in after playing football all day to have an adult ask, "who won?" "Don't know," the child answers, "we didn't keep score."

Creativity for young children is usually about the process of doing things. The reason they can throw away their work is because they do not perceive their work in relation to models or standards, the way adults do. Adults have a goal or end product in mind in almost every activity, and any action that doesn't take them to that end seems wasted.

> Don't focus on the results. Focus on and enjoy the process. If you do, the results will come eventually

Our culture is far more interested in goals and results than in the process of doing things. A yet to be produced screenplay, an unpublished novel or poem is looked upon as a miscarriage, or, at the very least, a waste of time.

No matter how old you get, if you can keep the desire to be creative, you're keeping the man-child alive.   *John Cassavetes, American actor*

No matter how old you get, if you can enjoy the process of whatever you do, you're keeping your childlike creative spirit alive.

Process and result

"Autotelic" is a Greek word, which means something that is an end in itself. Activities such as art, music and sport are usually autotelic. There is no reason for doing them except to feel and enjoy the experience they provide. Most activities in our adult life, however, are "exotelic," we do them not because we enjoy them but in order to achieve some later goal. To be successful at many of our exotelic activities, it is necessary to make them autotelic. Some examples are learning a language, losing weight and physical therapy. All three activities can be painful. If you let them be so, you won't do them very well. What you'll end up doing is spending a great deal of time fighting against the very notion that you have to do them at all.

Many adults drop out of courses they enroll in before the course is over. The principal reasons are:

- They feel lost. They don't grasp the course, but don't want to admit it.
- They don't enjoy it.
- They don't see enough progress.

They don't see enough progress because they don't enjoy the process. To attain significant results, the process needs to be embraced.

We've all experienced the sensation of trying to lose weight, quit smoking or get into better physical shape. We start out motivated and set our goals. For a while everything works well. We're dedicated and want to improve. Then, slowly, perhaps so slowly that we don't even notice it, we start to slip. We skip just one workout, or have just that one piece of chocolate cake. Before we know it we're right back where we started. It's not that we lack the motivation or willpower to set goals, it's how to maintain that motivation that's the problem. The solution is that you have to come to love the process which takes you toward your goal and not the goal itself. If you don't love the process, you'll always find reasons to duck doing what you really don't want to do.

The process is what's important. The result is secondary and for a creative person it's often a let-down.

The problem with learning a foreign language, for example, is that people feel awkward in a new language, they don't relate to it, they don't like it and they don't want to learn. Most students are there only because they feel they need to be, not because they want to. In fact, most people equate language learning with taking medicine. They know it will make them better, but they hate having to do it. The head may say, "yes I want to learn this," but the heart is silently screaming, "no way! Why isn't my own language good enough? Why do I have to learn this?"

When you don't like what you're learning, you don't really learn. Instead, you sit in the classroom, you look at the words in front of you instead of really reading them, your mind wanders, you don't concentrate, and you don't learn. In order to really learn something you've got to love the process.

Creative people engage in far more autotelic activities than non-creative people. There are two reasons for this. First, like children, they desperately try to avoid all activities they don't like. Second, they embrace the processes of many of the exotelic activities they undertake, thereby making them autotelic.

Don't assume you can't

Art Gogatz relates the following incident:

> I recently taught a creativity seminar at one of the universities in northern France. When it was over, I fell into conversation with several students. One commented that he must be the intellectual creativity type because he had absolutely no talent for anything artistic.
>
> "How do you know?" I asked him.
>
> "Because I can't draw," the student replied.
>
> "Were you ever taught to draw?"
>
> "Taught? We all drew in school, when we were kids, but no, I don't remember ever really being taught. Some of us were naturally better than others, that's all."

All children draw and paint in school but few are actually ever taught to draw. Instead it is assumed that the ability to draw is a natural talent, which some children have and others don't. Not so. Anyone can be taught to draw. It's the same with sport. Some children are naturally better at certain sports than others, but they all can be taught to play.

Art went on to ask the French student, "What about writing? If you can't draw, you can always write. What about photography, or film? Art isn't only about drawing, you know."

The student fell back on the classic answer.

"I don't have any talent."

"How do you know? Have you ever tried to take photographs that weren't snapshots? Have you ever attempted to make a film or write fiction? Have you ever really tried?"

The answer, of course, was no. The student assumed he didn't have any talent. His teachers never encouraged him, nor did this family. His case is typical.

There's nothing mystical about art. It can be learned. You may be a better writer than you are a draftsman, or a better photographer than a musician, but you can do it. The bottom line, though, is that you've got to want to. You've got to try and you've got to keep trying. If you do, you'll get better and better. You can't listen to the people who'll rush to tell you you're wasting your time. You've got to keep at it, and to keep at it anything you've got to love the process.

In creating, the only hard thing's to begin. A blade of grass is no easier to make than an oak.   *James Russell Lowell, American poet, diplomat*

If you're describing a blade of grass, you can just say, it's a blade of grass. If you think about it, however, a blade of grass has ingredients. Color is one. Do you want your blade of grass to be a dark, lush green, or would you rather a light, pale green? Is it one solid color, or is it multi-hued? A blade of grass has texture. Will your particular blade be moist, supple and fresh or will you choose to describe it as stiff, straw-like and parched? You choose the blade's form, shape, and size. Is it fragrant or resistant? Does it bend with the breeze or drown in a deluge?

What people fear most is taking a new step or offering a new word.
                                        Fyodor Dostoevsky, Russian novelist

People usually find that it's not hard to begin, once they've begun. In creating, the hard thing is to overcome the fear of taking that first step, a step we somehow always perceive to be a giant step.

In the dim background of mind we know what we ought to be doing but somehow we cannot start.   *William James, American psychologist*

In the dim background of mind we always know what we *want* to be doing, but we have difficulty expressing that desire. The reason we can't is that we're embarrassed and afraid that we won't be able to achieve what we want, and also that those desires won't conform to the norms of society, that they'll shock, offend and or disappoint our relatives and friends. This fear is one of the things that prevents the majority of adults from becoming highly creative.

We know what we ought to be doing. What we ought to be doing is what we most want to do. The problem is finding the courage to start. Creating anything is not easy. A blank sheet of paper, a virgin canvas, a lump of clay, it's all not easy. You decide what words to put on the page. You decide what images to put on the canvas. You decide what form the clay should take. Before you begin, it seems so overwhelming. The hard part is to begin, and then the hard part is to keep going, because to keep going you have to justify your meager results to yourself and others.

Wouldn't it be easier if you didn't have to justify the results? As a child, you didn't have to. As a child, you didn't have any problems starting or continuing, because it was the process that mattered, the creative process, not the result.

Father Alfred D'Souza is supposed to have once said:

For a long time it had seemed to me that life was about to begin, real life. But there was always some obstacle in the way, something to be gotten through first, some unfinished business, time still to be served, or a debt to be paid. Then life would begin. At last it dawned on me that these obstacles were my life.

There is no way to happiness. Happiness is not a place, but a process. So stop waiting until you lose ten pounds, until you finish school, until you have children, until you retire, until you get married, until spring, until you can afford it, until next week or next year, or until you have time. People make time for everything they want to do and use the excuse of not having time for the things they don't want to do or are afraid to do. Not having time is just an excuse. If you want to be more creative, you have to start! You can't worry about the results, just enjoy the process.

Don't focus so much on the plans but enjoy the processes which take you there, all the moments in between events. In the final analysis we spend most of our lives getting somewhere, so we might as well make the trip a happy one.

Childlike adults

In Lewis Carroll's *Through the Looking Glass*, Alice meets a lion and a unicorn:

> "What is this?" the Unicorn asked.
>
> "This is a child," the Messenger replied. "We only found it today. It's large as life and twice as natural."

Think back to when you were a child. Were you curious? Of course you were. So are creative adults. Were you easily bored? So are creative adults. Were you blunt, sometimes to the point of being rude? Were you idealistic? Were you adventurous? Are you still that way?

French writer and philosopher Simone de Beauvoir once defined an adult as a child blown up by age. It should be noted that the word "blown-up" has two meanings, enlarge and also destroy. De Beauvoir's quote actually refers more to creative adults than to adult-adults.

> ## Who has it better, the child or the adult?

Most adults say the child has it better. In fact the older one gets, the more likely one is to think so. The reason most cited is, no responsibility. No responsibility means no worries and no stress.

While adults overwhelmingly think that children have it better, the kids think it's the adults who have it made. Remember back to when you were ten? Remember how you couldn't wait to be eleven? Remember how long the year between your fourteenth and fifteenth birthdays seemed? Children think adults have it better for the same reason that adults think kids have it better, responsibility. Kids crave it. Adults hate it.

While adults overwhelmingly think children have it better, creative adults tend to like it the way they are. They generally answer that adults have it better. That should come as no surprise. Creative people are more childlike than regular people. In effect, they're childlike adults.

Most children enter adult life with personalities which are more conformist than creative and become adult-adults. Childlike adults have strong nonconformist streaks. They play more. They let their imaginations run into areas which adult-adults avoid. They also have a different idea of responsibility. Creative people seek responsibility. They want to be the one driving, piloting, building, taking charge, deciding. In fact, most of their creative lives are spent deciding what to paint or photograph or how old this character should be and what should happen to them. The problems that creative people face stem not from having too much liberty and responsibility but, like children, from not having enough of it.

Ask an adult to create a character (as a writer of fiction must do), and you will see that it causes them enormous problems. First you need a name for the character, and then you must describe them mentally and physically. You must create a history for your character, a present and a future. If you are writing a screenplay, you may easily have twenty or more characters. If you're writing a novel, you'll have many, many more.

Children easily create characters, playmates, places and situations. They play roles, something which adults have enormous difficulty doing. To watch a child grow is to be a spectator in a theater. Children pretend, imagine and talk to imaginary characters, much the way screenwriters and novelists do.

> Authors are easy to get on with, if you're fond of children.
>> *Michael Joseph, English publisher*

Is writing a lonely job? You sit in front of a computer for hours on end. You see no one, talk to no one. It's lonely, yeah, really lonely. Well, writers don't think so. Writing isn't lonely when you have your characters for company, they'll tell you. Pathetic, you immediately think. Pathetic is an adult reaction. A child would never say that. A child creates characters for company all the time. Remember that the child uses his or her imagination every day, while the adult tries his best not to. Adults suppress all ideas, thoughts and desires which aren't practical and then wonder why they're not creative.

Although adults introduce and encourage their children to believe in characters such as the Easter bunny, the tooth fairy, Barney, Mickey Mouse and Santa Claus, they go on to quickly channel those very same kids toward the practical and the reasonable, toward reality and away from the impossible. Creative adults are those who have resisted this push toward the reasonable and who are able to perform, not just in their daydreams or for their friends and families, but also for countless numbers of their peers, who are able to maintain their childlike sense of wonder and who have their own unique ideas of what's possible and what's not.

In the book *Alice Through The Looking Glass* there is an excellent example of how a child's imagination differs from that of an adult:

"I can't believe that!" said Alice.

"Can't you?" the Queen said. "Try again. Draw a deep breath and shut your eyes."

Alice laughed. "There's no use trying. One can't believe impossible things."

"You haven't had much practice," said the Queen. "When I was your age, I always did it for half-an-hour a day. Why, sometimes I've believed as many as six impossible things before breakfast."

Inventors and people in the arts have almost always been regarded as fools at the beginning of their careers and also sometimes at the end. A person who believes impossible things gets labeled gullible, if not an outright fool, yet once upon a time the idea of a car seemed impossible, so did electricity, television, nuclear energy, space travel and countless other things.

An adult looking at the drawing of a young child will inevitably ask the child what the drawing is supposed to be. This is an adult question. The child often doesn't know what it's supposed to be, nor for that matter does he or she care. The adult judges the work by comparing it to the real world, overlooking the fact that mere duplication of reality may not have been the child's goal.

If a child colors someone's hair violet, or a tree blue, an adult will say, "trees aren't blue. Trees are green." Adults are pleased when their children begin to color within the lines in their coloring books. Within the lines, however, also means within the boundaries. Teachers certainly don't encourage their students to draw off the paper and across the table and then down onto the floor. Neither do parents. In fact, if children do, adults are horrified.

Art Gogatz remembers:

One of the first things they told us in art school, was to go home and paint a room in your house white, then draw on one wall, covering it, drawing larger than life, then paint it white and do another drawing, then repeat the process again and again, then draw on the ceiling and down over the other walls, then draw on the floor and on the furniture. At this point you'll be inside your creation and you'll have a different and totally unique perspective from the one you had initially. The point of the exercise was to get us to push out our boundaries, to free ourselves.

* * *

When I was their age, I could draw like Raphael, but it took me a lifetime to learn to draw like them.   *Pablo Picasso, at an exhibition of children's drawings*

Why would Picasso, or anyone else for that matter, want to draw like a child, one might ask. Okay. Let's rephrase Picasso's quote to make it a little easier to understand:

- When I was their age, I could draw like Raphael, but it took me a lifetime to learn **to think** again like them.
- When I was their age, I could draw like Raphael, but it took me a lifetime to learn **to be as curious** again as they are.
- When I was their age, I could draw like Raphael, but it took me a lifetime to **be as free** again as they are.

> **The creative process is about eliminating boundaries, previously held perceptions and limitations about how something looks, functions or should be**

That's a very important statement, so important that we suggest you read it again.

From *Alice Through the Looking Glass*:

"The messengers have both gone to town," said the King. "Look along the road and tell me if you see either of them."

"I see nobody on the road," said Alice.

"I only wish I had such eyes," the King answered. "To be able to see Nobody, and at that distance too! Why, it's as much as I can do to see real people!"

Most people are afraid to look beyond what is considered normal. Why aren't we all more naturally and consistently creative? Fear, inhibitions, negative personal judgment, concern for self-image, the need to impress, anxiety over living up to the expectations of others, and the pressure to conform – these are the invisible nets which keep us from being creative. Those are the things which Picasso admits took him the better part of a lifetime to shed. They're the things we learn in adolescence and they're the things which ninety-eight percent of us carry to our graves.

It takes a very long time to become young.   *Pablo Picasso*

The child finds it natural to be with or without clothes, to wear costumes and look different. Children take life naturally, while adolescents are told they no longer can. Adolescents have to grapple with doing things in the culturally accepted way. New fears and doubts are created, along with concern for self-image and the pressure to conform. The child in the adolescent makes them want to rebel against all this new negativity. Each generation has had its rebellion, and we've seen everything from swing to beboppers to hippies to acid rockers. The current fad of piercing noses, navels, tongues and other body parts is in the same mold, one last stand before the uniformity of adulthood swoops in and takes over.

From *Alice Through the Looking Glass*:

"One can't help growing older," Alice said.

"One can't, perhaps," said Humpty-Dumpty, "but two can. With proper assistance you might have left off (growing) at age seven."

The best time to learn the theories of creativity is between years seven and ten, before fears, inhibitions, concern for self-image, the need to impress and the pressure to conform fully establish their tenacious roots. Desmond Morris has this to say in his book, *The Human Zoo*:

Many people have puzzled over the secret of creativity. I contend that it is basically no more than the extension into adult life of vital childlike qualities. The child asks new questions; the adult answers old ones; the childlike adult finds answers to new questions. The child is inventive; the adult is productive; the childlike adult is inventively productive. The child explores his environment; the adult organizes it; the childlike adult organizes his explorations, and, by bringing order to them, strengthens them. He creates.

Most adults don't like to be thought of as childlike adults. What they want to be are logical, rational, adult-adults, and that's exactly what they succeed in becoming. Creative people don't mind being called childlike, or almost anything else for that matter. They realize that there's nothing wrong with being childlike. There isn't, you know.

> ## The greatest thing you can do in life is to keep your mind young

I'm —— years old now and I still feel like a child, an adolescent. I still have lots to do. In fact, I do more and more every year.

Is this you? If it isn't, why isn't it?

While we're asking questions, let's try some more.

- Would you mind being called a childlike adult?
- Would you mind being called a childlike adult in front of other adults?
- Would you mind being called childlike?
- Would you mind being called childlike in front of other adults?

Imagine that you had some sort of terrible accident in which you lost your memory. You awake in a hospital room. There's nothing in the room but a bed. You've no idea who you are or how you got there. Everything is a blank. Someone enters and asks you how old you are. You've no mirror to see your reflection. What would you say? How old would you say you were if you didn't know how old you are?

Most adults have a difficult time answering this question. In fact, most insist that they cannot answer it, while creative adults quickly come up with a number. The question here is, how old do you feel? In fact, how old *do you feel*? Most highly creative people feel far younger than they actually are. It's normal. After all, they're really childlike adults.

How to break through invisible barrier two

The best way to break through barrier number two is by doing things, so we've put together a list of activities. It's not necessary to do them all, and you don't need to do them before moving on to the next barrier. Remember what we said at the end of the last chapter, that since all invisible barriers are linked, working to banish any one will also help you to break through others. You can also go back to any of these activities at any time.

ACTIVITIES

1. Make a collage. A collage is a good way to ease back into the arts. To make a collage you don't need to know how to draw. All you need are some old magazines, a pair of scissors and a glue stick. It's easy to do, easier than it would be to write a poem or take photographs. There's no limit to what you can do with your collage. Also keep in mind that your result will not be as important as the process of doing the collage. What we want to do is reintroduce you to activities that you enjoyed as a child, and get you into the habit of doing them more frequently. This is a good activity to do now because collages will be discussed in the next barrier.

2. Get a kids' coloring book and crayons and color everything wrong, make the grass any color but green, or brown, make the sky a color you've never seen before, keep going, make everything a different color, then go to a different page and let your coloring go beyond the lines. Color on the front page, the back page, anywhere you're not supposed to.

3. Look at your list of the things you did for an entire day (activity at the end of the first chapter). How many of the things on your list were autotelic and how many were exotelic? Except for watching television or listening to music, did you have at least two or three activities during the day that were purely playful? Did you do anything that day that wasn't practical, reasonable and rational? If you didn't, why didn't you?

Note: Not having enough time is not an excuse. We always make time for things we really want to do and use the excuse of being too busy for the things we'd rather not do.

"Decent, sensible people will agree with me"

Things don't change. You change your way of looking, that's all.
CARLOS CASTANEDA, PERUVIAN ANTHROPOLOGIST, WRITER

The preceding illustrations are examples of how we perceive things. In the first illustration you see either a young woman or a very old one. It doesn't matter which you see first. What's interesting is that when you see one you lock onto it and have difficulty seeing the other, even though you know it exists.

The young woman, much in the style of a Toulouse-Lautrec drawing, is in profile, turned away, looking from right to left. She wears a feather in her hair and a choker around her neck. The old woman's face is much larger. She is shown in profile. Her eye is the young woman's ear, her nose the line of the young woman's chin. The younger woman's choker now becomes the old woman's mouth.

The second illustration is at once that of a rabbit and/or a duck. The rabbit looks from left to right, the duck from right to left.

In the third illustration you will either see the plane moving away or coming toward you. If you imagine that you are looking up at the plane, it's moving away from you. If you imagine, however, that you're looking down at it, you find it coming toward you.

In all three illustrations, what changes is not the picture, but your perception of it. Things don't change. You change your way of looking. Creative people are consistently capable of changing their way of looking at something, while non-creative people are not.

Invisible barrier three is the notion that your way of looking at the world is enough to see you through. It's not. The secret to becoming creative lies in your ability to drop your way of seeing the world and tune into another person's point of view and see things from that person's perspective as well as your own. It requires practice, but it can be done.

When you enter a classroom, or for those of you who have finished school, where did you choose to sit? Statistics reveal that the students who perform best in classes sit in the front. Students who do the worst sit in the back. Teachers know that those who sit in front rarely ever fall asleep in class. Sleepers always lurk somewhere in back. Psychologists go on to contribute that students who sit by the windows want illumination or knowledge, while those who sit by the door have a defensive attitude and don't really want to be in class. Therefore the best place to sit is front row window and the worst rear row door-side. Actually the best place to sit is anywhere you've never sat before. People tend to sit in the same seats every class and that gives you the same perspective of the course. It's the same thing at home. Members of a family tend to take the same places at the kitchen or dining room tables. The same thing happens in the car. Changing your seat, wherever you are, changes your perspective and your attitude and that's what you want.

The adequate

One of the problems the preceding illustrations reveal is that of "the adequate." Once you decide the picture is that of a rabbit, your brain shifts into neutral, its work done. The same thing happens when we're confronted by a problem. Once we get an answer, any answer, an adequate answer, we tend to stop, even though the answer may be only one of a number of answers, and there may well be a better answer. We only go on to look for another answer when someone comes along and tells us we have the wrong answer.

Education trains us to look not for the best answer, or even the best right answer, but for the *one* right answer. What we are looking for is the one answer, the one road, the one way.

Have you ever found a better way of doing something (a way of getting to work, or a new feature on your computer) or a better product or service, only to realize that there was nothing to prevent you from finding it months or even years before, nothing to prevent you except the adequate.

It is said that the first step in psychotherapy is to recognize that it's something you do need. Psychotherapists continually wrestle with the same paradox. People go to therapy wanting change then spend most of their time there resisting it. The same is true for many of the things we do. In order to use our creativity to solve a problem, we first must recognize that a problem exists and that entails going beyond the adequate.

Many people could find solutions to their problems if first they realized that those problems existed. It isn't that they can't see the solutions. The problem is that they can't see the problems.

There's a way to do it better. Find it.   *Thomas Edison, American inventor*

There's always a way to do it better. Most people don't find the better way because they don't look for it. They assume that their way or their perspective is the only way or the only perspective. It is, of course, only one of many. The creative person is aware of this and seeks other perspectives, while the non-creative person looks no farther than his or her own point of view.

Give someone a camera and tell them to photograph a standing model. Unless the individual is a professional or has had training, the person will take the camera and hold it first horizontally, then after snapping off a frame or two, vertically. After a few more frames, the person will move in a little closer, take another photo or two and stop.

What people generally will not do is move in very close to the subject or, conversely, move way back. They also won't move vertically, by either bending the knees, kneeling or lying on the ground, or climbing on something. They won't move around behind what they are photographing, but will treat the subject from one angle, without venturing to even consider other angles or perspectives.

Most people approach life from one perspective, the obvious one, the uniform one, the safe one. That's what society teaches us to do. We thus tend to fall into ruts that limit our thinking. We glide through time on some kind of automatic pilot, happy when people and situations are predictable.

Remember what we said earlier. In order to think creatively, we must be able to look afresh at what we normally take for granted. In order to be creative, you must look at things from multi-perspectives. Take the time to see and feel what something looks like from the top, the bottom, the back, the sides, inside out, outside in.

Cubism, the art movement made popular at the turn of the twentieth century by Picasso, Georges Braque and Juan Gris, did exactly that in its portrayal of three dimensions on a two-dimensional surface. A cubist painting of a woman will have the eyes in front view, the nose in profile, and the lips from yet a different angle. You see the top, the back, the bottom, all on a two-dimensional surface. The idea behind cubism and most subsequent art movements was to free the artists, to get them away from the pure duplication of reality on flat, two-dimensional surfaces and look at things from multi-perspectives.

In *Alice Through The Looking Glass*, Humpty-Dumpty raises a classic problem that all creative people face.

"Good-bye! Till we meet again!" Alice called cheerfully.

"I shouldn't know you again if we did meet," Humpty-Dumpty replied. "You're so exactly like other people."

"The face is what one generally goes by," Alice said, thoughtfully.

"That's just the problem," said Humpty-Dumpty. "Your face is the same as everyone's. Now, if you had both eyes on the same side of your nose, or the mouth at the top, that would be some help."

"It wouldn't look nice," objected Alice.

"Wait till you've tried," said Humpty-Dumpty.

Dykstra's law: Everyone is someone else's weirdo

Wouldn't look nice? That's part of the problem. We want things to look nice and we want our ideas and our work to look and seem nice, and yet if everything we do pleases people, we won't be very creative. Picasso, Van Gogh and Dali are just a few of a host of famous artists who have stated that to be creative you can never worry about whether what you do will be judged to be in good taste or not.

> It is good taste, and good taste alone, that possesses the power to sterilize and is already the first handicap to any creative functioning.
>
> *Salvador Dali, Spanish artist*

It is difficult enough to produce a meaningful work of art without handicapping yourself with the notion that the work needs to be tasteful. If you're worried about offending, you'll never get anywhere. Your work must be capable of offending. Your work, any creative work, whether it be art or ideas, must be capable of disturbing people enough to wake them up, enough to make them start to become more aware of things they routinely see but still don't see or don't want to see.

All artists know that art is meant to disturb. It is not meant to please. Entertainment does that. True art may entertain, but its primary purpose is to stimulate, to provke a reaction.

Every creative work is meant to disturb. Creativity threatens the structure and suppositions of our rational orderly society and way of life. That's one of the main problems for businesspeople. Businesses don't want people to threaten the established structure. They want their businesses to run smoothly and in unison. They want and expect tomorrow to be a carbon copy of yesterday and it's not, it's just not.

The 18th horse

There was a man who left 17 horses to his three sons when he died. He left half the horses to his eldest son, a third to his second son and a ninth to his youngest. The sons tried to divide their inheritance but couldn't because 17 cannot be divided by 2, 3 or 9. None of the brothers wanted to compromise. Finally, after a heated argument, they turned to a wise old man.

> "Take my horse and your problem will be solved," the man told them. The sons were humbled by the old man's generosity, but accepted the horse. They now had 18.

The eldest son took half, 9 horses.

The middle son took his third, which amounted to 6 horses.

The youngest son took his ninth, 2 horses.

What do you get if you add 9, 6 and 2?

You get 17, of course. The brothers had one horse left over, which they returned to the wise old man.

There are times when a problem seems unsolvable. You need to step back, look at if from a different perspective and find the 18th horse. In order to do so, you must avoid framing the problem, which limits your perspectives and thus limits your solutions.

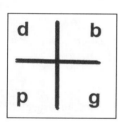

In the diagram, which letter is most out of place?

The normal tendency is to go into the problem, instead of backing up. When you go in, you frame the problem, which creates boundaries, and when you create boundaries, you limit your solutions.

When you go into something, you tend to spend all your time rearranging what is already there. Only by moving outside the framework are you able to add, subtract, substitute, magnify or simplify what you have. If you're too close to something, you won't see it, like the timeless example of not seeing the forest for the trees.

The answer to which letter is most out of place in the above diagram is, of course the t or, if you turn the page slightly, the x. Children don't see the structure in the center as a separation for four letters, but as a letter in itself, and a letter which is much larger than the others.

Children see the t or the x faster than adults. That's because adults immediately go into a problem, while children and childlike adults look for the simple solution first, which often means looking at the whole picture before going in. Creativity denotes the ability to put a larger frame than you are used to around all situations.

Some people are always grumbling because roses have thorns. I am thankful thorns have roses.   *Alphonse Karr, French journalist, novelist*

Putting a larger frame around something often means putting a simpler frame. It often means stepping back and making sure that you don't opt too quickly for the detailed or the complicated.

IF YOU SEE A FIRE, YELL FIRE!

This sign, which hangs in the computer room of the business school of a major university in Hong Kong, is so simplistic, it's striking. If a fire were to break out, the obvious reaction would be to yell, fire. Wouldn't it? Wouldn't it? Are you sure?

Sherlock Holmes and Doctor Watson went on a camping trip. As they lay down for the night, Holmes turned to Watson and said:

"Look up into the sky and tell me what you see."

Watson said, "I see hundreds of stars."

"And what does that tell you?" the famous detective asked.

"If there are hundreds of stars there must be thousands of planets. It is almost certain that there's life on another besides our own."

"Fine, Watson, but what else does it tell you?"

"Theologically, it tells me that God is great and that we are small and insignificant."

"What else does it tell you?" Holmes pressed.

"Well, since the sky is clear, I assume we'll have good weather tomorrow. What does it tell you?"

"It tells me," Holmes said slowly, "that somebody stole our tent."

> The obscure we see eventually, the completely apparent takes longer

When you look at a situation only from within your established way, you draw boundaries and then work within those boundaries. Whatever answers you come up with can only lie within those boundaries. To be creative you have to push out or enlarge those boundaries.

A tale of a father and his son

A father and his son are out driving on a highway. Their car is involved in a horrible accident. The father is killed and the son critically injured. The son is rushed to a hospital and prepared for emergency surgery. The doctor comes in, sees the patient and proclaims: "I can't operate! It's my son!"

Is this scenario possible, and if so, how? Keep in mind, of course, that doctors never operate on close relatives because of the emotional involvement.

Many answers are possible. The simplest is that the doctor is the patient's mother. It's the answer that most women quickly come up with. Men, however, immediately think of stepfathers, godfathers, adopted children and babies being switched at birth. Some even opt for complicated tales involving space ships and aliens.

Look down right now and describe what you see. Unless you're reading this book outside, your answer will probably be something like: "I see the floor."

If we were to ask for a further description, you might reply: "I see the rug," or "I see the patterns in the tile," or "I see the grains in the wood." Stop! You're going in. Back away. Look at the floor from a different perspective. Unless you're in a basement, or a house without one, the floor you're looking at is also the ceiling of the room beneath you.

One man's ceiling is another man's floor

Look at this diagram of a Necker cube.

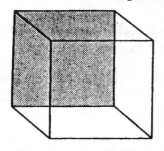

The Necker cube is another example of how we perceive things. Is the shaded part of the cube in the back or in the front? It depends how you look at it. If you look down into the cube, the shaded part will be at the back. If you imagine that the cube is above you and that you are looking up at it, the shaded part will be in the front. Its location depends on the perspective you assume.

$$XI+I=X$$

The equation of Roman numerals is incorrect. Correct it without moving any of the existing numbers and without adding or subtracting new numbers.

The reversal procedure

> ### If a string has one end, then it has another

Here's another wonderfully simplistic statement, one that illustrates what is called the reversal method. With it, one takes things in reverse order rather than the normal, one, two, three, approach that everyone adopts.

If you have a piece of string, which end is the beginning and which is the end? It depends on your perspective, or perhaps how you pick it up. It also can be argued that it may not really matter.

We are taught always to start at the beginning and go on to the end. Why? Why not start at the back and work your way forward? Why not start in the middle and jump backwards or forwards? If you start at a different point from everyone else, you may be able to see the one key thing they all miss. Many creative thinkers get their most original ideas when they challenge or reverse things, when they take things out of sequence, when they turn things upside down, when they turn things inside out.

It is said that this type of thinking prompted Ford's invention of the assembly line. Instead of the usual, "how can we get people to the material to work on it," Ford asked, "how can we get the work to the people?" From this emerged the idea of the assembly line.

If you haven't already figured out the answer to the equation problem, simply turn the book upside down. You will find that the equation has corrected itself.

A simple scheduling problem

Imagine you're working for a tennis tournament and you have to figure out how many singles matches to schedule. There are 64 men entered. How many men's singles matches will you need? The normal way to find the answer is as follows:

The 64 entrants play. Therefore, you will need 32 matches.
Then the 32 winners play, giving you 16 more matches.
Then the 16 winners play, using up 8 more matches.
Then the 8 winners play, in 4 more matches.
Then the 4 winners play, in 2 more matches.
Then the 2 winners play, in 1 more match.

$32 + 16 + 8 + 4 + 2 + 1 = 63$. The correct answer is 63 matches.

There's an easier way of finding it if you apply the reversal method. In order to end up with one final winner, you must have 63 losers. In order to be a loser, you have to have lost a match. Therefore, to get 63 losers, you will need 63 matches.

Almost everyone attacks this problem the same way, by counting winners instead of losers. As long as your method gives you an answer, you never bother to look for a better or simpler method. It's just not something we think of doing.

From *Alice Through the Looking Glass:*

> "How can you go on talking so quietly, head downwards?" Alice asked, as she dragged the Knight out of the ditch by his feet.
>
> The Knight looked surprised at the question.
>
> "What does it matter where my body happens to be?" he said. "My mind goes on working all the same. In fact, the more head-downwards I am, the more I keep inventing new things."

The reversal procedure helps us to escape from our normal way of looking at situations. It doesn't matter whether the new way makes sense or not, for once one escapes, it is easier to move in other directions. Although the reversal method is often useful in itself, its main purpose is that of provocation. We need a push or even a jolt most of the time in order to escape our normal tendencies and thought patterns. Reversing the order of things is one way of achieving it, but only one way.

Try this problem: You have a circle which contains the following letters: A, E, F. Outside the circle are B, C and D. Where do you put the letter G, inside or outside? Where do you put the H, I, J, K and L and so on?

Most adults look for a complicated, mathematical solution. They begin by going into the problem. A child will look for a simplistic solution first, before going in, which is what the creative (childlike adult) person also tends to do.

The answer? The G goes outside. The H and I inside. The J outside, the K and L inside. Straight letters go inside, while the curved letters stay out. We told you the solution was simple.

> Everything should be made as simple as possible, but not simpler.
> *Albert Einstein, German-born US physicist, mathematician*

Collages

One of the exercises we proposed at the end of Chapter 2 was to do a collage. A collage is often one of the first exercises Art Gogatz has his university students do when they take his creativity course. He gives no other instructions other than to bring a collage to the next class. The collages always fall into the following categories:

- Almost all are images cut out of newspapers and magazines and pasted onto a two-dimensional rectangular surface.
- The sizes of the rectangles don't vary much.
- The rectangles usually contain 15–40 pasted images.
- The borders of the rectangle are rarely trespassed.
- The collage is rarely three-dimensional.
- The collages rarely mix pasted images with those drawn or painted.

The dictionary definition of a collage is as: *An art form in which images are pasted together on a surface for their symbolic or suggestive effect*. The surface does not have to be a rectangle or even a square, but could be a triangle, a circle, or even free form. The surface does not have to be two-dimensional. The surface can be moving. The surface can be alive. The size of the surface can be anything you want. A collage can be done on the side of a car, on the top of a mountain or the head of a pin.

The images don't have to be cut from newspapers or magazines. The images don't have to be numerous, but can be as few as one. The images can be three-dimensional. The images can be moving. The images can be alive.

Anything can be used in a collage, yet almost everyone shows up with the same thing, cutouts pasted onto a flat, rectangular surface, because that's the first thing that comes to mind. Since this is a perfectly adequate solution, the students don't go any further. They stop thinking as soon as an adequate or satisfactory solution to something is found. That there may be other, perhaps better solutions doesn't even come up for consideration.

Are women as creative as men?

Think about your answer before reading on. Most people tend to answer this question with the simple word, yes. Others say, no. Still others declare, yes, even more so! The other answer that people often give is, it depends. It depends on the woman. It depends on the man. It depends on the circumstances. In other words, they feel they can't answer the question.

Rarely does anyone in a group or class ever challenge this question. Those who do challenge it are almost always women.

What is the challenge? The challenge is, *who said men are creative?*

The question, "are women as creative as men," is a biased one. In answering it, you focus only on whether the women are on a par with men. Men's creativity is not questioned. If you reverse the question and first ask, "are men as creative as women," you tend to get a higher percentage of people in a class situation who challenge the question. These people, however, are almost always men.

Creativity means changing some aspect of the problem, topic or field you're working on, and in order to do that you have to challenge conventional thinking about that problem, topic or field.

Creativity is the ability to think beyond convention and to look at our traditional constraints with nontraditional thinking.

Creativity is observing. It's rearranging. It's challenging accepted practices. It's resisting the seduction of the adequate. It is asking, is this the only solution? Is this the best solution? What would happen if I put this with that? What if?

What if an alien came down from another world and instead of trying to conquer the earth, was just trying to get back home? You'd have a film called *E.T.* All prior films in this genre assumed that if extraterrestrials came to earth, it would be for one purpose and one purpose only, to conquer.

What if the bad guys were really the good guys? You'd have a film called *Bonnie and Clyde* or *Butch Cassidy and the Sundance Kid*. Until these groundbreaking films (which were released in the same year), good guys were always good guys and bad guys were always bad guys. It never dawned on anyone that bad guys could also be heroes.

What if a tree could talk? Do you remember the Disney film *Pocahontas*? Creativity often consists of merely turning over what is already there, adding a twist, turning things around, changing just one aspect of something. Which popular children's film was a takeoff on the earlier World War Two action film *The Great Escape*? Replace Steve McQueen, James Garner and Charles Bronson with chickens and you have a film called *Chicken Run*.

Try this problem: Two soldiers, a tall, muscular one and a short one with thick, curly hair are walking through a forest. They resemble each other and indeed are related. The short soldier is the son of the muscular soldier, but the muscular solider is not the father of the short soldier. What is their relationship?

The solution to this problem should now be quite simple. In fact we've already seen it, in a slightly different form, earlier. The relationship is, of course, mother and son. A mother can be a soldier, and can easily be someone tall and muscular. Creativity is often just changing or realigning one aspect of something, but that one thing is usually enough to throw the vast majority of people.

The eagle

The following story comes from a small town American newspaper:

> An eagle has escaped from the zoo and is proving difficult to catch. It is perched on a high branch and is resisting the efforts of the keepers and zoo management to lure it back to its cage. A small crowd has gathered and a local television news team is on the way.

What can you say about this article?
Some typical reactions to the story are as follows:

- It's not a very important story
- It's local news
- The bird may not survive if it escapes
- We don't know where the zoo is. The location may have an effect on the bird's chances of survival
- Someone should call the police or fire department.

These are normal observations, but they are all from one perspective, the reader's, which is, of course, your perspective. Now try looking at it again from other perspectives.

- Damn bird! If it flies off it's gonna mean my job. It wasn't my fault it got out. Some idiot left the door open, and it wasn't me, but you know who they're gonna blame. I've put in over ten years here, but do you think that's going to matter? They're gonna fire me, and then no other zoo will take me! What am I going to tell my wife? What am I going to tell the kids? Damn bird!

The perspective is that of the zoo keeper.

- Damn keeper! How could he have let that bird out? Doesn't he know how much that eagle is worth? Damn! The publicity is going to cost us a fortune in donations! If that bird flies away, I'm going to catch hell with the mayor's office. Damn keeper! I should have fired him years ago! Well, he better catch that thing before the television people get here, or he's going to be out on the streets this time for sure!

The perspective here is zoo management.

■ Damn bird! He's just sitting there. Why doesn't he do something? Fly away, bird, before they catch you! Look out! The keeper's got a ladder and he's going to climb up after you! He's going to get you, and when he does he's going to make you pay! Don't let him get you! Do something! Fly, fly! Wait! Shit on his head! That's it! Shit on his head!

Perspective? Someone in the crowd!

■ Damn bird! I hope he stays put till we get there. That's all I need, drive all the way out to the zoo for nothing. I shouldn't be doing this anyway. I'm being wasted on these stupid assignments. I ought to be doing something important, like covering the White House, or some new Middle East war! Damn! I just hope that bird doesn't fly off before I get there, or I won't have any story to cover!

Perspective? A local television reporter. Are there any more perspectives? No? Are you sure?

■ Damn! What's all the commotion? What's all the fuss? Can't they leave a bird in peace? Boy, my old keeper sure looks mad. Why is everyone down there yelling at me? People never yelled before. What's going on? Will someone please tell me what's going on? Why can't they just leave me in peace?

The perspective is, of course, that of the eagle.
Are there any more perspectives? Of course there are.

■ Damn! All those lights and people pointing up at me, and now they're putting a ladder up against me! Ouch! Don't they know that hurts? Why are they here? Why can't they all go away and leave me in alone?

Perspective? The tree. Ridiculous, you snort? Trees don't have perspectives. What about Mother Willow in *Pocahontas*? Disney gave her the personality of a kind, wise grandmother and the audiences believed it. So why can't trees have perspectives?

■ Damn bird! I'm glad he's gone! He was a pig anyway, biting my bars and doing you-know-what all over me! Whew! What a relief! Am I glad he's gone! Good riddance! Do you hear me up there? Good riddance! Hey, wait! If he flies away, they'll put something else inside me, something ... something worse, like a rat or maybe something slimy like, ugh, a big snake! Hey, get that bird! Damn, don't let him go!

Perspective? The cage. The cage? Are you kidding? Well, if a tree can have a perspective, why can't a cage? In children's films all sorts of inanimate things, tables and chairs and cars, come to life. The purpose of this little story about the zoo is to remind you that your perspective is just one of a number of perspectives. Just because it's yours doesn't mean it's the only one or even the best one. There may well be a better one. There will *always* be another one.

How many times have you heard, she doesn't understand me, or my boss just doesn't understand me, or, I just don't understand that kid? People don't understand because even though they're both looking at the very same situation, their perspectives are different.

You can't be a good bullfighter until you first learn to be a bull.

Just as you can't be a good teacher without having been a student, you can't be a good student until you also learn what it's like to teach. One of the first tasks a student should be given upon entering a university is to actually teach a class. Experience in front of a classroom would help students see the reverse perspectives, and would give them better understandings of what it's like to be in a classroom.

Men and women who are going through divorces always fail to understand their partner's positions. A marriage counselor can see both sides. The children of a marriage can as well, but the two people most involved just can't. A child of a couple undergoing divorce will often say: "I see mommy's side, and I see what daddy means, but all they do is argue and fight." Divorcing couples are always urged to listen to each other, and they do try. Unfortunately, they usually revert to: "I understand what you're saying, but you're wrong." What they really mean when they say this is: "I hear what you're saying, but I don't understand it." To understand, you have to go beyond listening, and actually begin to feel what the other person is feeling. To do that you must avoid comparing the other person's position to yours, but rather suspend your judgment and forget about yourself. That's the tough part.

> Two points of view? Of course there are two points of view, mine and one that is misguided and wrong

How many people do you know who think this way? How often do you think this way?

In a divorce a woman may complain that her husband never communicated his feelings, while the man may feel that the woman was being overly sensitive. It isn't a question of who is right and who's wrong. What's important is that each person understands why the other person feels the way they do.

There are no facts, only interpretations.   *Friedrich Nietzsche, German philosopher*

Management–labor disputes are similar (but in many ways easier) to marital disputes. You start with offers, concessions, negotiations and threats, then follow them up with more negotiations, stalemate, the hardening of positions, strikes, more threats, then additional concessions and so on until both sides eventually reach an agreement. There's always an agreement. It's the same thing with war. Every war in history has been followed by a peace and an eventual reevaluation of positions that were once non-negotiable and etched in stone. We all come around to see the other point of view eventually. E-v-e-n-t-u-a-l-l-y. The problem with war is the sheer, utter madness that reigns between the "E" and the "y." After the final no there is always a yes, and on that yes the future of things, most times the future of the world, depends.

The difference between a traitor and a defector depends purely on one's point of view. The difference between a hero and a villain also depends on one's point of view. Even the difference between a genius and a madman depends on the prevailing point of view.

They called me mad and I called them mad, and damn them, they outvoted me.
   Nathaniel Lee, English dramatist, on being interned in an insane asylum

"You can't negotiate with terrorists. They're not like us. They're all crazy!" The behavior of a terrorist may seem irrational from our perspective, but our position is only one way of looking at the issue. The other person's values may differ radically from yours, which may lead him or her to reject something you consider acceptable. One needs to ask oneself, if I were a terrorist, would I agree to this? If not, why wouldn't I?

The problem in asking yourself the question, "if I were a terrorist would I agree to this?" is that one tries to answer the question as a terrorist but with non-terrorist values. In order to really answer the question, one needs to *understand what it feels like* to be a terrorist. It's similar to what an actor does when called on to play a role, or what a writer does when he or she is developing a character.

An actor playing an historical character develops his role by asking, what if I were living centuries ago? What would I feel as I walked the streets of London in Shakespeare's time? What would Florence look like, feel like, smell like, as I stood on a bridge over the River Arno in the year 1496? Would I, as Savonarola, a simple, Dominican friar, have the courage to lead my city against the abuses of Rome, and risk dividing the Church?

These questions don't encourage the actor to think what he would do in those circumstances; instead they take him out of himself and immerse him totally in his character's world. Only when he becomes his character does his portrayal seem real.

One of the keys to creativity is to forget about yourself and your way of looking at things long enough to emotionally understand someone or something else.

Henry Mintzberg, McGill University professor and one of the world's most influential teachers of business strategy, often asks:

> What does it mean to think globally? To become a global-minded manager, you have to learn how people from other countries and other cultures think and act in various situations.

It goes beyond learning how people think and act. Instead, it involves understanding how other people *feel* in various situations. Understanding what someone else feels is at the very heart of all creativity training.

Switching roles

> A Texan was visiting a farmer in Maine. The Texan asked, "How big is your farm?"
>
> The farmer answered. "It goes from the road to that stand of trees and across to the creek. Tell me, how big is your farm?"
>
> "Well," said the Texan. "I can get in my car and drive for an hour before I get to the edge of my farm."
>
> "Oh," said the Maine farmer. "I used to have a car like that myself."

Humor involves switching over from one way of looking at things to another. A punch line hits us without warning and reverses for a moment the way we normally look at things.

Even as a kid, I always went for the wrong woman. When my mother took me to see Snow White, everyone fell in love with Snow White. I immediately fell for the Wicked Queen.   *Woody Allen, American comic and film director*

One can never assume that one's point of view is the only point of view. Instead, one must seek other points of view. When one does, it is not merely to establish that one's point of view is correct, but rather to welcome equally valid alternatives.

Every man takes the limits of his own field of vision for the limits of the world.
Arthur Schopenhauer, German philosopher

Like the actor, the writer must also be able to feel everything his or her character is feeling. In order to create a character, whether that character be in a book or on the screen, you have to have that character inside you and you have to be able to get it out.

Art Gogatz relates the following incident from his studies:

When I was studying fine arts in New York, one of the professors gave us a strange and challenging assignment. For the next class, he announced, "I want all the men to come dressed as women and all the women dressed as men."

The university was located in downtown Manhattan, and while a couple of the students went to school dressed normally and then changed in the bathroom, most of us naively trooped in from our homes (me, via subway from the Bronx), looking quite different. In class the professor said nothing, and to our surprise the class went off as usual. At the end of the session he said, "you all look wonderful. Now stay like you are until next week's class." And so we did.

The idea, of course, was to begin (a week is virtually nothing, though at the time it seemed an eternity), to begin to understand what it *might, just might feel like* to be the opposite sex.

Why on earth would I ever want to do that, you may ask? Well, if you're a writer, half your characters will be of the opposite sex, yet all your characters must be believable. Your characters must live and breathe with such intensity that your audience identifies with them.

Your audience must lose themselves so much in the story and characters that they forget their audience status. They *are* in that boxing ring, *driving* that car, or *on* the Titanic.

An actor who plays the role of a handicapped person must understand what if feels like to be handicapped. When they play the role, for a certain amount of time, they are handicapped. A writer who creates the part of an old man must understand what it feels like to be old.

> Each morning my characters greet me with misty faces, willing though chilled to muster for another day's progress through the dazzling quicksand of blank paper.
> *John Updike, American novelist*

An acting student in New York recalls his first role.

> My first acting role was back in high school. I played a tree. It was one of Shake-speare's plays. *A Midsummer Night's Dream*, I think. Me and the other "trees" had to try to feel what it might be like to actually be a tree. We stood in the forest for hours on end trying. I'm not sure if I totally succeeded, but to this day, I'm a lousy gardener. It breaks my heart to pull up weeds. I feel they've as much right to be there as the flowers.

If you think it's difficult trying to feel what it's like to be a tree, consider that Albert Einstein imagined he was a beam of light hurtling through space, and this helped to lead him to the theory of relativity. If Einstein could imagine himself hurtling through space, don't you think you could imagine what something might feel like from someone else's point of view? If you're a man, ask yourself what this would feel like from a woman's point of view. You need to say "feel" like and not "seem" like or "look" like. You're dealing with emotions; you're not trying to be you as a woman, but as someone who exists independently of you. Actors and actresses have to learn to do that. Most people, however, have enormous difficulty becoming someone else, even for the briefest periods of time.

If you're a woman, ask yourself, what would this situation feel like to a man? How would a child feel if he were here? The question is not, how would I feel if I were a child? but, how would a child feel. They're different questions, and they lead you to vastly different answers. How would a teenager feel? How would an old man or woman feel? How would a handicapped person feel?

Perception begins with seeing

> Berra's first law: You can observe a lot just by watching

Many times when we read a text, or an article, we understand it immediately, while several hours later, the same text may require several readings. There is a difference between reading and looking at the words. When we read, we give the text our full attention, when we look at the words, we don't. Many people think they're reading, when in fact they're just looking at the words. Many people think they're listening, when in fact they're just spending their time comparing what they are hearing to their own beliefs.

A great many people think they are thinking when they are merely rearranging their prejudices.   *William James, American psychologist*

Have twenty people walk down the street, and then ask them what they saw. Even though they all saw the same things, their answers will vary greatly. Just as there's a difference between reading and looking at the words, there's a difference between looking and seeing.
Frederick Franck offers this in his book *The Zen of Seeing*:

Looking and seeing start with sense perception. When I look at the world I make immediate choices, I like or dislike. I accept or reject what I look at, according to its usefulness to me. On the other hand, when I see, I suddenly am all eyes, I forget this me, and liberated from it, dive into the reality that is before me.

**If you can teach a person how to see, that person will be more creative
If you can teach a person to forget about himself,
that person will begin to see**

It's observing things. It's rearranging things. It's changing things. It's enlarging things. It's reducing things. It's substituting things. It's combining things. It's reversing things. It's eliminating things. It's questioning things. It's challenging things. It's creativity, but it begins with observation.

The real voyage of discovery consists not in making new landscapes, but in having new eyes.   *Marcel Proust, French novelist*

Exercise

Draw a picture of yourself. It doesn't matter if you can't draw, and it doesn't matter if the final drawing doesn't look at all like you. Just try your best. When you're finished, take a look at your picture, and answer these questions:

1. Is your picture drawn on standard size paper, or were you lazy and drew it here in the book?
2. Is your picture drawn on white paper?
3. Is your drawing in the center of the page? Does it float? Is there a lot of space around it?
4. Did you begin your drawing with the head?
5. Is there a lot of detail in the face, and not much anywhere else?
6. Did you draw yourself from memory, rather than look in a mirror or use a photograph of yourself?
7. Is your drawing contained by the edges of the paper?
8. Is your drawing on paper, rather than some other material?
9. Is your drawing two-dimensional?
10. Are you unhappy with your drawing?

If you're like most people, you answered yes to all ten questions!

Your drawing doesn't have to be on standard white paper. If you put yourself in the middle, and failed to use the edges, you let yourself be confined by the page.

When most people start to draw, they begin with pencil or pastel. When they try painting, they begin with watercolor. All three are tight, restrictive media. That's not the way to start. You have to start by loosening up, by embracing freedom.

Look at the picture you just drew. Does it make you look smaller than you actually are? Does it represent only a part of you, the head perhaps? If it does, it represents just a fragment of the actual you, and that's a shame, but that's exactly the image of you that you share with the rest of the world, the real you, ah, that you never really let others see.

If you think about it, aren't you cruising through life in third gear? How many times do you really test yourself? How many times do you go all out? How many times do you challenge things? How many times do you create things? Think about it.

How to break through invisible barrier three

This invisible barrier may not be as easy to smash as the first two. It will, in fact, take sustained work. The important thing is to become more consciously aware of the existence of other, equally valid points of view. To do that you will have to begin to identify your patterns. By patterns we mean things you do without thinking, things that you do over and over, things that you've done for years, maybe even all your life. For each one of them, see if there may not be other and perhaps better ways.

ACTIVITIES

1. Take a camera, it can be any kind, a simple automatic camera will work just as well as a single lens reflex or digital camera. You also don't necessarily need to put any film in the camera. It's the action of taking the pictures that's important. Select a chair in your home and train your camera on it. You'll now have the chair with a frame around it. Be conscious of the frame. It's your frame, your normal frame, your everyday way of looking at that chair from your everyday height and your everyday angle. Now take a picture of the chair. Now sit on the floor. Your frame (or perspective) will be different. Take another picture. Now stand up and move back a couple of paces. Now there's more space around the chair, more space but also more things, maybe the rug, a table, a painting. Snap. Move further back. Snap. Move around to the side of the chair. Move in, move back. Drop your angle. Get something and climb up on it. You will now be looking down at the chair and you'll have a new, different yet equally valid perspective.

    Move around to the back of the chair. Snap. Crawl under it (if you can). Snap. Stand on top of it. Snap. Sit in it, and take yet another picture. This time you'll probably have to photograph yourself in the chair, but maybe not, try taking a picture over your shoulder of the back of the chair. Now get in real close, take the seat cushion off (if it has one). Snap. Turn the chair upside down. Move it into another room. You've now changed its environment. How long has it been since you moved that chair? It's been months, hasn't it, maybe even years? Why?

    This is a very simple exercise, but an important one. We usually have one way of looking at (and photographing) everything we come into contact with, and it is only if we make a conscious effort to look for other, equally valid ways and perspectives that we become aware that they exist.

2. Most of us start to walk by taking a step with our left foot. What about the right foot? How often do you use it to begin? From time to time, be conscious of which foot you first use to move forward when you start to walk. Just being conscious of things you do automatically reminds you to be consciously aware of the need to see things differently.

3. Think about some of the simple things that you do every day, things you do without thinking, things you do in the same order. If you share a bed with someone, which side of the bed do you sleep on? Your answer will probably be the same side, night after night. Why?

   Which seat at the table is yours? Which seat in the car do you always take? When you go to your local shopping center, which door do you enter by? It depends where you park, doesn't it? Well, where do you usually park? It's generally the same place, isn't it, even though the lot is huge?

   In the morning, do you brush your teeth before washing your face, or do you comb your hair first? You may not even know. Start to become more consciously aware of the sequence in which you do things. Why do you need a sequence anyway?

4. This activity is one which comes from performing arts classes. The idea is to try to experience what it might feel like to be something different or someone else. To begin with you need to accept that this is a serious exercise. If you find yourself laughing or feeling foolish, it won't work. If you do feel foolish, put the exercise aside and come back to it later.

   Okay, now we want you to begin by imagining what it would feel like to be a chair. To do that you will have to get into a chair's position and that will mean squatting down with your arms extended.

   Don't rush this. Take your time. Let the sensation of feeling foolish dissipate. Close your eyes. Let your senses and feelings take over. Forget about your surroundings, forget yourself, forget that you exist. You are a chair, you have become a chair. Lose yourself in chair-ness, give yourself over to it, smell it, wallow in it. Take your time. This is not something that you can do in a few seconds. It will, in fact, take several attempts. What do you feel? Maybe it's bored, or lonely, or maybe it will be feelings of calm and peace, or maybe nothing at all. Oops! Someone just sat on you. Can you feel the weight? Did you sag a bit when they did it? Who sat on you? What do you feel?

   Next try to imagine that you're a flower. What kind of flower are you? What color are your petals? How many do you have? Where are you? What can you see? Can you see at all? Maybe you can only sense things. What's around you? Take some time. Don't just imagine you're a flower, feel it. To do that you will surely need to be outside, down on the ground, close to the earth. Do you feel the wind, the rain, the night, how does the dawn feel?

In this activity you can work yourself up from inanimate objects to plants, animals and eventually to other people. In this case you'll be doing a form of role reversal, an exercise they often do in family therapy. Even though, you may not think so initially, it's easier to feel what it's like to be a chair or a tree than it is another person. When you're a flower, you can block the person in you out, but when you become someone else, that's difficult to do.

Feel what it's like to be someone different, someone much older, someone blind, someone handicapped, someone who lives on the other side of the world, someone of the opposite sex. Don't say you can't do it. Try. If you can't right away, work up to it. Most of these activities are ones that you'll have to come back to again and again, because you probably won't be able to accomplish them the first time you try.

If you have difficulty with this exercise, ask yourself a question. If someone were paying me a lot of money to feel like a flower or a chair, could I? Your answer will be "maybe." In fact, you may not succeed, but at least you'd take the exercise seriously and you'd sure try a lot harder. Well, unless you become a professional actor, no one is going to pay you a lot of money to feel like you're a flower, but you can help yourself with this exercise if you offer yourself a reward (maybe something you want to buy that's a little over budget) if you succeed.

Don't hurry. The process is a slow one. It takes time to feel like someone else might feel. If you're married, or have a partner, what would it feel like to be that other person? How would you, as them, feel to have to deal with you, eat with you and sleep with you? Now we are getting into difficult but interesting territory.

Men are crap. I came to this conclusion when I realized that if I were a woman, I wouldn't take myself out or go to bed with me.
Dustin Hoffman, American actor in the film Tootsie

The key in all this is to be able to forget about yourself, your thoughts, your desires, your fears, and your very personal and precious way of looking at everything. For the time you become something or someone else, you don't exist. Like an actor playing a part, or a writer creating a role, for a certain period of time you become that other person, thing, being or creature.

To do that you will need to clear your mind, which in effect means to stop thinking (stopping thinking, by the way, is the best way to fall asleep. If you have trouble sleeping, just stop thinking and you'll quickly fall asleep). Clear your mind. Let your feelings take over.

How would a child feel? How would a handicapped child of the opposite sex living on the other side of the world feel? Once you are able to do it, and then come back, you will have changed the way you look at that thing or person forever. Hopefully you'll also have changed the way you look at the world in general, for that's the essence of creativity, to be able to look at things differently at a certain moment in time.

Freedom in art

Impressionism started in the early 1870s in France. It was the first major art movement to deviate from realism. One of the reasons why artists at that particular time were free to move away from realism was the invention of photography. A camera duplicated reality far better than any human hand could. The artist was now free, free to go beyond the traditional boundaries, free at last.

Our intention here is not to give you a course in art history, but to make you aware of how important freedom has always been to both art and creativity.

The other great influence on impressionism came from science. For centuries everyone had assumed that light was white. Scientists in the mid-1800s discovered that light was made up of the colors of the spectrum, red, orange, yellow, green, blue, indigo and violet. The impressionist's use of color was an attempt to recreate the light bathing an object.

The name "impressionism" has caused a lot of confusion. It stems from an 1874 painting by Claude Monet entitled *Impression: Sunrise.* Most people mistakenly assume that impressionism refers to the artist's idea or impression of something, but that wasn't the aim. The impressionist was merely attempting to reproduce the quality of light that existed at the moment he or she painted the picture. Was it revolutionary? In the 1870s, it certainly was.

Impressionism: *A theory and school of painting whose aim is to capture a momentary glimpse of a subject, especially to reproduce the changing effects of light by applying paint to canvas in short strokes of pure color.*

Until impressionism, most painting was done indoors, and was executed slowly, often laboriously. Impressionists painted outdoors, and quickly, before the light changed. The artist recreated a quality or condition of light by using small dabs of pure color. The best way to look at impressionist art is to squint at it. If you squint at an impressionist painting, you'll see that it crystallizes into an almost three-dimensional splash of light and air.

Impressionism was radically different from anything which came before. Only when we compare it to later movements do its fully discernable images strike us as traditional. Although each art movement owes much to its predecessor, you should keep in mind that each movement in the history of art represented a radical change from that which came before it.

Cubism, surrealism, abstractionism and expressionism were all movements which initially shocked, offended and alienated far more people than they pleased.

It's boldness, audacity, the desire to push out boundaries, the need to question everything, and the desire to live rather than merely mark time, which blesses and stains each and every creative person.

> You are not alive unless you know you are living.
>
> *Amedeo Modigliani, Italian artist*

You've got to go for it! You can't worry about the results. You can't worry about who you might offend. You have to trust your intuition and go for it! That's what the creative person feels, and that feeling overcomes whatever fears he or she may have.

The movement which followed impressionism was fauvism. Here the emphasis shifts from light to form. The influence of Cézanne, Gauguin and others is obvious. Color is strong, indeed even rampant. Rather than being bound by color, the artist is now free to use it as he or she wishes.

Cubism followed fauvism. The cubists were also concerned with form. As mentioned earlier, the idea behind cubism was to free the artist from concentrating on only one angle of a subject. The cubist painting gives the viewer three dimensions on a two-dimensional surface. Many cubist works were collages, or paintings with three-dimensional images pasted on them.

After cubism came Dadaism and surrealism. There is a significant difference between these movements and all those that preceded them. Up to this point, art was based upon the observation of reality. In other words, you were drawing or painting what you saw, rather than what you imagined. With both Dadaism and surrealism, the artist began working for the first time with imagined versions of reality.

Dadaism, which means babble, or baby talk, was a provocative movement designed to free the artist from conventional ways of looking at the world. In the irrational arrangement of objects, the artist was saying, "why does one thing have to follow another?" Why can't we turn things around and upside down? What if? Why not? Everything was permissible as regards materials, subject matter and location. The more banal the object, the better. Marcel Duchamp turned a urinal into a work of art simply by isolating it from its normal environment. It was a short-lived movement meant to disturb, jolt and, of course, liberate.

Surrealism plunged the artist into the depths of his imagination. In his book *The Age of Surrealism*, Wallace Fowlie explains:

> This detaching of objects from their usual surroundings can be viewed as a gesture of freedom from the rules of society, family and the state and represents the limitless possibility of salvation through dream, love and desire.

By isolating, combining and distorting everyday objects, surrealism forces you to consider them differently and that's exactly what creativity is all about, whether it be in art or in idea generation.

Abstractionism has come to be a generic term that encompasses various non-realistic schools of art. In its pure sense, however, it refers to a type of art which abstracts or draws the essence out of things. It reduces and simplifies. It forces you to examine things as they are in their barest, most basic terms.

In abstract art you are now working with images that are often indefinable. In surrealism and Dadaism the images were out of context, or distorted, but they were identifiable images. In abstract art, the image of reality is often altered to the point where it becomes indiscernible.

> What I want to show in my work is the idea which hides behind the so-called reality. I am seeking the bridge which leads from the visible to the invisible.
>
> *Max Beckmann, German expressionist artist*

In expressionism the artist is free to show his emotions – anger, frustration, indignation, joy. The artist hurls paint at his canvas, drips the paint onto his canvas, swirls it onto bodies then pushes them onto the painting surface. All this is done with one purpose in mind – to convey emotion.

August Endell, in *Definition of Expressionism*, puts it this way:

> We stand at the threshold of an altogether new art, an art with forms which mean or represent nothing, recall nothing, yet which can stimulate our souls as deeply as only the tones of music have been able to do.

Pop art of the 1960s was a movement, which, like Dadaism, took things out of their normal context. The idea in pop art was to isolate and magnify common everyday commercial things, things we see again and again, things we see and don't see. How many times have you seen a can of Coca-Cola? You know it's red. You know it says Coca-Cola, but what else is written on it? What other images does it have? Could you duplicate it if you had to? How about a dollar bill? You touch one every day, often several times a day, yet most people can't remember what's on one. Pop art forced us to look differently at things we see but really don't.

From the fragmentation of color by the impressionists to the mixture of surfaces and planes by the cubists to the surrealists' destruction of space and time, and the abstract expressionists' attack on form and pigment, the idea of the creative person at the vanguard of change comes through.

> No artist is ahead of his time. He is his time. It is just that others are behind the time.   *Martha Graham, American dancer, choreographer*

Look at these questions and answer them as honestly as you can:

- Would you rather be in the vanguard or in the pack? (If you have to know where you're heading, you belong in the pack.)
- Would you rather be on stage or in the audience? (If you have to know what you'd be performing to answer the question, you belong in the audience.)
- Would you rather be the writer or the reader? Of what, you ask? Of anything, a textbook, a screenplay, a poem or a love letter!
- Would you rather be the one dreaming or watching the dreams of others flicker by in some dark, musty movie theater?
Remember that if you aren't the lead dog, the view never changes.

From *Alice Through The Looking Glass*:

> "I declare it's marked out just like a large chessboard," Alice said. "How I wish I was playing. I wouldn't mind being a Pawn, if only I could join, though of course I should like to be a Queen, best."

> "You're in the second square now. When you get to the eighth square you'll be a queen."

> Just at this moment, somehow or other, they began to run. The Queen went so fast that it was all Alice could do to keep up with her.

"Faster, faster," the Queen cried. And they went so fast that they seemed to skim through the air, hardly touching the ground with their feet, till just as Alice was getting exhausted, they stopped.

Alice looked around in great surprise. "Why I do believe we've been under this tree the whole time! Everything's just as it was!"

"Of course it is," said the Queen. "What would you have it?"

"Well, in our country," said Alice, "you'd get to somewhere else if you ran very fast for a long time as we've been doing."

"A slow sort of country," said the Queen. "Now here, it takes all the running you can do to keep in the same place. If you want to get somewhere else, you must run at least twice as fast as that."

That takes us back to something we said at the end of the last chapter about gears. Cruising in third gear just maintains the status quo. If you want to get somewhere else, it requires the courage to push yourself into fourth gear, to risk seeing and trying new things. It does not mean working harder or burning the midnight oil, but rather having the courage to try new things.

How fast do you want to run? Fast enough to be free of the pack? Remember that the pack runs pretty slowly. Who determines how fast the pack runs? You certainly don't! Do you want someone or something else to decide how fast you can run? Do you really?

PART II

Toward the Edge

"Suppress all provocative thoughts"

*The artist, like the idiot or clown, sits on the edge of
the world, and a push may send him over it.*
SIR OSBERT SITWELL, ENGLISH AUTHOR

The highly creative person also sits on the edge of the world, but he or she
wouldn't have it any other way. There is an advantage to sitting on the
edge of the world. You get to see what's on both sides. Remember that
creativity is the ability to see the things that everyone else sees and more;
the ability to see other perspectives; the ability to go beyond the limits
which society says you should respect; the ability to enter and leave the
worlds of reality and imagination without a passport.

Invisible barrier number four is the idea that you mustn't dare to be
different and that includes looking, thinking and acting differently.

If a man is a minority of one, we lock him up.
Oliver Wendell Holmes, American physician, author

Don't you want to look different?

The answer for most people is, no way! Okay. Don't you want to be
different? The answer here is a qualified, and thus somewhat timid, yes.
Don't you want to think differently? Ah, now the answer is, of course!
This is because someone who thinks differently still looks like everyone
else. Someone who is different may not always look the part, but someone
who looks different puts him or herself on display.

You won't think differently unless you're capable of being different
and you won't be different if you're capable of looking different. Students
in art schools often look and dress differently. One of the reasons they do
this is that it's easier to look different than it is to think or be different.
Their looking different is an exercise and nothing else, an exercise along
the way back toward creativity.

Many people are frightened at the thought of having a slightly mad
side, a part of them that may be out of control. Because of this they struc-

ture their lives in the most rational possible ways. The creative person adroitly manages to sit, or walk, on the edge of two worlds, the worlds of imagination and reality.

> Creativity: Stuff your conscious mind with information then unhook your rational thought process.
>
> *David Ogilvy, founder Ogilvy & Mather advertising agency*

Adrian Furnham, University College of London professor of psychology, said this in a 1999 review of the book *When Sparks Fly*, by Dorothy Leonard and Walter Swap:

> It is well known that creatives and psychotic patients have common information processing patterns – these seem unable to inhibit irrelevant information from entering consciousness. Unrelated ideas become interconnected – and we have creativity.

It is not that creative people are unable to inhibit irrelevant information from entering consciousness, but rather they welcome, and actually consciously look for, that irrelevant information, first, simply because it is irrelevant and therefore lets them mentally "throw cold water on their faces" from time to time to refresh tired thought patterns, and second, because creative people are less afraid of all thoughts, their own as well as those of others.

Freud recognized two fundamental principles, the first, which he called the "pleasure principle" and the second the "reality principle." The pleasure principle tells us to do whatever feels good while the reality principle tells us to subordinate pleasure into what needs to be done, which translates into work. Subordinating the pleasure principle to the reality principle is done through a psychological process that Freud calls "sublimation," where you take desires that can't be fulfilled, or shouldn't be fulfilled, and turn them into something productive. But the desire for pleasure doesn't disappear, even when it's sublimated into work. The desires that can't be fulfilled are repressed into what Freud called the "unconscious." Because it contains repressed desires, things that our conscious mind isn't supposed to want or even know about, the unconscious is by definition inaccessible to the conscious mind.

There are, however, some indirect routes to the contents of the unconscious. The first is by dreams, the second by slips of the tongue, and the third by humor.

Freudian psychoanalysis often uses a technique called "free association." The purpose is to have a patient express his or her thoughts spontaneously, without any self-censorship. When successful, it allows images, feelings and thoughts to come freely into consciousness.

Psychoanalysts maintain that the ability to regress into the unconscious while still maintaining conscious ego control is one of the hallmarks of the creative person.

The reason why creative people are less afraid of their own thoughts is because they hold fewer things and consequently fewer thoughts to be forbidden. They have fewer inhibitions, fewer taboos. Creative people need to be able to consider and cope with any subject, no matter how strange or disgusting. The world of the highly creative person revolves around *expressing*, instead of *repressing*, their thoughts, emotions and desires.

Creative people, like children, also manage to do more of what they want to do. Most people accept that in the course of a day there will be many things they will have to do, even though they may not want to. Creative people never fully, and we stress the word, fully, accept this.

> **The creative person is less afraid of his own thoughts because he is less afraid of all thoughts**

It has been said that we are all born mad. We learn to be sane, at least the vast majority of us do.

Creativity and originality are often associated with people who do not fit into mainstream culture in some way. This does not necessarily mean that their creativity is, however, the product of any neurosis.

We can also say that we are all born children. Some remain so. We are all born creative. Some of us also remain so.

In tests such as the Rorschach, or inkblot, highly creative people give answers that run from the normal to the original, but they rarely give bizarre answers. A bizarre answer is one that could not be seen in the illustration. If the inkblot looks like a butterfly and someone says it looks like a typewriter without being able to say why he thinks so, that answer would be considered bizarre. Non-creative people rarely give original answers, but they sometimes give bizarre answers. Creative people are original without being bizarre. The novelty they see stems from the reality they also see. They are able to consider the boldest ideas and mold them into solutions to problems. They are able to fit their ideas to the exacting demands of reality. It is this juggling of the fantastic and the real, which adults manage better than children. Creative adults are sometimes able to turn childlike dreams into rallying cries for change.

In the story about the eagle in the last chapter, students will sometimes come up with bizarre perspectives (always toward the end of the exercise), such as other animals, flowers, rain and clouds. These answers are bizarre because they are not mentioned in the story. All the perspectives cited were mentioned in the story.

When it comes to observing reality, people often do not see what is in front of them. Instead, they see their concept of what reality should be. They are not seeing what is before their eyes, but what they expect and want to see.

A person with a particular way of looking at the world will find that everything he encounters will reinforce that fixed idea.

The zombie

A man woke up one morning convinced that he had turned into a zombie overnight. Try as she might, his wife could not convince him otherwise:

"Why do you think you're a zombie?" she asked.

"Don't you think zombies know they're zombies?" the man answered.

"You're just having a mid-life crisis," his sister chided him, upon rushing over.

"Zombies don't have mid-life crises," the man calmly replied.

His wife got him an emergency appointment with a psychiatrist.

"So you think you're a zombie," the doctor began.

"I know I'm a zombie," the man answered.

"Do zombies bleed?"

"No. Zombies are the living dead. They can't bleed."

The doctor took a pin and pricked the man's finger. Blood immediately oozed from the puncture. The man stared in disbelief.

"There," said the psychiatrist in triumph. "Now do you believe me?"

"Well, what do you know," the man finally said. "Zombies do bleed."

We rarely see things as they are, but rather as we are. When it comes to supporting our ideas, we simply ignore the things that don't fit and select the things that do. Evidence to support absolutely any belief is amazingly easy to find. If you don't think so, just ask any person who is wracked by jealousy.

Positive and negative space

People tend to concentrate on the positive and ignore the negative. When someone first begins to draw, he or she has a difficult time grasping the dynamic interaction between positive and negative space. He or she concentrates on the object and not the space around it, which, in terms of composition, has equal importance. Without a relationship between positive and negative space, the drawing will never work as a unified image.

Can you read the word that is written here in negative space? Because of our tendency to look for the positive rather than the negative, it's often difficult to read, yet once you shift and look for the negative, it becomes easy. In fact, it becomes so easy that you'll have a difficult time not seeing the word, which, by the way, is "fly".

> The intervals between the events are more significant than the events themselves. *Albert Einstein, German-born US physicist, mathematician*

Learning to see the negative as well as the positive (not only what happens but also what doesn't happen) is a fundamental part of creative problem solving.

In the following scene from one of the Sherlock Holmes films, Holmes asks Doctor Watson about what he did not hear, rather than what he did:

> "Watson, do you remember hearing the dog bark last night?"
>
> "Come to think of it, no."
>
> "Precisely. It's the fact that the dog did not bark that's important. It means that the murderer must have been known to it."

People are afraid of the creative process. They're afraid of empty spaces, afraid of the enormity of starting a task from scratch, afraid of not having enough ideas. It is not the lack of ideas which usually blocks our thinking, however, but the ideas we do have. It's easier to find a new way of looking at things if there is no fixed way already established. This is another reason why children are more creative than adults. Children tend to arrive fresh at a problem and can ask questions that go to the heart of the matter, thereby restructuring it.

Experts tend to define what is new in terms of what is old, what is unknown in terms of what is known and to put new ideas into existing and well-established frameworks. Beginners aren't married to established ways of doing things. Hence, they'll often see things the experts will miss. The future doesn't have to be linked to the past. People always try initially to evaluate something new by comparing it to what they already know. It's a method which doesn't always work. The creative process includes disrupting, even dismantling the old as much as it does spawning the new. Fresh, innovative thinking is impossible if we are locked into the way things have always been done, and if we always believe that what happens tomorrow will approximate what happened today.

In brainstorming sessions there is a tendency to include only people who are familiar with the problem for which the group is trying to generate ideas. This tendency is wrong. Brainstorming groups should also include people from outside the organization, people whose perspectives are fresh, people without strings, preconceived ideas or internal or political causes to promote.

> I had an immense advantage over many others dealing with the problem inasmuch as I had no fixed ideas derived from long-established practice to control and bias my mind, and did not suffer from the general belief that whatever is, is right.
>
> *Sir Henry Bessemer, English engineer, on his discovery of a new method of producing steel*

We are not saying that novices are preferable to experts when it comes to the generation of ideas or problem solving. What is indeed preferable is to have experts who are capable of putting aside their expertise long enough to look at what they are working on with fresh, novice-like attitudes.

Assumptions

In problem solving, as in life, one always assumes certain boundaries, even when no boundaries are mentioned. If someone solves the problem by stepping outside those assumed limits, the reaction is often, hey, you can't do that! Well, why can't you? The difference between creative people and non-creative people is that creative people are capable of trespassing assumed limitations when they need to. Let's take a look at some problems.

Problem one
Arrange four blocks so that each is touching two others.

The solution is not very difficult. An example of one solution is the following:

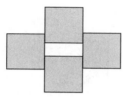

Problem two
Now arrange the four blocks so that one is touching one other, two are touching two others and one is touching three others.

Again the solution is not too difficult. This is one of several:

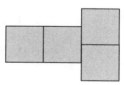

Problem three
Now try to arrange them so that each is touching three others.

One of the first solutions people come up with is this:

The solution is invalid because each block is actually only touching two other blocks. Try it yourself with four blocks if you don't believe us. To solve the problem, you need to place *one* of the blocks on top of the three others which are touching.

There is nothing in the instructions to say that you can't, yet most people don't think of it simply because they *assume* the blocks to be two-dimensional. The assumption is self-imposed and the exclusion of a three-dimensional solution is automatic.

Problem four
Now arrange the four blocks so that each is touching only one other.

This arrangement too causes many people problems. The solution is to separate the blocks:

Again many people assume that the blocks cannot be separated. The assumption inhibits the solution.

In problems like these, one often needs to look away, step back, do something else for a few minutes then come back to it. When one returns, it is often easier to adopt a fresh approach. Most people do the opposite, they concentrate and go into the problem, rather than step outside.

Problem

NSAIFSPARSELAEL

Cross out six letters in the above, so that the remaining letters, without altering their sequence, spell a common English word.

It is often said that the second attempt to solve a problem should come from a totally different direction and the third from still another direction, yet that's exactly what people don't do. When confronted with a problem their second solution is inevitably a carbon copy of their first. In fact, all their initial solutions tend to be variations of that same first failed attempt. It is only by consciously looking for solutions that don't mirror your first attempt that you will finally be able to make progress.

Whenever Thomas Edison was going to hire a new employee, he would invite the applicant over for lunch and the first course would always be soup. While the soup was being served, Edison would casually mention that he was on a salt-free diet. If the person salted the soup before tasting it, Edison would not offer him the job. He did not want to hire people who had too many assumptions built into their lives.

To assume is to take something for granted, to expect that something will be a certain way because it has been like that in the past or because you want it to be that way. It's natural to make assumptions. We all make them every day, yet while assumptions help us to cut corners and save time, they can also function as artificial, and all too invisible, boundaries that keep us from exploring new and different paths and doing new and different things.

After crossing out six letters in the word above, what word were you left with?

NSAIFSPARSELAEL

Cross out the N   1st letter
Cross out the S   (all 3)   2nd letter
Cross out the A   (all 3)   3rd letter

Cross out the I	4th letter
Cross out the P	5th letter
Cross out the L (both)	6th letter

You are left with the word FREE, a word which lies at the heart of creativity. If you had trouble with the exercise, it is because you made an assumption; you assumed that the instructions, cross out six letters, meant a total of six characters.

We're starting to see a pattern. Creativity differs from many other things in life, because when it comes time to turn on your creativity, what you know can sometimes actually handicap you. Speed can handicap you. Experience can handicap you. Even knowledge can sometimes handicap you.

> Imagination is more important than knowledge.   *Albert Einstein*

Like the glass of water that is too full to accept yet another drop, we usually have to get rid of the invisible nets we all lug around, nets woven out of our prejudices, fears and inhibitions, if we are to become creative again.

The road to creativity will force you to take a hard look at a lot of the excess baggage (rules, habits, security blankets, clothing and customs) that you have acquired over the years. It will mean considering things you usually reject and trying things you always dismiss as crazy. It will mean examining your habits and distancing yourself from the conventional. It will lead you away from a lot of what you've learned and from what others expect you to do. It will mean change, and with that change will come a feeling of confidence and liberation.

Lateral thinking

> In order to invent, one must think aside.
> *Etienne Souriau (Hussain, 1968)*, The Theory of Invention

Lateral Thinking was the title of a book published in 1973 by Edward de Bono, a British doctor and educator. The premise of the book is that there are two kinds of thinking, vertical and lateral. We are all trained to think vertically, to go from one logical step to the next, moving all the time towards the one correct solution to a problem. We are not usually taught to think laterally, to go beyond the adequate and generate idea after idea.

This process of idea generation, which is similar to brainstorming, helps us see other perspectives.

Patterns

De Bono points out that the mind is especially good at organizing information into patterns. Once the patterns are formed, it becomes possible to recognize them, react to them, use them. As patterns are used, they become firmly established. The pattern system, however, has certain limitations. It is easy to combine patterns or add to them, but it is very difficult to restructure or eliminate existing patterns.

Lateral thinking is closely related to humor, insight and creativity. The four processes share common ground.

> I used to make obscene phone calls to her collect, and she used to accept the charges all the time.
>
> *Woody Allen, from his film, Take the Money and Run*

Since humor takes things out of their normal context and turns them around, it forces us to look at everyday things differently, thereby restructuring set thought patterns. Creativity also involves the restructuring of patterns but with creativity there is more emphasis on the escape from restrictive patterns.

> Every act of creation is first of all an act of destruction.
>
> *Pablo Picasso, Spanish artist*

Creative thinking is not only constructive, it's also destructive. You have to break out of one pattern to discover another. It is that ability to break out, trespass, go further than other people are willing to that separates creative people from non-creative people. Remember that the limits we are talking about are not laws, but social restrictions, invisible limitations, which one adheres to voluntarily.

Lateral and vertical thinking

In vertical thinking, one moves forward by sequential steps, each of which must be justified. In lateral thinking, one uses information not for its own sake, but for its effect. In lateral thinking one may have to be wrong at some stage in order to achieve a correct solution. In vertical thinking, this would be impossible. One of the basic principles of creativity is opening yourself up to influences that have no connection with what you're doing. In lateral thinking one often seeks out irrelevant information. In vertical thinking one selects only what appears relevant.

Vertical thinking selects a direction by excluding other directions. The system uses judgment. In lateral thinking the judgment is deferred, while ideas are being generated. Lateral thinking, like brainstorming, does not select or judge but seeks to open up other directions. With vertical thinking one selects the most promising approach to a problem, the best way of looking at something. As soon as an approach is adequate, the looking tends to stop. With lateral thinking, one generates as many alternative approaches as one can, since one is not selecting. Judgment is the basic function of vertical, while movement is the basic function of lateral thinking.

Lateral and vertical thinking are fundamentally different. It is not a matter of one process being more effective than the other, for both are necessary. It is a matter of realizing the differences in order to be able to use them effectively. Lateral thinking is useful for generating ideas and approaches and vertical thinking for developing them.

Vertical thinking moves only if there is a direction in which to move. Lateral thinking moves in order to generate a direction. One does not have to be moving towards something, one may be moving away. It is the movement or change that matters. Vertical thinking is sequential. Lateral thinking can jump.

With vertical thinking one has to be correct at every step, if not, there is a blockage, one ceases to move, except backwards. With vertical thinking one uses the negative to eliminate certain directions. With lateral thinking there is no negative. With vertical thinking one concentrates and excludes what is irrelevant, with lateral thinking one welcomes outside influences for the ideas they create. The more irrelevant such influences, the more chance of restructuring the established pattern. To only look for things which are relevant means perpetuating the pattern.

> **First rule of pathology: Most well-trodden paths lead nowhere**

It is the willingness to explore the least likely paths that's important, for often there can be no other reason for exploring such avenues. At the entrance to an unlikely trail, there is nothing to indicate that it is worth exploring and yet it may lead to something useful. With vertical thinking one moves ahead along the widest, most frequently used boulevards, which point in the safest direction.

Problem

How many squares are there in the diagram below?

The answer to how many squares are there in the diagram is 30. Most people come up with less (17 is a common first answer), because the adequate kicks in with the message, that's enough. You don't need to look further.

One is often blocked by the adequacy of a present arrangement from moving to a better one. There is no point at which one can focus one's efforts to reach a better arrangement because one is not even aware that there is a better arrangement. The problem is to realize that things can be improved and there may be a better way. There will *always be another way*.

> Do not go where the path may lead, go instead where there is no path and leave a trail.
> *Ralph Waldo Emerson, American writer*

How to break through invisible barrier four

This barrier is also a difficult one to break through and like barrier three you may find this thought lurking around even when you think you have finally broken through. Basic to eliminating this barrier is the acceptance of the notion that you can look, think and act differently and still maintain your role as a well-respected professional, parent, civic and community leader. If you want to be creative, you will need to express more of your thoughts. Some of them may be provocative and may disturb the people around you. Then again, they may not. What seems provocative to you may be treated mundanely, indifferently or scandalously by those around you, but that is something you can't worry about or you'll keep on suppressing most of your thoughts. Have you ever had what you thought was a fantastic idea in the middle of the night (or when you were drunk), only to see later that it wasn't so hot? Provocative thoughts are like that. They appear stronger when they're rolling around in our minds than they do once we actually express them. Remember too that what was provocative today will look very different tomorrow.

ACTIVITIES

1. What thoughts do you have that actually frighten you? Who have you told them to?

2. Make a list of your provocative thoughts. Stop at seven, then over the course of the next week tell three people (they don't have to be friends or family) some of the things on your list. See what their reactions are. See what your reactions are. Start a new list. Continue the process. You will see that the more provocative thoughts you express, the easier it is to have them, while if you suppress them you're suppressing not only the thoughts but the entire thought generation process.

"I don't want to have to get to know you"

Television won't be able to hold on to a market. People will soon get tired of staring at a plywood box every night.
DARYL ZANUCK, HEAD OF 20TH CENTURY FOX
FILM STUDIOS, 1946

The surrealist artist André Breton said: "It is at the movies that the only absolutely modern mystery is celebrated." You enter the theater willingly, eagerly. You look around you, and are aware of everything except the huge rectangular screen in front of you. The moment the lights are lowered, however, that screen will become your whole universe. What you see, in bursts of light and darkness, you will accept as life, the images will reach out and capture you completely.

The very darkness which envelopes you is more complete than you realize, for the world of the cinema is not light, but a balance between light and darkness. Half of all the time in the movies is spent in darkness. There is no image on the screen at all. In the course of a single second, forty-eight periods of darkness follow forty-eight periods of light. A filmstrip is run at twenty-four frames per second. Twenty-four still photographs, which are shown to the audience twice each. The film comes to a stop in the projector forty-eight times every second. Given the retina's inability to adjust quickly to differences in brightness, an illusion of movement is created by this rapid, start-stop projection of still photographs, each slightly different from the one before.

When you watch a film you accept that the actions on the screen do really exist, that the dangers and events you are seeing are really unfolding. For a certain period of time, you enter an imaginary world, where anything is possible, anything conceivable.

To use your creativity, you also must accept that for the time you need to be creative anything is possible, anything is conceivable. The worlds of reality and fantasy can overlap to a far greater extent than you now permit them. Creative people take real situations and shake a little fantasy on them, turning them upside down, or inside out. It doesn't take much. Fantasy is precious. A little goes a long way.

> The horse is here to stay, but the automobile is only a novelty, a fad.
>   *President of the Michigan Savings Bank, advising against*
>   *investment in the Ford Motor Company, 1905*

Invisible barrier number five is restrictive or defensive thinking. It's the idea that what I need to do first and foremost in life is to protect myself. It stems from the ancient concept that man's first and only mission on this earth is to protect himself, his family and his tribe. When you are in the defensive mode, you regard all the actions, words and ideas that come from strangers as potential threats. If you were a soldier manning the fortifications of some medieval fortress, or peering out from the muddy trenches on the eve of the Battle of Verdun in World War I, you would rightly interpret all sounds and movements as potentially hostile ones, yet this is the way most of us live our lives, constantly on guard, constantly vigilant, constantly defensive.

> There is no likelihood man can ever tap the power of the atom.
>   *Robert Millikan, Nobel prizewinner in physics, 1923*

> Who the hell wants to hear actors talk?
>   *Harry Warner, president of Warner Brothers Studios, 1927*

History is filled with examples of restrictive thinking. People have a difficult time imagining the value of anything new, anything different, anything which comes from outside the fortress or the trench.

Don't need it, and besides, probably won't work anyway! That's a phrase you hear a lot, if not out loud, then in your thoughts. There's judgment at work here, snap judgment it's often called, which says I won't waste my time considering it. For some of what we do, that kind of thinking works, but not when you need to be creative.

Creative thinking teaches us to defer the automatic "no" we use to deflect everything new. By turning the "no" into a "maybe", we make sure that we've considered the idea not only from our perspective, but also from every perspective. If we can do that, we're well on the road back to creativity.

When Daryl Zanuck said in 1946 that television wouldn't be able to hold onto a market, he was looking at things from a film producer's perspective. He neglected to take the perspective of the audience into account. We get so used to seeing things the way they are that any totally new situation seems improbable and impossible and because it does we feel justified in tearing it apart.

X-rays will prove to be a hoax. *William Thomson, Lord Kelvin, British physicist*

Avoid using the automatic and defensive word "no", so that ideas can be used as stepping-stones to other ideas. Replace the word, "no", with the words, "what if"

Subjectivity has doused many a good idea. It happens every day, countless times every day. Someone comes up with a new idea, and everyone around the conference table starts thinking and fretting.

What is this? What's in it for me? Does it really have a chance of going anywhere? If it gets approved, how's it going to affect me? How should I react to this?

What you're judging is not the idea but your relation to it. Behind "am I for it or not" lurks the question "is there anything in it for me?" If there's nothing for me, then why should I support it? If I'm not for it, then I must be against it, for if it does succeed, the guy who thought of it will look good, and I'll look bad in comparison. The "detect threat" bells go off in your head, and the sides of your mouth twitch nervously as you assemble your rationalizations as to why it can't possibly work. If it doesn't do me any good, you selfishly reason, why have it around at all? The result is another potentially good idea slain before it had a chance to breathe.

We don't like their sound, and guitar music is on the way out.
Response to the Beatles' music, by the giant American recording company Decca Records, 1962

You would make a ship sail against the wind and currents by lighting a fire under her decks? I have no time to listen to such nonsense!
Napoleon Bonaparte to Robert Fulton, inventor of the steamboat

Sensible and responsible women do not want to vote.
Former American President Grover Cleveland, 1905

Again we encounter the problem of the adequate. We get used to things being the way they are and we get used to seeing them in the same way, which is, in effect, not seeing them at all. When something new comes along, the adequate jumps in and tells you, hey, we don't need it. What we already have is fine. You thus tend to regard the new thing negatively and from only one narrow perspective. Your decision becomes, it won't work!

A plumber in Nottingham, England submitted a design for a tank to the British War Office in 1911. The design was studied and filed, and was not discovered again until World War I was over (the first war in which rudimentary tanks were used). The filed document bore the following official comment: "The man's mad!"

People like new ideas. They like to point out what's wrong with them so that they'll have a reason to reject them. After all, people aren't interested in you or your ideas. They're interested in themselves and will embrace your idea only when they see that it will not harm but in fact help them.

> **Law of the individual: Nobody really cares or understands what anyone else is doing**

Most people regard new ideas as powerful threats to their elaborate, invisible fortification systems, and refuse to even consider them. We are so sure of how things are that we lose all perspective of how things could be. It has often been said that the man with a new idea is considered an idiot until the idea succeeds. Since most people hate to be considered idiots, most good ideas get swallowed. Gulp! Think about it. You're flushing all your best ideas down the toilet.

> Every time a man puts a new idea across, he finds ten men who thought of it before he did, but they only thought of it.   *Anonymous*

Chester Carlson invented xerography in 1938, but companies, including IBM and Kodak, weren't interested in developing his idea. Why bother to spend money on a copy machine, they reasoned, when carbon paper was so plentiful and cheap?

> **Howe's law: Every man has a scheme that will not work**

This is true. Every man does have a scheme that will not work. They also have a scheme that will work.

In 1959, Ruth Handler approached several leading toy manufacturers with an idea for a new doll. "It's twelve inches tall", she told them, "and very lightweight." In response to the question, what does the doll do, she replied:

> You can move her arms and legs, and her head turns, but her eyes don't open and close, and no, she doesn't say mama, or anything else. She doesn't drink milk and she doesn't have a bottle. Actually this doll isn't a baby, but a grown-up woman and, like all women, she comes complete with her own wardrobe, which you have to buy separately. I named her after my eldest daughter, she added, after the toy executives finally stopped laughing. "Dolls are all babies," the businessmen pointed out. "Little girls will never buy this." After being turned

down by everyone else, she finally sold her idea to Mattel, a California-based company. Today, two Barbies are sold somewhere in the world every second.

*   *   *

Rail travel at high speeds is not possible because passengers, unable to breathe, would die of asphyxia.   *Dionysius Larnder, English scientist, (1793–1859)*

Can't act, can't sing, slightly bald. Can dance a little.
                Comment by a Hollywood executive on Fred Astaire's first screen test

What is now proved, was once only imagined.
                                William Blake, English poet, painter

If people stopped imagining all the reasons why things can't work and put their thinking to use to make them work, more things would work.

The person who says it can't be done should not interrupt the person doing it.
                                        Chinese proverb

In 1978, Sony Enterprises tried to design a small, portable stereo tape recorder. They failed. Instead they came up with a small, stereo tape player that couldn't record. The speakers also posed a problem, so they gave up the idea. Masaru Ibuka, then honorary chairman of Sony, saw the invention and remembered that they were working on developing lightweight headphones for a different project.

Even if we adopt headphones instead of speakers, the Sony executives reasoned, it still doesn't record. The idea that tape players record was so well established that no one ever contested it. Who would ever buy a tape recorder that couldn't record?

Sony finally decided to produce a limited quantity. The marketing group received only $100,000 for advertising and nothing for promotion. The anticipated target group was young people, but they failed to buy them. Instead, affluent, young couples (yuppies) responded and the rest is Walkman history.

William Harvey's discovery that blood circulated through the body was rejected for years by the medical community and he lost much of his medical practice as a result. When introduced, Joseph Lister's pioneering of antiseptic surgery was dismissed as bothersome housekeeping.

They couldn't hit an elephant from this dist…
        Last words of US General John Sedgwick at the Battle of Spotsylvania, 1864

Everything that can be invented has been invented. *Charles Duell, commissioner of the United States Office of Patents in a letter to US President McKinley, 1899*

In 1824, Louis Braille, then a French teenager, invented a new alphabet system to enable blind people to read. Previous efforts all suffered from a common error. All imitated the alphabet of people who had sight. Braille, who had lost his vision in an accident when he was three, based his method on a system which had been invented by French army Captain Charles Barbier de la Serre, called sonography. This system represented words phonetically so that soldiers could pass instructions at night without the need to speak or use lights. The system, which used 12 raised dots to represent different sounds, had been rejected by the army as being too complicated. Braille simplified Barbier's system into one of 6 raised dots so that a fingertip could feel all the dots at once. In 1834, he demonstrated his code to the world at the Paris Exposition of Industry. King Louis-Philippe, who presided over the opening, like others, did not understand the significance of the invention and judged it an amusing trick. When Braille died in 1852, not a single Paris newspaper noted his passing. His invention has now been adapted into nearly every language on earth, from Albanian to Zulu and is still the major medium of literacy for blind people.

Many new inventions are basically improvements on older ideas. The key in this case was simplification. In other instances, it's addition, substitution, enlargement or a reversal of the normal order of things. It is foolish and dangerous to say that something that does not work will not work, yet we do it all the time. Other medical researchers had observed that penicillin mold checked the growth of bacteria on an agar plate, before Alexander Fleming did. Fleming, however, realized that the mold might also inhibit the growth of microorganisms in the human body. His work paved the way for antibiotics.

> Make it a habit to keep on the lookout for novel and interesting ideas that others have used successfully. Your idea needs to be original only in its adaptation to the problem you are working on.   *Thomas Edison, American inventor*

When Nicolas Copernicus presented his idea that the sun rather than the earth is the center of the solar system, he was ridiculed. Martin Luther commented that Copernicus wanted to reverse the entire science of astronomy and called the Italian a fool. When Galileo took up Copernicus's idea, he fared no better. He was called a madman and would have been executed as a heretic if it weren't for the intervention of influential friends.

> The human mind treats a new idea the way the body treats a strange protein. It rejects it.   *Sir Peter Medawar, British zoologist*

Restrictive thinking in education

With rare exceptions, schools do little to encourage creative thinking. American schools are often rated among the best when it comes to stimulating creative attitudes. Schools in developing countries and Asia tend to be among the strictest and among the worst. Still, the majority of schools in the USA have a long way to go.

> Modern education has made great strides in encouraging inventiveness, but it still has a long way to go before it can completely rid itself of the urge to suppress creativity.   *Desmond Morris, British zoologist, anthropologist*

The real purpose of education is to replace an empty mind with an open mind, yet this goal is rarely achieved. Instead, we cram information into students and to be sure it is retained, we test them. The emphasis is on data retention instead of data application. In today's changing world, a world in which data is more and more abundant and available and the need to apply data more and more important, most teachers still cling to the classic notion that data retention exams are the only way to evaluate students.

> Tell me and I'll forget. Show me and I'll remember. Involve me and I'll understand.   *Confucius, Chinese philosopher*

Traditional education is based on the need to be right all the time. Throughout education, one is taught the correct facts, the correct deductions to be made from them, and the correct way of making these deductions. One learns to be correct by being very sensitive to what is incorrect. This is true outside the classroom as well, when children are taught what is and what is not socially correct. Emphasis on the need to be correct all the time (not to be wrong, look silly or be different) shuts out creativity because it stops you from taking illogical pathways, and prevents ideas from forming and linking. People hate being wrong or ridiculous, even though they might accept it in theory.

Teachers often frame an answer to a question so that only the particular word or phrase they are thinking of will be accepted. The students may come near the answer without actually hitting it. To expect a precise answer to most questions and tolerate no other is a shame, yet teachers do it all the time.

How many times does two go into four? The answer "twice" is a fine, acceptable answer, and most people believe it to be the one and only answer. "Every time" is just as good an answer, however. By insisting on narrow and rigid answers the teacher may think he or she is getting results, while in fact they are stifling invention and creativity.

Which comes first, marriage or divorce? The normal answer is marriage, but that's not the only answer. Divorce can come before marriage if someone is already married, falls in love with someone else and wants to remarry. It's perhaps not the majority of cases, but it does represent a significant amount. Can you think of another way of justifying the statement that divorce always precedes marriage? One answer: In the dictionary. You will always find divorce before marriage in the dictionary. A philosopher may also point out that divorce from one's parents or from a single type lifestyle always precedes marriage.

Let's look at yet another simple problem. Women who are citizens of Country A and are at least twenty-one years old all have the right to vote in Country A. So:

- My secretary is twenty-eight years old.
- My secretary is a citizen of Country A.
- My secretary has beautiful hair.

Therefore my secretary has the right to vote in Country A. True or false? How can you justify the answer, false? The secretary could be a man, and there is no mention that men in Country A have the right to vote. Ah!

This problem is one of many that are used to demonstrate logic. It is widely assumed that highly creative people aren't logical, yet many of the same principles apply. Lewis Carroll, the author of *Alice in Wonderland*, was also a mathematician and logician.

Edward de Bono has this to say about traditional education in *PO: Beyond Yes and No:*

> There is an absolute insistence on the need to be right all the time. Status in the classroom is tied to being right. It is tied to self-esteem. Being wrong is a matter of shame. In this way being right all the time acquires a huge importance in education, and there is this terror of being wrong. The ego is so tied to being right later on in life that you are reluctant to accept that you are ever wrong, because you are defending not the idea but your self-esteem.

Later in this book we will discuss direct, honest communication and cite instances when famous people, among them our elected leaders, were caught doing things they shouldn't have been doing. The reaction in almost every instance is initially to deny any wrongdoing. Only later does the real truth come out, and by then the public, even though they may have been inclined to forgive, has had to grapple with the dilemma that the official not only "erred" but lied.

When we take a position, our pride stops us from admitting that we could be wrong. When someone objects to our views, we are more concerned with fending off those objections than looking at how much truth there may be in them. We become defensive and search, often desperately, for fresh support for our position.

If you are right, anyone with an opposing view must be wrong. Therefore you will inevitably want to point out how right you are and how wrong he or she is. Naturally the other person will want to do the same. That's how arguments start. That's how fights start. That's how wars start. Both of you may be right. You may be simply starting from different points or different perspectives.

Most of us spend enormous amounts of time analyzing differences. We compare what we find or what is offered to us with what we know and have. We compare something that may be better with something that we know already works. We look for differences instead of looking for similarities. When we judge, it is usually between things, not among things or within things. People who begin to travel internationally are always struck initially by how different everything is. What they are doing is comparing what they find with what they know at home. If they go on and travel extensively, they eventually reach the conclusion that things are not so much different as they are the same. They do this when they stop comparing everything they find with one specific home base, and begin to look for similarities rather than differences. When you look for differences, you are rarely happy with what you find. When you look for similarities, the opposite is true.

Creative thinking is appreciated when it works. In academic settings that are based on empiricism and research, however, it is often looked upon with enormous skepticism.

In our universities, people want to be all equal. That means you cannot excel. Maybe that's good for stability, but it's not good for creativity.
Heisuke Hironaka, president of Yamaguchi University, Japan

Confidence and respect play important roles in learning. People who feel an emotional bond, and with it a high degree of confidence, with their teacher feel freer to be curious and therefore ask questions. Unfortunately, curiosity and questioning are qualities that aren't always rewarded in the classroom or, for that matter, in the workplace.

What's important in most careers isn't how much material you know, but how easily you can access information and apply it to the task at hand. Most education today is still directed almost solely at making students score high on exams. In other words, test scores have become almost the only academic performance of students in schools. Test-oriented teaching is a major culprit hindering the development of children's creativity and imagination in almost all disciplines of teaching.

The grading and testing processes focus on getting a preset answer that does not allow alternative ways to accomplish things or alternative results. You getting a particular right answer is then used to prove that you've learned something. That something may or may not be of use to you in the future. It will only be useful if you are confronted with a very similar situation that requires a similar answer. Exams should not simply test what you've been taught, but rather if you can apply that knowledge to other sets of circumstances. Schools cannot possibly give you all the answers. They should teach you how to go about finding the answers when there is no one there to provide them.

When it comes to assessment, teachers need to understand that a student who can only spit back facts cannot be expected to solve an unfamiliar problem or create something new.

Restrictive thinking in the workplace

Like schools, the business world also does what it can to hinder the development of creativity. Although freedom and change form the basis of creativity, try telling an interviewer that you left a previous job because you needed a change, or that the environment on the job was not giving you the freedom you needed. People are supposed to leave jobs for more money or opportunity, not for a change, yet change is absolutely vital if you want to be creative.

In the creative departments of large advertising agencies you will find art directors and copywriters. Art directors are people with fine arts backgrounds, who are responsible for the idea and concept of the ad as well as the visual image. The copywriter's responsibility is the written or spoken word. Art directors and copywriters tend to change jobs frequently, every two to three years on the average. The advertising agencies know this and encourage it. Why? It's done to keep their people fresh and creative.

It's very difficult to operate on a highly creative level if your environment is routine, and the same people, the same offices and the same tasks make for routine. To be creative, you need change. Most office situations restrict an employee's creativity by restricting their freedom. The first thing that's restricted is physical freedom. You have to be there, if not everyone assumes you're not working.

Art Gogatz was once working for a direct-mail advertising agency in New York, when one of the vice-presidents asked for Fred C., one of the firm's account executives:

"He's out taking a walk," the vice-president was told. "He said he needed to think."

The vice-president's answer?

"Tell him to think on his own time!"

The following comes from Dostoyevsky's novel, *The Possessed*:

"What do you do?"

"I work."

"What kind of work?"

"I think."

Too often we have the feeling that we're not being paid to think, just to have our bodies in a certain place for a specified amount of time.

To be creative, you need distraction. You need to break your concentration.
You need to take walks. You need to move. You need freedom.
Most of all you need freedom

To think is to differ.   *Clarence Darrow, American lawyer*

The trend among some advertising agencies today is not to give their creative people offices, but instead give them the freedom of working wherever they choose. In traditional companies people get very upset if you tell them they don't have an office, or a desk, or a half a desk, or a space, just a job to do.

"Where am I supposed to work?", they usually blurt out.

"Anywhere you want. Just bring me the work on time."

In the new type of agency one is like a freelancer, except one is on staff. The freedom which comes from a lack of physical restraints and managing one's own time is essential for creative people, but is still something which non-creative people (both employer and employee) don't handle very well.

Procedures and meetings have more to do with mistrust, control and monitoring than with motivating or innovating. Every office has its self-appointed sheriffs, people whose main preoccupation is tracking down and keeping tabs on everyone else. A lot of executives are also sheriffs. The role of the sheriff is a tiring one because it is steeped in negativity and based on mistrust. Trust forms the basis of all relationships, personal and professional, yet the work system which insists that some supervisor monitor where we physically are between nine and five shows very little trust indeed.

> The purpose of any good system is to liberate people to do their most creative work, to free them up, not tie them down, to give them power, not to control them

What most companies seek from outside consultants is a better way to control others. "How do we get those people to...?" is what the consultant often hears which really means "how do we get them to do what we want?", or "how do we control them?" The disease that is still afflicting most firms today is overcontrol, and control is most exercised by the people who are defining reality.

Managers are taught to control and manipulate people, to get them to do what they (and the corporation) want them to do. Executive comfort derives from order, stability, predictability and focus – but the focus is on conformity, the conventional and implicit intolerance for new ideas. Predictably enough, behaviors become formalized, operations rigid, relationships autocratic, and vision shortsighted.   *Pedro Cuatrecasas, president, pharmaceutical research, Parke-Davis, in an essay in Ford and Gioia's* Creative Action in Organizations

Have you ever gone to your boss with what you thought was a terrific idea, only to be disappointed when the idea was given less than a minute of the person's time?

Fact: People hate change. Those same people work for companies. Those same people are the ones evaluating your ideas. How receptive do you think they're going to be to a new (and because it's new, it will seem radical) idea?

Physical and intellectual freedoms are inseparable.

> You are not going to be creative if you feel either physically or mentally restrained

Forty reasons why we/it/they can't change

1. We've never done it before.
2. Nobody's ever done it before.
3. It's never been tried.
4. We tried that once, years ago.
5. Someone must have already tried it.
6. We've always done it this way.
7. It won't work in this company. We're not big enough.
8. It won't work in this company. We're too big.
9. It doesn't fit our operation.
10. What we have works fine.
11. You'll never get it approved.
12. We can't afford it.
13. It needs more work.
14. Production says it's a bad idea.
15. We don't have the personnel.
16. We don't have the equipment.
17. The union will scream.
18. We don't have the time to test it.
19. Customers hate change.
20. It's great, but ...?
21. You're on the wrong track.
22. The market's not ready yet.
23. With the market the way it is, we can't take a chance.
24. It needs committee study.
25. It's too radical.
26. It's too visionary.
27. It may work on paper, but ...?
28. How do you know it'll work? You're not an expert.
29. It's too simple.
30. I don't like it.
31. It's against all combined logic.
32. It'll take too long to pay out.
33. I already thought of that. But it dawned on me it wouldn't work.
34. If it fails, we'll all look stupid.
35. Not in this industry.
36. Marketing says it can't be sold.
37. Who is going to do it?
38. If it's so good, why isn't everyone else doing it?
39. It's not new.
40. It's impossible.

How to break through invisible barrier five

Barrier five is restrictive thinking. You can only break through this barrier if you make a conscious effort to consider things rather than rush forward the limiting word, "no."

When Albert Einstein was confronted with something, he would often say, "let me think about it," instead of giving an opinion or answer. In the US we rarely say, "let me think about it." Instead we hurry to answer every question posed, even if we have little knowledge of the topic, rush to give our opinions, rush to make decisions. We like things to be clear and simple, black or white, for or against, yes or no. This rush to judgment means that more often than not we rush the word "no" forward more than we do the word "yes". It's that sharp, snap, defensive "no" that destroys not only our own creative ideas but those of others as well.

1. Start to be aware of how many times you use the word, "no." Be aware too that the word, "no," comes disguised in many forms. Words like "difficult," "fail," "complicated," "problem," "poor," "hard" and "bad" are all ways of saying "no." Let me think doesn't mean let me think about it later, it means let me take the time to consider it and that's what you need to be creative, you need to look at something from as many angles and perspectives as possible before judging it.

2. Tell some of your good ideas (it could be for anything, a new business perhaps) to your family and friends. If you don't have any ideas, borrow some from books, magazines or the Internet. The purpose is to see how many and how quickly the ideas get shot down. Be careful how you present the ideas. If your friends think you're not serious about pursuing an idea, they'll probably humor you and go along with it. Once they believe you're serious, however, they'll hurry to point out all the problems.

    It is often said that if you believe you have a good idea, try it out on your friends and family. If they say you have a wonderful idea, you may be in trouble. An idea which people recognize as great probably is too late to have much impact. But if your friends look confused and shrug their shoulders, things are looking up. If they laugh and tear it apart, you know you're on to something. At least you'll know your idea is new.

    A few years ago someone got the idea of sending Hollywood film studios the original screenplays of some of the all-time most successful films. There was only one catch; the names on the screenplays were changed as well as those of the authors. You'd expect that the studios would have quickly recognized the ruse or that they would have been eager to produce the scripts, but no, almost all were quickly and unceremoniously rejected.

"Never ask"

We know what we are, but we know not what we may be.
WILLIAM SHAKESPEARE, *HAMLET*

Restrictive thinking starts at home. It is difficult to accept someone else's innovative idea when one's own life is governed by restrictive thinking.

A new idea is delicate. It can be killed by a sneer or a yawn. It can be stabbed to death by a quip and worried to death by a frown on the right man's brow.
Charles Brower, former president, Batten, Barton,
Durstone & Osborne advertising agency

A system of values, which comes from your heart rather than your head, will lead you to do things because you want to rather than because you feel you *should*. This is vital for creativity. Shoulds reflect what society wants, what others, your husband, your wife, your parents, your friends want, not what you want. You will automatically be more creative when you live from your own truth and values than when you adopt what others may think is right for you.

Most people don't ask themselves what they want, not what they really, truly want. Fewer people still ask their partners what they want.

How do you like what you have?

When was the last time you asked yourself this question? Try asking your partner from time to time what you can do to make him or her happier. It's a simple question, but people don't ask it. Is it because they feel they don't have to, the question embarrasses them, or deep down they really don't want to know? Try asking yourself. Stop every now and then and ask yourself, "Am I doing what I really want to do?"

Most people avoid the question because they are not in the habit of separating what they want from what they think is possible. Most people avoid the question because they know what they are doing is not what they want, and that what they want is impossible to attain.

If you find yourself limiting what you want based on what seems possible, you are censoring your vision. If you don't admit to yourself what you want simply because it does not seem possible for you to have it, you're censoring yourself.

If you can dream it, you can do it.   *Walt Disney, American film maker*

Dreams fade. When we're young, we don't worry that our dreams may be somewhat fantastic; in fact the more fantastic they are the more we like them. When we grow up, we get disappointed and hurt when we don't realize our dreams. To compensate, we scale them down. Realism dominates our thoughts and we are proud to have our feet on the ground. Too often this means that we no longer have any dreams at all.

Unfortunately dreams are our first casualty in life. People seem to give them up, quicker than anything, for a reality.   *Kevin Costner, American actor*

Janice R. is an educational assistant in one of the universities in southern England. Last time Reuben Mondejar was teaching there she mentioned that she was going through a divorce after many years of marriage. They got to talking and she revealed that she had always wanted to be an actress, but her parents (her father had been a career army officer) refused to let her.

"I regret it to this day," she revealed. "Even though my parents are dead, I still blame them."

"Well, you're on your own now," Reuben told her. "Your children are grown. There's nothing to stop you pursuing your dream."

"You're right," she agreed. "Maybe I will finally do it."

If you wait for the perfect moment, when all is safe and assured, it may never arrive. Mountains will not be climbed, races won or lasting happiness achieved.
                Maurice Chevalier, French actor

Sensing that Janice was just agreeing that it was something she could do, but probably would not do, Reuben pressed on.

"You can study in the evenings. I know a group that meets on Tuesdays. Why don't you call them?"

"No," she sighed. "I couldn't do that. With the divorce and all, I'm not ready emotionally. Maybe next year."

Her answer really wasn't surprising. She blames her parents for not letting her study acting, yet she herself never tried.

"Even as an adult, I didn't want to disappoint my family," she said, thoughtfully. "For them being an actress was like running off to join the circus or becoming a prostitute. Later, my husband never encouraged me, so here I am."

> Experience is what you get when you don't get what you want

Most people pretend that they don't really want what they want because they're not ready to risk what it would take to get it. Instead they look for excuses so that they don't have to act on their dreams and visions. Not acting out our dreams is the easy way. It lets us skirt failure. Don't sell yourself short. Your potential is undoubtedly much greater than you have ever realized. Next time you think you won't be able to do something, remember that the past does not dictate the future.

The saddest summary of a life contains three descriptions: could have, might have and should have.   *Louis Boone, American educator and writer*

We all have things we could have done, might have done and should have done. Creative people just seem to have less "coulds, mights and shoulds" than other people. They manage to do more of the things they want to do. Think about that! They're doing more of the things they *want* to do. Why aren't you? Don't blame other people. Don't blame situations. You're holding yourself back you, and no one else!

Twenty years from now you will be more disappointed by the things that you didn't do than by the things you did do.   *Mark Twain, American novelist*

> Pay attention to your dreams. Nurture them. Look after them. Treat them as if they were your children. Don't give up on them. Never abandon them. They are part of you. They are you

But aren't all dreams childish? Don't we make fun of people we call dreamers? Why wish for something when you know you can't have it or achieve it? The reason is that without the wish, the reality would have no chance of ever happening.

A man will never do everything he dreams, but he will never do anything he doesn't dream.   *William James, American psychologist, philosopher*

The moment we label our dreams as fantasies we kill them, for dreams may be nurtured but fantasies must be abandoned.

Carl S. is a professor of information technology at a US university. His profile is typical of many others:

> I tried several of the fine arts, with little success. In grade school, I tried painting but soon realized that I'll never become a Michelangelo or Picasso. In college, I tried the guitar but realized that I won't be a Carlos Santana. Finally, I gave up my pursuit to be someone "different" and decided to carve out a boring life studying and working, which were less demanding of special skills.

You don't need to be a Michelangelo or a Carlos Santana and you don't need special skills. What you need is desire, the burning desire to do what you want to do, not only what you think you can do. In fact, most people don't know what they can accomplish, simply because they are never encouraged. The sad reality is that people don't encourage each other. Deep down, they're jealous, in fact, deeply jealous that someone else may exceed them, so they will rarely encourage you to do something they couldn't do.

> Any man who selects a goal in life which can be fully achieved has already defined his own limitations.
> *Robert Cavett, American writer*

Pay attention

Creative people observe and listen. They pay attention. Attention to what? To everything, but especially what they are feeling, what they are sensing, (intuition), what they are thinking, the subtle things around them, but more importantly what they want. They always try to do what they want, not at the expense of others and not on an everyday basis, but in the long term.

> Being entirely honest with oneself is a good exercise.
> *Sigmund Freud, Austrian founder of psychoanalysis*

All dreams are difficult to realize. How much effort do you think it will take to achieve your dream? It could be securing a scholarship, playing a sport to at a certain level, or maybe losing weight. How much time do you think it will take you to achieve your goal? After you have an answer, apply the "100 rule." You can achieve your dream but it will require 100 times your estimate. Are you still willing to try? A successful person is someone who tries, who focuses and pours all his or her energy and devotion into a single dream. Unsuccessful people pour part of their energies into the dreams of others. Which one do you want to be?

"I want to change jobs."

"Why?"

A simple question, but what a question! The question demands that you come up with rational reasons. Many things we want, really want, don't make sense, yet we've been taught that everything we do should make sense, and that everything should have a logical sequence and meaning.

It is often said that reasons and shoulds are the whores of society.

"I want to change jobs."

"Why?"

"Why? Because I'm bored. I'm not going anywhere"

"Yeah, well. You think I'm not bored in my job?"

"I'm bored, but I'm not going to change, therefore you shouldn't change either." We hear this kind of argument all the time. It is a type of argument that pushes you toward conformity, and away from doing what you really want.

> I'm not to listen to reason. Reason always means what someone else has to say.
> *Elizabeth Gaskell, English writer*

The major decisions in life should be made with the heart, not with the head. The heart reflects your true personal desires, while the head tells you what you, as a member of society, think is good for you.

> When making a decision in vital matters, such as choice of a mate or a profession, the decision should come from the unconscious, from somewhere within ourselves.
> *Sigmund Freud*

People aren't jealous of those who dream, people are only jealous of those who follow their dreams. Tell someone you plan to open your own business and you'll hear something like this:

> Do you have any idea how many new businesses fail every year? Eighty percent! I've heard that eighty percent of all businesses end up going under. It takes money to start a business, and a lot of it. Who's going to lend it to you? Someone must have tried this idea of yours before, you know. You're not a

genius. You don't know beans about marketing. What are you going to do if it fails? If I were you, I wouldn't waste my time even thinking about it.

In less than a minute the person, perhaps one of your best friends, has already opened and closed your business and is feeling sorry for you. What they're really doing is feeling sorry for themselves. It's not so much that misery loves company, it's more, no one has the right to do what I won't do. People who don't own stocks, and who ought to be indifferent to the fluctuations of the market, are often secretly happy when the market goes down, for they're able to tell themselves, "see, stocks are a gamble. I may not have gained like some of the people I know, but at least I haven't lost anything either."

> All men dream, but not equally. Those who dream by night in the dusty recesses of their minds wake in the day to find that it was vanity, but the dreamers of the day are dangerous men, for they may act on their dreams with open eyes, to make it possible.   *T.E. Lawrence, British soldier, known as Lawrence of Arabia*

People are jealous of dreamers because in the quest for their goals, dreamers often don't adhere to reason, etiquette, or the rules that society imposes. Reasonable people feel that everyone else should be reasonable too. Timid people feel that everyone should be timid too. Fearful people feel that everyone else should be fearful too. In fact, most people feel that everyone else should do exactly what they do. The advice they give pertains to what they would or would not do, and not to what's good or not good for the person asking for the advice.

Ask some of your friends what they dream about achieving over, say, the next three to five years. A lot of the answers you get will be vague. This is because the question is not one which people like to think about. It's a difficult question for a lot of people, first because you're combining words which people don't usually put together, dream and achieve, and second because of the time frame. Most adults are convinced that they won't be able to achieve their dreams, and so they scale them back to the point where they become attainable (at that point they rarely resemble the initial dream), or peg them so far into the future that they never have to deal with them. The majority of the answers will reflect reasonable goals which the person believes to be fully attainable. If you point this out and press your friends for things which they dream about achieving, they may even become annoyed. The subject is one they just don't want to think about. While they're fully convinced that they're not going to get what they want out of life, they have yet to accept responsibility for it.

I'd rather regret the things I have done than the things I have not.

Lucille Ball, American actress

Listen to thyself

The basis of Greek philosophy was, know thyself. The basis of creativity is, listen to thyself.

On a scale of 1 to 100, how good a listener do you consider yourself? On the same scale, how do you think the following people would rate you as a listener?

- Your best friend
- Your boss
- A business colleague
- Your husband/wife or partner

The average answer for "how good a listener do you consider yourself" in the USA is slightly over 50. The highest rating is bestowed on the person's best friend, the lowest given to one's husband or wife.

When the same question is asked of highly creative people, the initial answer (how good a listener do you consider yourself) jumps to slightly over 80 and is the highest answer. Best friends now come in second. All answers are higher than the average. This says that highly creative have more self-confidence than non-creative people. It also affirms their faith in their ability to listen. Listening demands openness, trust and respect. It's more than patiently hearing other people out. It's being able to forget about yourself and what interests you and forge an emotional bond with someone. In conversation, it means listening instead of impatiently waiting to add you own thoughts or experiences.

Listening, like most things, starts at home. You can't really listen to someone else if you don't listen to yourself.

I think deep down all of us know what we want to do, but most people say, before I do that I'd better do this in case that doesn't happen, so I'll have something else to fall back on.

Eddie Murphy, American actor

Michel and Helene D. live in northern France. They have two children ages 13 and 9. Michel is 47. He is the director of an art therapy studio that is part of a regional psychiatric hospital. Helene is a psychologist in the same hospital. Both studied art and continue to paint. Michel has had numerous exhibitions and some success with his painting. He feels fortunate to have a job where he can paint. He is, however, restricted in terms of what he can and cannot do there. Anything bold or provocative would upset the patients. Bringing in models from outside is also not permitted. Michel paints at home, but the environment with two children is also not conducive to anything provocative, or challenging.

"You need a separate studio," Art Gogatz told him, last time he visited. "You're also not working with other artists. You're working alone, in a vacuum and your work will soon start to reflect it."

Michel agreed.

"Have you considered going to one of the artist's colonies, where you have the benefit of interaction with different kinds of artists?" Art asked? "A lot of them are run in the summer."

"Yeah, but vacation has to be with the family," Michel sighed.

"What about your job? You're been there almost fifteen years. Have you ever thought about changing?

"All the time," he answered. "In terms of my painting I know I have to move on. You just keep putting it off."

"Putting what off?" his wife flared up. "Quitting? Oh no! Eight more years and you'll be eligible for an early retirement. After that you can paint all you want."

Michel and Helene don't have the same idea about his art. For him it's all consuming, it's what he loves, it's what he wants to do. She considers it his hobby.

> Hobby: Something that a person likes to do or study in his or her spare time

Many people are stopped from pursuing their goals because they fear they won't be successful. "You'll never make it," they convince themselves. "It makes no sense even trying!"

Compared to what we ought to be, we're only half awake. The human individual lives far within his limits.
                                                                    William James

There is nothing with which every man is so afraid as getting to know how enormously much he is capable of doing and becoming.

Søren Kierkegaard, Danish philosopher

Most of us never come to really completely know ourselves. We focus on what we think we are instead of what we can be and never appreciate how much more we could do if we just gave ourselves the chance. Most of what we are ignorant of we choose to be ignorant of. In most cases it's because we just don't want to know.

Let's suppose you won a staggering amount of money in the lottery. What would be the first thing you'd do? Say the first thing that comes to your mind, without censoring it in any way. What would you do?

The answer most people come up with is quit working, then take a vacation, but the answer we're interested in is what would you do next? What would you do for the rest of your life? Would your answer be impossible without the money? Probably, but think about it. You can have whatever it is, you really can, but you're going to have to work for it, because no one is going to give it to you. You're not going to win the lottery. The odds say that if you buy a hundred tickets a day for the rest of your life, you'll still never win. Whatever you mentioned, become a professional golfer or a fashion designer, or even live the comfortable life on the French Riviera, is achievable, precisely because it's the thing you want most. The sad part is that it is rarely what you are presently working toward. What we work toward is what we think we can achieve, not what we want. That's sad, very sad.

Youth gets together his materials to build a bridge to the moon, or perchance a palace or temple on earth and at length, the middle-aged man concludes to build a woodshed with them.   *Henry David Thoreau, American writer*

Cecilia R. is a senior in high school in Bogota, the capital of Colombia, South America. Cecilia comes from a wealthy family. She's attractive and speaks English well. She won't have any problems getting into a good university. She wants to study theatre, but her father, a lawyer, warns her to keep it as a hobby. He wants her to study a solid career like law or business, one that carries little risk.

Part two of the argument goes like this: You can't afford it. We can't take the risk. Keep it as your hobby until you can make it pay, then and only then can you consider doing it as a career. The problem is that if you never do it full time, you probably won't progress to the point where you can make it pay. It will always remain a hobby. The desire for approval dominates the career choices of many young people. There's tremendous pressure to conform to narrowly defined images of success and study safe careers.

Art Gogatz relates the following incident:

> I knew a fifty-year-old man in New York who was the principal of a high school. One day he came home and told his wife that he wanted to become a lawyer. His wife told him he was crazy, that he was too old, and that he ought be thinking about retirement not about becoming a lawyer. Well, the man quit his job and went to law school and five years later passed the bar and became a lawyer.

*   *   *

> Common sense is the collection of prejudices acquired by age eighteen.
> *Albert Einstein, US physicist, mathematician*

We're proud to have common sense. We gladly let it dominate our thinking and our lives. Common sense, reasonable, logical, safe, common, regular, ordinary sense is what we convince ourselves we want. We let ordinary thinking dominate our lives. That's what we want. That's what we strive for. Is it any wonder that only two percent of adults are highly creative?

All highly creative people have a natural, automatic urge to create. Does this urge ensure success? Not always. For the creative person, however, success is something that is separate from the creative process. It is not the goal.

Modigliani, the renowned Italian artist who lived in Paris at the beginning of the twentieth century, died in poverty at age thirty-five without having achieved any shred of success. For most of his life he couldn't even give his paintings away. Too poor to buy materials, or sometimes food, he often painted on both sides of the same canvas. Through it all it was the process, which sustained him. He never once considered abandoning his art to take up another profession.

The highly creative person may spend months and years working on projects for which they know they may never be paid. Joe Eszterhas, the screenwriter of films such as *Basic Instinct* and *Flashdance*, wrote nine full-length screenplays before selling one. As a screenplay takes approximately four months to write, Eszterhas devoted three years of his life in work for which he received absolutely no pay. Three years isn't much when we consider the struggles of a Modigliani or a Van Gogh, yet the average person will not devote months, let alone years, to anything for which there is no guaranteed payback.

The most common ingredient for success is that people love what they are doing.

> **If you truly love something, you'll be successful at it**

> **Do what you love and love everything you do**

If you really care about something, you are more able to take risks to achieve it. If you really care about something, you won't abandon it the first time you fail. If you really care about something, you'll pour everything you have into it, and your enthusiasm will inspire others. If you really care about something, you'll have a better chance of success.

I write (music) as a sow piddles.   *Wolfgang Amadeus Mozart, Austrian composer*

What Mozart means is that he wrote music naturally, automatically, it just flowed, he couldn't have stopped it even if he'd wanted to. Fine, you say, Mozart was a genius, but what about me? Well, it's not a question of genius or talent. It's a question of desire and courage.

> **Desire is what matters, desire and love for what you do**

People ask how can a Jewish kid from the Bronx do preppy clothes. Does it have to do with class or money? It has to do with dreams.
Ralph Lauren, American fashion designer

Wherever you go, go with all your heart.   *Confucius, Chinese sage philosopher*

Ask yourself the following question: If you weren't going to get paid, would you still go to work?
"No! Why should I?"
"Because you love your work."
"I sure don't love it enough to do it for free!"
Creative people do. They're working for more than just money. They're in it for the love of the process. Think about it the next time you're getting ready for work. Is there anything else you'd rather be doing? Is going to work what you most want to do?

I think a person who takes a job in order to live, that is to say, just for the money, has turned himself into a slave.

Joseph Campbell, American author, educator

An entrepreneur who starts a business usually ends up working 15–16 hour days. The breakeven point for a new business is usually a year or more after it opens. Therefore for at least a year the entrepreneur works like crazy and makes no money. Studies, however, show that entrepreneurs often consider the first year of that business to be the most exciting time of their lives.

I never did a days work in my life, in was all fun.

Thomas Edison, American inventor

Choose a job you love and you will never have to work a day in your life.

Confucius

It is astonishing how little people know about their feelings. Their lives pass by as a featureless stream of experiences, a string of events. Creative people are in close touch with their emotions. They always know the reason why they're doing something, although that reason may not always be a logical and therefore explainable one. They are sensitive to pain, boredom, joy and other emotions. They are quick to leave if they are bored and quick to get involved if they are interested. They are aware of their inner states without having to become self-conscious.

A student of Zen asks his master to tell him the three secrets of life:

"First, pay attention," the master replies. "Second, pay attention. Third, pay attention."

Pay attention to what? Pay attention to what you're feeling, to what you want. Most people don't ask themselves what they want because they are afraid to know, afraid that whatever it is won't be attainable, afraid that it will alienate their family and friends, or even afraid that what they truly want won't conform to the norms of accepted society.

Even the bravest of us rarely has the courage for what he really knows.

Friedrich Nietzsche, German philosopher

People who are frightened by their thoughts cannot express them. Instead they repress them, so they are not even aware they exist. Freud referred to this as the superego.

The creative person walks a fine line, for what he knows, what he really knows, his wants, his desires, his dreams and also his demons lie closer to the surface of his personality. This is his great strength, his inkwell of ideas, his waterfall of expression, but it's also a volatile cargo. For most people it's easier never to ask, easier never to know.

I didn't know I was a slave until I found out I couldn't do the things I wanted.
Frederick Douglas, American journalist

Most people would consider that statement an exaggeration. Not creative people. They understand exactly what Frederick Douglas meant.

Children and creative adults derive great pleasure from doing what people say they cannot do. They hate to be told they can't do something, they hate rules and restrictions, they hate limitations and they don't easily accept the word, "impossible."

Do you think I should do it? The important question is not really should I do it, but do I want to do it?

- Should I call him?
- Should I ask her out?
- Should I buy it?

It's obvious that the person wants to. They're just looking for a push, something to back them up, a reason, something that makes sense, some logical, rational, sane reason, in other words, a reason that other people can accept.

"What do you want, really, truly want?"

"I want to become an astronaut."

"Why don't you?"

"I don't have the qualifications. Besides, I'm too old now."

"The issue then, is not why don't you, but why didn't you?"

What do you want to be when you grow up? How many times were you asked that as a child? Plenty, if you grew up in the US and perhaps less often if you grew up elsewhere.

"Don't ask me what I want to be. The only thing that matters is what I can be."

That happens in the USA too, but only when the kids get a little older. Once they're in their teens, the "what can I be" begins to carry as much weight as "what do I want to be." By the time they reach decision-making age, "what can I be" dominates.

Don't let what you *think* you cannot do interfere with what you can do. Don't let what other people *think you can't do* influence what you can do. Don't let what they can't themselves do influence what you can do.

Edward de Bono has this to say in his book *Six Thinking Hats*:

> From the past we create standard situations. We judge into which standard situation box a new situation falls. Once we have made this judgment, our course of action is clear. Such a system works very well in a stable world. In a stable world the standard situations of the past still apply. But in a changing world the standard situations may no longer apply. Instead of judging our way forward, we need to design our way forward. We need to be thinking about, what can be, not just about what is.

Knowledge is based upon what happened in the past, while all the decisions you face are based upon what will happen in the future. It takes courage not to be overly influenced by the past. It takes courage to cross bridges and it takes courage to burn bridges. It takes courage to be creative, although some people don't refer to it as courage, but madness.

Many business school students in Europe, when asked why they chose to study business, reply that they wanted to study a field in which they'd be able to find a job. If you ask them what else they would like to have studied, you often get an answer such as:

"Music. I've played the piano all my life. It's what I love."

"Why didn't you study music then?"

The answer? "Too difficult," or the standard, "I just wasn't good enough."

Somewhere, someone convinced them not to do the thing they love most because they wouldn't be good enough at it.

If you can dream it, you can do it

That's the fundamental difference between creative and non-creative people. Creative people truly believe that if you can dream it, you can do it. They have a different conception of the word, "impossible."

We all shy away from the impossible dream. It is, after all, foolish to go after things that are impossible. That's what most adults think, that it doesn't pay to waste time trying to do things we cannot do. There's a vicious circle at work here. How do we know what we can do and can't do until we try? Most of us underestimate our talents. Most of us never give ourselves a real chance.

If you can't be free, be as free as you can be.

Ralph Waldo Emerson, American writer

We all have good ideas, just as we all have dreams. Most of us never do anything with our ideas. We shelve them and eventually abandon them. There has never been a lack of good ideas, but the number of people who are sufficiently moved by an idea and have the courage to risk taking a stand to defend and push the idea is relatively small.

Atkinson and McCelland researched why people attempt certain tasks in their book *Achievement Motivation*. Some people tend to anticipate and fear failure, whereas others have an optimistic determination to succeed. They found that people with a fear of failure tackle:

- An easy task – they go on doing easy tasks over and over because there is no threat of failure. It is comfortable but they don't learn anything.
- A moderately difficult task – they do not want to start and will avoid this task at all costs because it might show them up.
- A very hard task – quite against reason they may attempt this task because it has the built-in excuse of being terribly hard. They anticipate failure.

Atkinson and McCelland found that people who have confidence in achieving success tackle:

- An easy task – they often get them wrong. They don't pay attention, it is too boring and they feel it's a waste of time.
- A moderately difficult task – they really respond to this type of challenge. Here is something worth trying.
- A very hard task – they do not attempt it. They have a clear idea of what they want to achieve and are prepared to wait until they have enough experience to try it.

Highly creative people have enormous confidence in their abilities to succeed. It's true that they often get bored with easy tasks and it's also true that they respond well to moderately difficult tasks. The difference with respect to the above findings is that highly creative people often attempt tasks which are very hard, if they are interested in the subject. They don't expect to fail. They expect to succeed because they have a different way of looking at the word "impossible." They also have a different way of looking at failure. They don't view it as an utter waste of time because it isn't the result that counted but the process. They will thus look upon the failure as a learning process, while the average person will view it solely as a loss of time and energy.

Let's go back for a minute to the person who wanted to be an astronaut. Is there any hope for him? Sure. He could become a writer or an actor. Neither profession has an age limit. Perhaps he could write a screenplay about astronauts. In order to do so, he'd have to put himself on a space shuttle. He'd have to imagine what it would be like and that imagination would have to be so intensely vivid that he'd feel he was actually there. If not, the viewers won't be able feel it. If you truly want something, you'll find a way. If you can dream it, you can do it.

> If you let conditions stop you from working, they'll always stop you.
>
> *James Farrell, American novelist*

Take a look at the following profile:

- As a boy he was a mediocre student and was told by one of his early teachers that he'd never amount to anything.
- At the age of fifteen, he was asked to leave school.
- He failed his first university-level entrance exam. When he finally was admitted, he did only average work and was turned down for a post-graduate assistant's position and denied a recommendation for employment.
- He got a job as a tutor at a boarding school, but didn't last very long.
- He submitted a thesis on thermodynamics for a doctoral degree, only to have the thesis rejected.

If you haven't guessed the person by now, the next clue should give you the answer. Four years after his theory on thermodynamics was rejected, he submitted his special theory of relativity for a doctoral dissertation at the University of Bern, Switzerland. It too was rejected. The person was Albert Einstein.

> If you let conditions stop you from being creative, they'll always stop you.
> If you let other people stop you from being creative,
> they'll always stop you

Consider the following:

A man who was born in the USA in 1809, failed in business in 1831.
He ran for the legislature in his home state and lost in 1832.
He failed once again in business in 1834.
In 1836 he suffered a nervous breakdown.
He lost a second political race in 1838.
He ran for the US Congress and lost in 1843.
The same thing happened in 1846.
He ran again for Congress in 1848 and was defeated.
He tried for the Senate in 1855 and lost, then for vice-president in 1856 and lost one more time.
Any normal person would have given up. He didn't. Again, he tried for the Senate. Again he tasted defeat.

Who was this man? He was Abraham Lincoln, elected president in 1860.

It is said that a man is not finished when he is defeated. He is finished when he quits. In creativity he is finished when he gives up his dreams, when he settles for anything less than what he wants, when he tells himself, it makes no sense even trying.

Nearly every man who develops an idea works it up to the point where it looks impossible, and then he gets discouraged. That's not the place to become discouraged.
Thomas Edison

Success is going from failure to failure with great enthusiasm.
Sir Winston Churchill, British statesman, prime minister

The answer to, "who is creative," is *you are*, if not now, then as soon as you'll let yourself be.

What are the factors that we must overcome if we want to be more creative? They're the ones we acquired in adolescence. They're the ones that clip our wings. They're the ones that stop us from listening to our hearts.

Fear, inhibitions, negative personal judgment, concern for self-image, the need to outdo others, the need to impress, anxiety over living up to the expectations of others, and the pressure to conform are what we must overcome if we want to become highly creative once again.

How to break through invisible barrier six

This barrier, which includes, don't ask yourself and don't ask others, is another sturdy one. We all like to think we're honest with ourselves but in truth most of us are secretly afraid to admit that what we have, or what we probably will have, is really not what we most want.

ACTIVITIES

1. Make a list of the ten things that you most want in life. They can be things you want to possess or achieve. They can be anything at all, but it's important that your choice is not influenced by what you think you can do. If you do this correctly, it will take some time to put the list together.

    Now look at your list. How many of these things do you think you will succeed in doing or having? Your answer may be a scant two or three. Now ask yourself another question. How many of the things on your list do you think it's theoretically possible to have or accomplish? Your answer may now be the majority, even almost all. Then why don't you go out and accomplish the things you most want? Who or what is holding you back?

    Take another look at your list. How many of the things on it could you show to your friends and family? If your answer is most or all, you're probably self-censoring yourself. Many of the things we want, really want, we never admit to anyone, and often not even ourselves.

    Look again at your list. How many of the things on it have you ever really tried to do? How many times have you tried and failed?

    How many of the things on your list are what you personally want, and how many reflect what society or other people want?

2. Who are you? That's a good question. It has been said that the three hardest things in the world are diamonds, steel and knowing oneself.

    One of the creatures Alice meets in her wonderland is a caterpillar who sits on a mushroom and smokes a hookah. The caterpillar keeps asking her one question, who are you? If you had to answer the question, what would you say? In fact write down three words that you think best describe you as a person. Be honest. Don't be influenced by what people have told you in the past.

Once you've done that, ask yourself a couple of questions. Are you happy with all three words? Do you wish you could describe yourself differently? If your answer is yes, which words would you like to use?

Now ask other people, your friends, colleagues and family to give you the three words which best describe you. Compare your words with the ones you get from your friends. How does your image of yourself compare with the image others have of you? If there is a significant discrepancy it may mean that the real (or imagined) you is very different from the one you project. Creative people are pretty much open books; they share their thoughts and feelings with everyone. They keep very little inside. They don't hold back.

"What invisible defense shields?"

Fear is the biggest obstacle in life.
MOTHER TERESA, ALBANIAN-BORN CATHOLIC NUN,
MISSIONARY — NOBEL PEACE PRIZE

We all live behind invisible defense shields. They're the shields which protect us from potential slights and attacks upon our egos. Some of us have more extensive and elaborate shield systems than others. Keeping them up requires effort and there are times when we do let them, at least partially, down. When, where and for how long depends on the person we're with and the situation we're in, or perhaps how much we've had to drink. It's fear which forces us to live behind shields, and it's fear which stops us from becoming more creative. In order to become more creative, we have to let down our defenses.

If you ask people what they are most afraid of, the answers will range from spiders, mice and snakes, to ghosts, death, the dark, and the unknown. Often you will find the word "failure" on those lists. Rarely will you ever find the word, "freedom."

There is something uniform about the human race. Most of them have to work for the greater part of their lives in order to live and the little freedom they have left frightens them to such an extent that they will stop at nothing to rid themselves of it. Nothing has ever been more unendurable to man than freedom. *Fyodor Dostoevsky, Russian novelist*

This is a dictionary definition of freedom: *an exemption or liberation from the control of some other person or power. The absence of hindrance, restraint, confinement or repression.*

For an adult, freedom is linked to the acceptance of responsibility and that can be a frightening task. It means that to find a solution for any of the problems you face, you must ultimately turn to yourself and no one else. It means admitting that you, not circumstances, ultimately determine your success or failure. It means seizing control not only of time but also of your talents and weaknesses. It is you versus you, one on one. Nowhere in this world will you find a more worthy opponent.

Confronting a blank page or a blank canvas can be terrifying because you're confronting freedom, in fact, you're staring it in the eye. Most of the day is spent doing what we can, not want we want. But now, on that blank page or canvas, you suddenly have no restrictions. You can send men to the moon, bring them back, make them fall in love, bring their children into the world, or have them confront death. If you are writing a screenplay, novel or play, you are responsible not only for the characters and settings but also for the story, the action. Something has to happen. Will that something be interesting? Will the audience find your characters riveting? Where will your action take place? Can you make your audience or reader feel that they're actually there?

> Outside, among your fellows, among strangers, you must preserve appearances, a hundred things you cannot do; but inside, the terrible freedom.
>
> *Ralph Waldo Emerson, American writer*

The terrible freedom, the gay, mad, frantic freedom, the freedom that nurses you, seduces you, the freedom that owns you, that terrible freedom! Damn, is it precious! If you're creative, there's nothing more precious. Absolutely nothing in the world!

For the final project in his creativity class, Art Gogatz often gives his students a theme such as "22 centimeters below," and tells them to do whatever they want with it. The only instructions are that whatever the students do should incorporate and summarize the ideas and theories of creativity that were discussed in class, themes like perception, movement, boundaries, risk, taboo, intuition and emotionality. The students always bombard Art with questions. "Twenty-two centimeters below what?" is always the first question.

"Below whatever you want it to be below," Art explains. "You can use any media you want, photography, film, drawing, painting, sculpture. You can write something, you can do theatre, music. It can be as simple as a single spoken phrase. It can be anything."

"*Anything?*" they repeat, floundering for lack of guidelines, for lack of parameters, for lack of structure.

"What throws them," Art admits, "and you can see it in their eyes, is that you're not giving them enough instructions. It's the idea of freedom which makes them uneasy."

It has been said that there are millions of people who long for immortality who don't know what to do with themselves on a rainy Sunday afternoon. What stops them from creating? What stops them is the fear that whatever they create will not be accepted, and therefore they will not be accepted. In theory, everyone should be fully creative. People want to be, most just don't have enough willpower to overcome their fears.

For creativity to happen, something within us must be brought to life in something outside of us. What images do I put on a blank canvas? What words do I put on a blank page? What kind of business do I create? You are completely free to choose. That is either sublime or unnerving.

> A great wind is blowing and that gives you either imagination or a headache.
>
> *Catherine the Great, empress of Russia*

Breezes can give you imagination or headaches too, as can telephone calls, traffic jams, and virtually anything you encounter. Most people are afraid of having too much imagination. It's easier to deal with a headache.

That brings us back to the word "freedom." To be creative you have to want freedom, that terrible freedom, but in order to want it you have to overcome your fear of it.

One of the exercises we asked you to do at the end of the first barrier was to list three things you love.

When you ask people this question, the answers usually range from my family, my girlfriend, my husband and my car, to Venice in the rain, Central Park on Sunday afternoons, skiing, tennis, dancing, listening to music and sleeping. In fact, the answers run the gamut from A to Z.

There are two answers, however, which rarely appear, except when you ask highly creative people. These answers are:

- freedom
- my studies, my work, my career.

Over fifty percent of all Americans consistently report that they're dissatisfied with their work. That's staggering. In 1999, Monster.com, the international Internet job-search portal, asked its users this question: How long did it take you to find a job you like? Sixty percent answered that they were still looking. In another Monster.com survey in the same year, people were asked if they felt what they did at work made a difference in the world. Only eleven percent said yes.

People are generally only devoted to their work as a means to a materialistic end. Others may feel alienated, either by someone or some slight, a passed-over promotion, or an extra effort which was not appreciated. The fact is that most people do not like their jobs very much. Work is work and should not be enjoyable, they tell themselves. Wait! There's something very sad here.

The divorce rates in many industrialized countries are higher than they have ever been. That means more and more people in these countries are unhappy with the most basic, fundamental areas of their lives, and it's not something which is only confined to the industrialized world.

"I like my job, but I don't have to love it."

True, you don't have to, but you should at least love the career you chose. You should want to do it even if you weren't getting paid or, conversely, you should figure out a way to get paid for what you love. Creative people are lucky because what they must do is the same as what they most want to do.

"Thank God it's Friday."

"Why?"

"Because I don't have to work tomorrow. I can relax. I can do whatever I want. I'm free."

Do whatever I want? That's what creative people do all week long! For them a Tuesday is the same as a Sunday, except that the kids are home on Sundays. If your work is what you want to do, what do you care what day of the week it is?

> A man is a success if he gets up in the morning and gets to bed at night and in between he does what he wants to do.   *Bob Dylan, American singer/songwriter*

Concern for self-image

How am I doing? Is anyone noticing? Has anyone noticed how well I did, or how badly? Do these questions sound familiar? They should. They're ones we ask ourselves all the time. They're ones that inhibit our creativity. If you are overly concerned about what people think of you, you will avoid any topic or behavior that lies outside the realm of accepted thinking. Thus you will be excluding pathways that may lead to ideas and solutions. You will be shutting down your creativity.

A man who trims himself to suit everybody will soon whittle himself away.
Charles Schwab, American industrialist

Pressure to conform

Growing up means learning to live in the world, learning that we're a part of a family, a neighborhood, a community, a nation. We submit to the kind of judgment that has conformity as its goal. This judgment condemns, criticizes, attaches blame, makes fun of, assigns guilt, punishes and buries anything that, or anyone who, happens to be the least bit different.

I prefer my children to my cousins and my cousins to my neighbors and my neighbors to my countrymen.
Jean-Marie Le Pen, leader of National Front, French right-wing political party

And I prefer my countrymen to people from other nations, and people of my faith to those of other religions, and so on. This natural but dangerous attitude permeates the world and is the principal reason why war and violence continue to plague us.

> **The creative person shuns the group, the clique, the brotherhood, the gang and the mob**

For a creative person, the easiest thing to be is herself. The most difficult thing to be is what other people want her to be. For the non-creative person, the easiest thing is to be what others want her to be. To be yourself, in a world that is doing its best to bully you into being somebody else, is not easy. If everyone is thinking the same, then somebody isn't thinking.

For most people the desire to blend in overwhelms the desire to be unique and leads to the suppression of any personality traits that could be considered different. In effect, you let the world see only part of the real you. Creative people don't care what people think of them, so they're not afraid to bare everything, talents as well as weaknesses. Most people are afraid to show themselves to others and take refuge behind their invisible but highly effective defense shields.

By the time each generation has reached the point where its members could be fully creative adults, they are already burdened with a heavy sense of conformity. This prevents the vast majority of them from living up to their creative potentials.

Children are influenced by their parents, their teachers, the media and their friends and classmates. When peer acceptance becomes more important, they say and do many things not because they want to, but because those things gain them acceptance. Most adults still select their words and actions at least in part by what others want or expect from them.

Not all conformity is bad. For most of what we do each day, we need to conform to the rules of society. The shame is when we digress from what we believe in, in order to impress someone, be accepted or avoid appearing different. Once we begin to conform, we find ourselves saying and doing not what comes naturally but what we think others want or expect us to say.

Society instills us with values, which include ambition, consumerism and security. It gives us a plan for how to live our lives. To want something different is to walk a very lonely path, yet the notion of creativity is to seek out those paths. Being creative does not mean being lonely, it means being the first to strike a path, a path which will improve and better everyone who subsequently takes it.

> To be independent of public opinion is the first formal condition of achieving anything great.   *G. W. Hegel, German philosopher*

> A man is not hurt so much by what happens as by his opinion of what happens.
> *Michel Montaigne, French philosopher, writer*

And that opinion is entirely up to us. It's not up to others, it really isn't. That's something that creative people realize and when they do the feeling is electric and changes them forever.

Your opinion of what happens is yours and yours alone

Art Gogatz sometimes draws a group of stick figures on the board at the beginning of one of his creativity seminars, and then draws one lone figure outside the group:

> I then ask several participants to choose which of the figures on the board represents them. Almost everyone chooses to be someone in the group. To be creative, you don't have to always distance yourself from groups. What you need to do, however, is be *capable* of stepping away from groups from time to

time. You have to feel comfortable both inside and outside the group. This stick figure exercise is an absurdly simple one, yet one which demonstrates just how hard it is for people to stand by themselves.

When you conform, you're being intimidated into doing something because you're afraid to stand alone.

In modern society, the opposite of courage is not cowardice; it is conformity.

Rollo May, American psychologist

We are discreet sheep; we wait to see how the drove is going, and then go with the drove. We have two opinions, one private, which we are afraid to express, and another one, the one we use – which we force ourselves to wear to please Mrs. Grundy, until habit makes us uncomfortable in it, and the custom of defending it presently makes us love it, adore it, and forget how pitifully we came by it.   *Mark Twain, American writer*

Negative judgment

There are three levels of negative judgment that inhibit creativity.

Self-judgment

This is a voice from your past, a parent, a teacher or an adult. It's a voice of reason telling you to think and act the right way, meaning the way everyone else thinks and acts. You get many ideas every day that never come into your conscious awareness, because your own judgment so quickly and almost automatically rejects them.

In every work of genius, we recognize our own rejected ideas.

Ralph Waldo Emerson

Judgment from others

This is when another person labels you as you might refer to yourself. Because it sounds so much like your own voice of reason, you accept it as a confirming truth.

Collective judgment

Fashion dictates the way we dress, nationality establishes food preferences, social class establishes tastes. These invisible voices operate in your lives as sources of judgment. You are likely to conform to their dictates or feel guilty if you don't. The creative person must overcome conformity and the guilt associated with it.

> Conformity is the jailer of freedom and the enemy of growth.
>
> *John F. Kennedy, American president*

> Most of the things we do, we do for no better reason than that our fathers have done them or our neighbors do them and the same is true of a larger part than what we suspect of what we think.
>
> *Oliver Wendell Holmes, Jr, American jurist*

Becoming more creative is not easy. It involves getting rid of inhibitions and embracing subjects (taboos) which everyone else avoids. It involves seeing the world differently, and to do that you have to be the same as everyone and more. In order to see differently, you have to be capable of being different. People who are different all the time get locked up. Creative people are normal people who live in society, but who are not afraid of being different. Most people are not capable of being different because the desire to blend in overwhelms everything.

> **Nothing destroys creativity more than fears, concern for self-image, negative judgment and the pressure to conform**

> The one who follows the crowd will usually get no further than the crowd.
>
> *Anonymous*

One of the important characteristics of creative people is their refusal to define themselves and their work by other people's assessments. People in the arts do this all the time. They have to. Other examples from history are Thomas Edison, who was urged to quit school because he was considered dumb and Winston Churchill, who was labeled a slow learner.

> Creative people are different. This is not to say that they don't enjoy having the acceptance and support of others or that the possibility of losing friends doesn't bother them. It means that, however much they may want acceptance

and support and friendship, they don't need them the way others do. Instead of looking to others for approval of their ideas, they look within themselves. For this reason, they are less afraid of appearing eccentric and odd, are more self-confident, and are freer to speak and act independently.

Vincent Ruggiero, The Art of Thinking

The fashionable uniform

So many men, so many suits, dark suits, solid suits, blue suits that look some how gray, gray suits that look blue. So many suits, so many white shirts, so many dark ties.

Think about it next time you're getting ready to go to work. Are you wearing what you really want to wear, or are you wearing a type of fashionable uniform. The sad reality of it all is that most people actually want to wear a fashionable uniform.

Colmena is a large, South American savings and loan corporation. Like many companies, it has, and vigorously enforces, a dress code. All employees must purchase mix-and-match outfits from the company. Women have to buy four blazer-type jackets, seven blouses, three skirts, two pairs of pants and several pairs of shoes. Every morning they consult the company's calendar that tells them the jacket, blouse, skirt and shoes that must be worn that day. The company says the idea is to maintain a sense of harmony. Harmony, which is aesthetic uniformity, comes at the expense of creativity.

A lot of adults had to wear uniforms when they went to grade school. Private schools and religious schools are the largest proponents of the uniform idea. In the US children who go to public school don't usually have to wear one, but in the majority of countries round the world it's still the norm. What does it inhibit? It inhibits personal freedom and with it creativity. Highly creative people hate being told what to wear and how to look. They want to make those decisions themselves, rather than have fashion, society or business tell them what to wear.

The expression a woman wears on her face is far more important than the clothes she wears on her back.   *Dale Carnegie, American writer and educator*

Over the last few years many companies have adopted a casual dress day, usually Fridays. Casual dress day? What about the rest of the week? Ah, the rest of the week you wear the fashionable uniform.

Why can't you wear casual clothes whenever you want? Why can't you dress up on Fridays? Shouldn't that be your decision? Don't you think you're qualified to make it? Your job is telling you, even though we're paying you a lot of money, we don't think you're responsible enough to know what to wear. We're afraid you'll show up looking goofy, so we'll organize it for you. Monday to Thursday you dress up, and one day a week, the day we choose, you can wear the same casual uniform that everyone else here will wear. Creative people hate being told what to wear. They just can't stand it!

Casual dress Friday is, in effect, a dress code. It says, four days a week we all look the same, well dressed, and one day a week, the day the company chooses, we all look the same, casual. It's regimented, it's decided and it makes creative people scream.

It's the same mentality that says, even though we hired you, we don't trust you. We think that the moment you're not being watched, you'll goof off, so to prevent that we'll make you work in our offices, where we can keep our eyes on you. How much confidence does that show? Not much. Most people accept it. Creative people don't. They just don't!

The *International Herald Tribune* published an article on April 6, 2001 about the Cerner Corporation, a company which develops software for the healthcare industry, based in Kansas City, Missouri. The company's CEO had sent an internal email, which was leaked and subsequently posted on Yahoo! It read:

> We are getting less than 40 hours of work from a large number of our Kansas City-based employees. The parking lot is sparsely used at 8 am and the same at 5 pm. It should be substantially full at 7:30 am and 6:30 pm on weekdays and half full on Saturdays.

The memo shows a simplistic and all too prevalent gauge of success, measuring worker productivity solely by worker presence.

Some companies today, especially Internet companies, have permanent casual dress codes. Most of these companies are small, and most of the people who work there spend their days in front of their computers. A computer doesn't care what you wear. As soon as you have to go out and meet people, however, ah, that day you have to haul out the fashionable uniform.

I don't want to look different. I want to look distinctive

We're talking about degrees. Distinctive is a guy who wears a strange tie with his suit. Why wear a tie at all? Why wear a suit at all? Why not wear what you want to wear? You wear a suit because:

- It's expected.
- Everyone does. If you don't, you'll feel different.
- You feel secure in it. You feel that you'll be accepted.
- You have to.

Because you have to! Remember what we said before about things you have to do versus things you want to do?

Because it's expected. Who expects you to? All the other people who are wearing suits and ties expect you to. They have to wear them, therefore so do you. It's like the person who said, you think I'm not bored with my job? Just because you're bored doesn't give you the right to do something about it when the rest of us aren't doing anything.

Because everyone else does, and if you don't, you'll be different. Conform! Conform, or be looked at! Conform or be stared at! Conform or be talked about! Conform or be whispered about! Conform or be turned out, separated, excluded, alienated!

My God, don't let that happen to me, we all panic! Please let me blend in! Please let me run with the pack! Please let me swim with the school! Please let me follow the crowd!

> I would rather sit on a pumpkin and have it all to myself than be crowded on a velvet cushion. *Henry David Thoreau, American writer*

Because you feel secure. You feel secure because you look the same as everyone else. The thought of being naked might repulse you, yet if no one wore clothes, you'd soon want to get rid of yours. The clothes would make you feel different. That's why visitors to nudist parks often feel uncomfortable in their clothes. It's not the clothes or modesty or nudity that makes them feel uncomfortable, but the fact that they now look different from everyone else.

> Whoso would be a man must be a nonconformist. *Ralph Waldo Emerson*

That's a wonderful, but somewhat idealistic statement. Let's rephrase it. Whoso would be creative must be a nonconformist.

I don't know the key to success, but the key to failure is to try to please everyone. *Bill Cosby, American comedian, actor*

When you're faced with a decision, you can always follow someone's lead, do what others expect you to do, or do what you feel is best. The first and second are initially easier to do but, in the end, harder to live with. Always keep in mind that you are unique, and that what works for someone else may not for you. People can give you advice but they can't decide for you. They can decide for themselves but they can't decide for you. Only you can do that.

When Albert Einstein bought clothes, he bought them by the dozen, not because they were cheaper, but because he didn't want to waste time every morning deciding what to wear. Pablo Picasso also didn't pay a lot of attention to what he wore. He didn't care about impressing people. Extremely wealthy people, who are sometimes deemed eccentric, also often don't care. Highly creative people don't care. Who does care? People who need to impress others are the ones who care. People who are concerned about their images care. The key word is need. Some people need to impress others, while others don't.

The English writer Elizabeth Gaskell wrote about the need, or rather the lack of a need, to impress others, when writing about the ladies of Cranford:

> What does it signify how we dress here at Cranford, where everybody knows us? And if they go from home, their reason is equally cogent, what does it signify how we dress here, where nobody knows us?

Solomon Asch conducted what has now become a classic series of experiments on conformity in the 1950s. In most of his experiments, a group of seven–nine university students were each asked to match the length of a line shown on one card with one of three comparison lines shown on another card. The comparisons were easy to make. A control group averaged slightly over ninety-nine percent correct. What the subjects in the experiments did not know was that in every group all but one person were assistants of the experimenter. In most sessions, the group contained only one real subject.

In the first part of the experiment, the standard line was 10 inches long and the three comparison lines were 8¾ inches, 10 inches and 8 inches. Students gave their opinions in clockwise order around the table, and everyone said that the 10 inch long comparison line was equal to the standard line.

In the second part, the students were shown a standard line 2 inches long and the comparison lines were 2 inches, 1 inch and $1^1/_2$ inches in length. Again the students matched the lines without difficulty.

Unbeknownst to the subject, who always sat near the end of the group, in the third part the confederate students were instructed not to choose a 3 inch line as being equal to a standard 3 inch line, but to choose instead a line which was $3^3/_4$ inches in length.

Asch found that three-quarters of the subjects conformed on at least one trial, and one-third were influenced on half or more of the trials. Most students rendered at least some judgments that contradicted their senses and many conformed on the majority of the trials.

> A man who wants to lead the orchestra must turn his back to the crowd.
>   *Anonymous*

In his book *The Psychology of Judgment and Decision Making*, Scott Plous relates an interesting experiment conducted in the 1970s by Bibb Latane and John Darley. They invited students to be interviewed on the subject of life at an urban university in the USA. When students arrived, they were seated in a waiting room, either alone, with two other people who were assistants of the experimenters, or with two other students who knew nothing of the experiment. As the students waited, white smoke began to pour into the room through a vent in the wall. Seventy-five percent of the students waiting alone reported the smoke, half of them within the first two minutes. In contrast, only one out of ten ever reported the smoke in the presence of the two other people (the assistants) who remained inactive. Of the groups of three students who waited together, only thirty-eight percent reported the smoke. The experiment was repeated several times in different circumstances, with similar results.

Is there any group of people who are immune from the inhibiting effects of other people? According to the results of a review by Bibb Latane and Steve Nida in 1981 (cited in Plous 1993), there is one such group, children under the age of nine. After that, the decision to intervene is heavily influenced by the presence of others.

How to break through invisible barrier seven

The first step in breaking through this barrier is to admit that you do use invisible defense shields to protect yourself. There is nothing wrong with having shields, in fact they are necessary. It's just that creative people use them sparingly, while most people have them up virtually all the time. Letting your shields down is actually easier than you think. All you really need to do is begin to be less concerned with what other people think of you, and to do that you will have to become less self-centered (or less interested) in yourself. The best way to do that is to become more interested in other people.

ACTIVITIES

1. Write your own epitaph. Some of you may find this exercise a touch morbid, but it's really not. Anyway, the creative person mustn't shrink from any subject, even death. An epitaph doesn't have to be long. It can easily be a paragraph, or just a few sentences.

    Okay, now look at what you wrote. Does the epitaph talk more about the things you accomplished in life or does it mostly describe you as a person? If it's heavy on description, it may mean that you are overly concerned with your image.

2. When you are invited to a business or social gathering, are you:

    - Concerned about your physical appearance?
    - Do you consciously change the way you stand and move?
    - Are you aware of who may be looking at you?
    - When someone is talking, do you listen or do you find yourself thinking about the impression you're making?
    - When someone is talking to you, are you listening or are you thinking about what you're going to answer or contribute?
    - Does concern for self-image prevent you from really seeing and listening to other people?

3. What did you wear yesterday? That shouldn't be too difficult to answer. Most people are able to remember what they wore the day before. How about your husband, wife or partner, do you remember what they wore yesterday? Ah, that's more difficult, isn't it? Most people, in fact, can't remember. How about your boss or teacher, your assistant or a colleague at work, your best friend, do you remember what any of them wore yesterday? If you can't remember what they wore, you can be sure they don't remember what you wore. Think about that the next time you're fretting about what to wear in the morning. Think about that the next time you start to worry about what people think about you.

4. The famous Russian novelist Dostoevsky would often briefly follow people he saw in the streets of St. Petersburg. If, for example, it was an old lady, he would begin to imagine where she lived, what her name was, if she had children and what kind of relationship she had with her family. He did it to help him create the vibrant characters of his novels, but you can do something similar to help you begin to heighten your powers of observation.

How many people did you see yesterday? Dozens or perhaps even hundreds, but how many did you really see? How many do you remember? You probably only saw (or paid attention to) the ones you know. The rest you didn't bother to look at. Start. Start being more interested in other people for their own sake, and not only for how they interact with you. Creative people are not at all concerned with their images when they need to be creative.

"I can conform from nine-to-five and still be a nonconformist"

The glass is half-full and the glass is half-empty are descriptions of the same phenomenon but have vastly different meanings. Changing a manager's perception of a glass from half-full to half-empty opens up big innovation opportunities.
PETER DRUCKER, AMERICAN MANAGEMENT CONSULTANT

The question is what kind of nonconformist will you be? You'll probably succeed in being a nonconformist among conformists, but you may not measure up very well among real nonconformists. It's the same thing with creativity. In every family, in every circle of friends, in every office, someone is more creative than everyone else. Whether that person is indeed highly creative, or only slightly creative depends on whom you compare them to.

We've been talking about highly creative people in this book and those people find it difficult to conform at any time of the day. Remember, if you are highly creative, it will touch everything you do.

Highly creative people can cope with business environments. However, they find many corporate environments restrictive and attempt to change them. Highly creative people generally do better in small businesses or entrepreneurial roles than they do in large corporations. Among businesspeople, the word "creativity" is a difficult one to tolerate because it is interpreted as being vague and undefined. They prefer the word "innovative" to creative. In business, the creative spirit is seen as being both volatile and valuable. Businesspeople want innovation, they just want it to come from normal (normal here meaning manageable) people and situations.

The glass is half-empty or half-full is an example of the ability to see other perspectives. Most managers cannot do that regularly because they have never been taught to do so.

A competitive advantage

A company's ability to innovate is an important competitive advantage. Firms which know how to encourage innovative thought are able to respond more rapidly to market changes and customer needs than firms who do not.

Most businesses would agree that creativity is important to their long-term survival, yet most also don't really know how to go about fostering it. Most don't have structures that encourage innovation. The people in the middle of most companies generally do not see the top executives acting as though they really want innovation. In fact, it's usually the opposite. Management says it wants employees who participate more and employees agree that they want to be more involved, but neither side really understands or trusts the other. The battle between autonomy and control is a bloody one. It is only when top management shows a willingness to take risks, and a tolerance for those who do, that creativity will flourish in the world of business.

In her book *The Change Masters*, Rosabeth Moss Kanter asserts:

> As long as segmented structures and segmentalist attitudes make the very idea of innovation run against the culture grain, there is a tension between the desire for innovation and the continual blocking of it, by the organization itself. Thus the primary set of roadblocks to innovation result from segmentation: a structure finely divided into departments and levels, each with a tall fence around it and communication in and out restricted, indeed carefully guarded. Information is a secret rather than circulating commodity. Hierarchy, rather than team mechanisms, is the glue holding the segments together, and so vertical relationship chains dominate interaction. Preexisting routines set the terms for action and interaction and measurement systems are used to guard against deviations.

Most corporations aren't good at long-range planning because their executives are too concerned with protecting their own personal careers.

One of the problems with companies is that we tend to consider them differently from people, yet in fact people are a corporation. We think of psychoanalysis in terms of individuals, their worries, their irrationalities and their fears, while we think of organizations as orderly places where people behave in rational ways. Only when we begin to realize that companies are as irrational and fearful as the people who work in them, does corporate policy begin to make sense. If people erect elaborate invisible defense shields to protect themselves from other people, what kind of defense systems do you suppose a company can build?

How can a company develop policies which welcome rather than resist innovation? If innovation is viewed by the organization as something negative, if it is considered something that goes against the grain, it will be impossible. Change must be made attractive or inevitable, if not, people won't sign on. There must be a clear understanding that innovation is the best way for each person to prosper, and that it is at the foundation of each person's success.

Developing a climate that encourages risk taking and encourages innovation requires both talk and action. One after another, firms have failed when trying to change policies because their basic approach to motivating people was focused on avoiding risk. The norm in the halls of corporations worldwide has long been fear. It's the fear of offending a superior, fear of being passed over for a promotion or a raise, fear of being reprimanded for mistakes and, of course, the fear of being fired. A fearful person will not dare trespass social rules. People who are afraid are never creative.

> **Fear is the greatest obstacle to creativity**

The dominant issue thus becomes not how can companies foster innovation, but how can they help their employees (meaning also themselves) become less fearful? Confronting fear is a subject we will deal with in invisible barrier ten, so let's put it aside and concentrate on something companies do spend a lot of training dollars on, communications.

People have a tendency to talk at each other instead of to each other. One person says something, and another will contribute something, based upon his or her direct or indirect experience. You might tell a friend that you're going to Singapore. Your friend will immediately search for something to say which relates to his or her future plans, travel or Singapore. What they finally offer may be pretty far afield. It could well be something like, "I had a neighbor once who came from Singapore, or maybe it was Hong Kong. Nice guy." You're not talking to each other; you're talking at each other.

> **Most conversations are, in truth, vaguely related monologues**

Horizontal communication

Who talks vertically? Teachers to students, parents to children, bosses to employees. Vertical communication follows the lines of power. Queen Victoria often complained that Gladstone spoke to her as if he were lecturing to the public, which was vertically. She preferred Disraeli, who talked to her like a human being, which means horizontally.

Today a lot of people are afraid to talk, really talk to each other. They're afraid that their remarks will be misunderstood, afraid of repercussions and lawsuits. Fear that a comment may be interpreted as a form of sexual harassment has placed a lot of people on guard. Horizontal communication scares people. They are worried about asking questions that appearing nosey, patronizing or offensive. Our excessive reliance on politically correct dialogue has unfortunately made us afraid to be open with each other.

"Hello. How are you?" "How are you," is a question that's really not a question. It's really saying hello twice. If someone actually told us how he or she really was, we'd be aghast. In fact, it would probably embarrass us.

Creative people express their thoughts, fears, desires, ideas and feelings easily. If the atmosphere in a company hinders this expression, innovative thinking will be held in check. Horizontal communication means having access to everyone. If your boss is too busy to listen to your ideas, you'll end up by never offering any. Most managers insulate themselves behind assistants and secretaries, behind walls of schedules and in offices. Most managers are never as accessible as they should be. They tend to listen to limited groups of people. Anyone in a company can have a good idea or may say something that leads to other good ideas. People, however, tend not to pay attention to someone they feel is of lesser status. If communication is horizontal rather than vertical, you will give everyone the same attention. Innovative thinking is the result.

Not only must there be accessibility, but also people must have the courage to say what they think, without fear of repercussions. If you criticize something in your company, will your boss take it as a personal attack? Too many bosses do, and many more employees fear that their bosses will take criticism badly. The result is that ideas don't get expressed. The losers are everyone involved.

"What can we do to make your job run more smoothly? What can we do to make you happier?"

When is the last time your CEO personally asked you these questions? Most of the time they don't ask, or if they do, it's buried in a survey circulated by the human resource department, a survey with multiple choice answers that don't really apply to you. When's the last time someone who wielded real power at work took an interest in you personally and listened to your suggestions as well as your complaints? If people don't feel valued or committed, they will withhold their knowledge, expertise and insights as a form of payback.

Limited praise and lack of recognition is one of the primary reasons why employees leave jobs. In fact, it is often said that people don't leave companies, they leave their managers. It's not really a lack of recognition but a lack of communication, in effect, a lack of caring, which drives not only employees but most customers away. Surveys of defecting customers in industry after industry show that most people leave not because of price or product but because they don't like they way they are treated. Companies who don't listen to their employees will have a difficult time listening to their customers.

It's very hard to know what people in an office are feeling. Over the past few decades, large firms adopted policies which effectively told employees to keep their emotions in check. It's difficult to find a balance between reasonable openness and respectful discretion. People are emotional beings and managers are beginning to realize that the ability to understand and manage emotions improves a person's performance, ability to work with colleagues and interaction with customers.

The role of a manager is to bring out the energy that's inherent in people.
Henry Mintzberg, Canadian business professor, writer

Bringing out the energy means bringing out the emotions, the enthusiasm, the desire and the drive. Companies who want more effective leadership need to work with their executives to develop emotional approaches to managing, instead of the traditional monitoring roles, which stem from mistrust and fear.

Creativity and emotional intelligence

Most MBA students are never asked to take a selling course, they are never taught how to give a presentation or how to make a speech, but they are experts in cost accounting, understanding manufacturing efficiencies and applying option pricing formulas. Companies today are realizing that the majority of MBA programs are teaching similar sets of skills, and that these skills don't always help their graduates become leaders.

Effective leaders all have a high degree of what has come to be known as "emotional intelligence." Without it, a person can have the best training in the world, an analytical mind and dedication, but still won't be a great leader.

The five components of emotional intelligence are:

- *self-awareness* – the ability to recognize and understand your moods, emotions and drives
- *self-regulation* – the ability to control or redirect impulses and moods, as well as a propensity to suspend judgment
- *motivation* – a passion for work that goes beyond money or status, in effect, sustainable enthusiasm
- *empathy* – the ability to manage meaningful relationships and skill in treating people according to their emotional reactions
- *social skills* – managing relationships and an ability to find common ground and support.

Do these points sound familiar? They should. Creative people possess high degrees of emotional intelligence. Are they then great leaders? In many ways, "yes," for the goals of creative people revolve around a desire to change the world, or at least a certain part of it. Creative people spend most of their lives not trying to lead but trying to wake people up, to make them aware of what needs to be done to make the world a better place. This task, no small one, consumes their time and energy and paves the way for others. This brings us to an often quoted comparison between creativity and innovation, which states that creativity is merely thinking about a problem or issue while innovation is actually doing something about it. In reality, creativity is making other people think about problems or issues that they've avoided. At some point a leader needs to come on board and say, "okay, now that you're ready, let's act," but without the process of making people aware that something needs to be done, leadership will fail.

Leaders don't need to be highly creative. They do, however, need to be able to recognize and act on the creativity of others.

Fostering a creative atmosphere

For decades the idea of promoting creativity in a company was tied to the suggestion box. Suggestion systems are still used in many companies worldwide. Although the value of a suggestion system cannot be denied, too much emphasis has been placed upon it.

There are different kinds of suggestion systems. The traditional entices employees to contribute ideas and offers them monetary rewards should the ideas be accepted. The other, modeled more on the Japanese *kaizen teian* which means continuous improvement proposal system, motivates employees to offer suggestions for the good of the company and thus for the individual employee who is a part of the company, and not merely for cash rewards.

Surveys vary but most show that the average Japanese employee proposes many more suggestions than his American or European counterparts.

What are some of the problems with the suggestion systems in use?

- Just because a company offers its employee's cash for ideas doesn't mean that the employees will be able to come up with any.
- Employees who offer suggestions that are not implemented often become disenchanted with the company and their roles in it.
- Suggestions tend toward improvement in the employees immediate workplace. Hence they are rarely radical or far-reaching.
- Suggestions tend to revolve around cost-saving measures.

That said, there is really nothing wrong with the suggestion systems in use. They just don't go far enough, because the people who are making the suggestions are not capable of going far enough. They are not working to develop and maintain their creativity and hence self-censor many of their suggestions.

The trend in the 1990s

The consensus in the 1990s was that the best way to build creativity was to create a free-spirited, casual work environment. The theory was, and still is, that once the rules are relaxed, people will quickly make use of their innate creativity. Some of the things which have been tried include:

- Put up funny art in the office
- Take everyone out to lunch every month
- Provide candy or snacks at meetings
- Casual dress Fridays
- Annual or semi-annual retreats

- Donut breakfasts
- Halloween parties
- Company-wide athletic contests.

The idea that when fun is part of your corporate culture, people are more relaxed and open to thinking about new, creative or innovative ideas does work, but a simple relaxation of the work environment also doesn't go far enough. You can't expect the vast majority of adults to be creative on demand, nor can you expect them to be creative simply by relaxing their work environment. If that were true, everyone would be highly creative at home, and they're not. Someone who is not creative at home can't be expected to turn on his or her creativity as soon as he or she gets to work. The environment alone won't make people creative. Some form of education, through a mixture of awareness, understanding and practice is needed. If we accept that creativity can be taught, or at least enhanced, we can also accept the idea of creativity training. If, however, we cling to the old notion that creativity is a talent that cannot be taught, we rally round the idea that it is the environment and the environment alone that releases or restricts our natural creativity.

> To change behavior, you must change feelings and beliefs, and this requires education rather than training

When you train people, you teach them a task, but when you educate people, you deal with them at a much deeper level. Companies need to do more than train their employees, they need to educate them, but this takes longer to accomplish and is difficult to measure.

Creativity seminars

There are two kinds of creativity education seminars. The first is an information seminar and the second is an activation seminar. When you do the first type of seminar, there usually comes a point when the group tends to say, "stop. Don't give us any more theory. We know what we need to do to become more creative, but we can't get there by ourselves. We need someone to take us there."

The activation seminar is composed of volunteers from the first group. In activation seminars the leader must be able to inspire the group to collectively and individually overcome their fears and take those all-important first steps forward. Just as in therapy, where people come wanting change and then spend the majority of their time fighting against what they came for, you get people who come to activation seminars and then spend most of the time resisting what goes on. Some in the group are ready and willing to run to first base. These people can easily be taken (without stopping at first base) on to second, for they have mentally rehearsed what would happen at the seminar before coming (people always mentally rehearse their performances at sporting events, interviews, dates and so on) and have accepted going to first while secretly hoping, but not expecting, to go any further. These people can indeed often be taken on (again without stopping at second) to third base. Once you get them to accept taking action, their resistance (akin to sales resistance) momentarily fades and it's easy to get them to go further, just as it is easy to get someone who consents to buy an article of clothing to buy a second article in a different color or an accessory to go with the first article.

> The purpose of therapy is precisely to take one out of the rigid grooves, the narrow compulsive trends which are blocks to freedom. Any good therapy is a method of increasing one's experience of freedom.
>
> *Rollo May, American psychologist*

The only way to get people to be more creative is to teach them to look for other perspectives and points of view, and to do that, you have to get them to expand their personal freedom. Can it be done in a short seminar-type environment? Surprisingly, a lot of it can. The ideal seminar brings together people who don't know or work with one another, but yes, the intensive hour seminar format has certain distinct advantages over a semester-type university course. When you take the mystery out of creativity, when you put it in real terms that people can relate to, and when you have a seminar leader who the group can emotionally identify with and trust, they respond. Enormous breakthroughs are the result.

> The mystery of togetherness, of minds meeting minds, but without the social anxiety that plagues many business encounters. Replacing that with a very basic trust is what lies beneath the best ideas.
>
> *Mary Wells Lawrence, American co-founder of*
> *Wells, Rich & Greene advertising agency*

Train everyone

That brings us to another point. Innovation training in industry cannot just be for managers. Anyone can have a creative idea. Creativity is not dependent on intelligence. It depends on personality. The person who cleans the floor can have as many creative ideas as the CEO, but that's a hard point for a CEO to accept. A firm will only be creative if everyone feels involved.

Innovation in business today is mostly associated with high-tech and Internet companies. That's because many are new companies working in new industries. It's always easier to break the rules if none exist. When a structure already exists it's difficult to change it. Most people who go to work for a company inherit a set of accepted practices. In fact, your first few weeks at a new job are usually spent learning how things are done. Because you're new and often unsure of yourself, you rarely challenge any of those procedures.

Before teaching your new employees how to do things your way, ask them to look at the company as an outsider. Their observations may be invaluable.

In an essay in Ford and Gioia's *Creative Action in Organizations,* Barry Straw, a professor at the University of California at Berkley, put it this way:

> First, instead of the normal recruitment process in which people are brought in who have the skills needed by the firm and the values it admires, innovative companies must let down their barriers. They must accommodate those whose skills are more peripheral and whose goals are suspect. Second, instead of socializing new members of the organizations to absorb the values and culture of the firm, the innovative corporation must encourage people not to listen, at least not too hard. There is nothing that kills innovation like everyone speaking in the same voice, even if it's a well-trained voice.

Think about the work you do. Who defines the tasks that you do, you or someone else? Who defines the behavior necessary to perform those tasks? Who defines your performance goals?

External and internal commitment

People will be more creative if you give them the freedom to decide how to climb a particular mountain, or do any particular task. In many jobs, however, people are given very little freedom to make decisions about how to accomplish the work. Their commitment to the work thus becomes external.

When the commitment is external:

- The tasks are defined by others
- The actions required to perform those tasks are defined by others
- Performance goals are defined by management
- The importance of the goals is defined by others.

However, when the commitment is internal:

- Individuals define their tasks
- Individuals define the actions required to perform them
- Management and individuals jointly define performance goals that are challenging for the individual
- Individuals define the importance of the goals.

If you're told what to do, when to do it and how to do it, your task is easy, because you bear little responsibility. People get used to having their thinking done for them. Internal commitment can be very threatening for people who aren't used to it.

Creative people hate to be told what, when and how to do anything. Take away their internal commitment and you take away all their desire. The result is that they'll be unhappy and look to leave.

The problem with creativity in a lot of companies (and a lot of individuals as well) is that they just don't want to go through all the necessary work and changes which will be necessary. They want creativity the easy way.

> Real creativity, the kind that is responsible for breakthrough changes in our society, always violates the rules. That is why it is so unmanageable and that is why in most organizations, when we say we desire creativity we really mean manageable creativity. We don't mean, raw, dynamic, radical creativity that requires us to change.   *Richard Farson*, Management of the Absurd

Manageable creativity means lukewarm, half-ass creativity, which unfortunately usually means no creativity at all. There is no easy way. Manageable creativity doesn't work. If you want creative people, you must be willing to put through the necessary radical changes. Is it worth it? Time will tell, but remember that time is not on your side. For companies entering the Internet age, the future is becoming the present at the speed of light. You can no longer rely on traditional practices for handling data and making decisions. You need to be adaptable, resourceful and open to change in order to stay ahead of the competition. You need creative people.

Classic examples of innovation

In 1904, Antoine Feutchwanger was selling sausages at the Louisiana Fair. He tried serving them on plates, but it was too expensive. Then he had the idea of giving his customers white cotton gloves, so they could eat the sausages without burning or soiling their fingers. That also was too expensive. Antoine's brother, a baker, was at the same time looking for ways to sell his bread. The brothers decided to try wrapping the sausages in bread and the hot dog was born.

A year later, Ernest Hamwl was trying to sell paper-thin Persian waffles at the World's Fair, without much success. Finally, when the popular ice cream stand next door ran out of dishes, he fashioned his waffles into cones so that the ice cream stand could go on selling. The ice cream cone was born.

Antoine Feutchwanger used a form of lateral thinking to invent the hot dog. His initial goal was not to sell bread, or sausages in bread. His initial goal was to sell sausages, period. His solution was to combine products. Many people don't think about combining things because they are too focused on their own product or problem. They keep going over and over the same set of criteria in their minds, without looking for anything new. Creativity often involves recombining or making connections between things that may seem unconnected.

> Combine, substitute, modify, isolate, eliminate, highlight, magnify, reverse, rearrange

The idea is to come up with a new idea. That new idea may well be an adaptation of an old idea, but it will always reflect a different way of looking at your present situation.

Antoine Feutchwanger and Ernest Hamwl combined their products with another to form something new. Their motivation was survival. They had to come up with something in order to sell their products. You've all heard the saying, "necessity is the mother of invention." Well, necessity is a surefire way of getting you around the adequate. Feutchwanger and

Hamwl were entrepreneurs. Neither had to take his idea to higher-ups to have them implemented. They did the work themselves. The problem in most businesses is getting someone to appreciate the value of your idea and getting the corporation to implement it. It's frustrating to go to your boss and have your idea squashed. After the second or third time, you stop doing it. Why bother, you bitterly remind yourself and shut your entire idea-spawning process down entirely.

The idea bank

All companies should have an idea bank. A form of modern day suggestion box, it would encourage employees, customers and even people from outside the company to contribute not suggestions, but ideas. Each idea could be given a tracking number, so that the contributor could see how much exposure the idea actually received. On implementing an idea, the company would be required to publicly acknowledge the source. Idea contributors would use those acknowledgements for their performance evaluations or their résumés (CVs), (remember that contributors need not work for the company). Companies could even post problems on their idea bank via their website, and see what ideas people from outside could produce.

Many of the good ideas used in business are not spawned by necessity, but originate due to creative thinking, luck or some combination of the two. For years when you rented a car, the rental agency told you to bring it back with the gas tank full. If you didn't, they charged you at a higher than normal rate. Most people took the time to fill it up just before returning it.

Then some years ago it dawned on the agencies that they were losing money by doing this. The idea of prepaid gas was born. Now you can prepay a full tank of gas, when you pick up your vehicle. If you do, they inform you, with a smile, you can bring the car back empty. The price of the tank is professed to be the going rate at stations in the area. Since the agency only needs to find one gas station selling gas at that price, the rate they quote is usually slightly higher than you would find on the street if you took a few minutes to shop around. Since it's impossible to bring the car back empty, unless you push it, cars are always returned with paid-for gas sloshing around in their tanks. Every drop of that gas is found money for the agency. People often miscalculate how much gas they need to get from one point to another, and bring cars back with the gas tank half-full. Multiply that by all the cars the agency rents and you can see why they try to push prepaid gas on you. The prepaid gas concept has been great for the agencies. Why didn't they think of it before?

For years when you went to the dentist you sat in a chair and the dentist stood. Today you lie down, and the dentist sits. The new "dentist chairs" are better for the dentist and better for you. You're both more relaxed. Your dentist is less tired and you're less tense. Why didn't someone think of having patients lie down years ago? It just didn't occur to anyone, because the "chair" was adequate. It worked. It just doesn't work as well as the recliner.

Recent examples of innovation

How many watches do you own? For years the answer to that question was simple. One! Watches were supposed to do one thing and one thing only, tell the time. They were supposed to be accurate and reliable. You wore one until it broke, and then and only then did you buy a new one.

Why can't your watch do something besides tell the time? Why can't it be fashionable as well as reliable? You wear it, after all, just like you do jewelry or clothing and you don't wear the same clothes every day. You change them, not always because they're dirty but because you want to look different. Then why do you wear the same old predictable watch, day in day out, year after year? Doesn't it bore you? Don't you get tired of looking at it?

That was the idea behind Swatch, and they caused a revolution in the watch-making industry. Instead of one watch, people now owned several. A plaid one, a black and white one, a red one! You bought a watch like you bought a pair of shoes or jackets, and each morning you decided which of your five, six or seven watches you'd wear.

Benetton, the Italian clothing manufacturer, was an innovative company from the start. Instead of selling its line of women's sweaters the traditional way, through department stores, or directly to the public via catalogs, it decided to sell them exclusively in its own stores. The stores, which were small, modern and well lit, carried, in the beginning, a limited line of products, mainly women's sweaters and tops. What Benetton did was offer its sweaters in a variety of colors and sizes. It knew that nothing frustrates a woman more than being told: "Sorry, we're out of that particular size." It also realized something very important. When someone consents to buy something they want rather than need, it is possible to sell them a second and even a third, for their sales resistance is momentarily low. Sweaters were the perfect product. If a woman liked the way she looked in a pink sweater, she'd also like the way she'd look in the same model in baby blue or yellow. Women also do something that men don't; they match colors rather than mix them. The belief by many women that certain clothes are only able to be worn with certain others give them a predisposition to multiple purchases.

Benetton's advertising strategy has also been radical. When it began, its advertising strategy featured the United Colors of Benetton message, a happiness-type idea and concept, featuring people of various races and ethnic origins. In 1984 it launched a series of controversial ads. One of the first showed a black woman breastfeeding a white baby. That upset a lot of people. Benetton followed that up with one showing a priest kissing a nun. The ads themselves are also not your traditional form of advertising. They say nothing about the product. They are photographs with the Benetton logo, nothing more. A subsequent Benetton shocker featured a man dying of AIDS. It was followed up with one showing the bloody clothes of a man blown to pieces in the war in Yugoslavia.

Benetton maintains that it has a social conscience, that its advertising focuses the attention on causes and issues we all know about but don't pay enough attention to. The company has stated:

> Benetton believes that it is important for companies to take a stance in the real world instead of using their advertising budget to perpetuate the myth that they can make customers happy through the mere purchase of their product. Unlike traditional adverts, our images usually have no copy and no product, only our logo. They do not show you a fictitious reality in which you will be irresistible if you make use of our products. They do not tell anyone to buy our clothes; they do not even imply it. All they attempt to do is promote a discussion about issues which people would normally glide over if they approached them from other channels, issues we feel should be more widely discussed.

Benetton's critics say the company is using sensationalism to sell its sweaters! It's fine to focus attention on world problems, they point out, just don't get rich from it!

Benetton went on in 1994 to publish a photo of the world's leaders dressed as women. Its explanation:

> If the world's leaders were women, global politics would be handled with more compassion and honesty and maybe some of the problems would get solved.

Another advertisement, a kaleidoscope of male and female genitals, was banned by most countries of the world.

Whether you agree or disagree with Benetton's advertising campaign, it has:

- had an impact on advertising worldwide
- made its logo one of the most recognized in the world
- demonstrated that a company of its size and stature can prosper without television advertising (it uses print media almost exclusively)
- shown that advertising campaigns do not have to be altered to fit perceived tastes and buying habits.

For years the trend in advertising, notably in North America, was: Don't take any risks! Don't offend anyone! Benetton's advertising disturbs, offends and shocks people. That is its intention. Few people in the advertising business thought Benetton's bold idea would succeed. Conventional wisdom at the time said that to run shocking ads, which say nothing about the product, directed at the twenty–forty-year-old woman, is nothing short of product and corporate suicide!

Other companies are now successfully using non-product advertising. Today consumers are inundated by advertising. Most of the ads they see they don't remember. In fact statistics tell us that up to twenty percent of the people fail to understand an ad on television when they see it, while another fifteen percent attribute it to a competitor. Televisions all come with remote controls. The average viewer no longer watches a single program but channel surfs from one program to another, watching bits and pieces of everything and nothing. No one sits through advertising anymore. You surf on, parachuting into sixty-second commercials in the 34th second and moving on in the 36th.

In the mighty struggle for the consumer's attention, Benetton-style ads more than hold their own. You remember them, which is far more than can be said for most advertising today. What, after all, is the worth of an ad if no one notices it?

Budweiser's successful television ad campaign, which began with ants, then spread to frogs and lizards is a result of Benetton's ground-breaking work. If you had gone to the people at Anheiser-Busch before Benetton and said: "I've got a great idea how to sell your beer! We'll use frogs!" The people at Anheiser-Busch would have replied, "frogs don't drink beer, people drink beer! Out!"

Companies like Anheiser-Busch and Coca-Cola have realized that they don't always have to show their products in their ads, that consumers know their products. Non-product advertising is effective at getting the consumer's attention. In today's advertising jungle, that's a hell of an accomplishment.

Benetton's logo is one of the most recognized in the world. Unlike Coca-Cola, McDonald's and Nike, which appeal to everyone, Benetton's clients are still predominantly women. Even though most men around the world don't use its products, they still know Benetton's logo. The Italian company has also managed to get worldwide recognition while relying on primarily magazine and billboard advertising. It's amazing what it's achieved when you think it rarely ventures into any other advertising media.

Oliviero Toscani, who took the photos used in the Benetton advertising campaign, has this to say:

> Research? We try to do the very opposite. We try to make our ads personal. If you do research, you get yesterday's results. If they did research five hundred years ago, they never would have discovered America. They would have found out the world is flat. You have to have the courage to make mistakes. Everything we do is about impulse, about guts. That's what built Benetton.

If you are creative, you have the courage to make mistakes. If you are creative, you have the courage of listen to your instincts. If you are creative, you have the courage to take risks.

> Regaining your creativity means finding the courage to try to make your dreams come true

How to break through invisible barrier eight

This barrier should no longer pose major problems. If you've accepted the fact that creativity is something which you have to commit to and that if you do it will touch every aspect of your life, then you've already begun to deal with this creativity obstacle.

ACTIVITIES

List all your major activities in the course of a recent average week, not a special week such as when you're on vacation, but an average week within the last month. Your list will probably include things like eating, sleeping, watching TV, sport, work, hobbies, sex, commuting, shopping, reading and housework. Now rate and group them to see how much pleasure each activity gives you. Consider your total pleasure to be 100.

■   How many of those 100 pleasure points do you get from sleeping, how many from eating, how many from work and so on?

     Do this honestly. Don't rate them according to what you think you should say. Evaluate them purely on what you feel.

You should now be able to identify where the principal pleasures in your life are coming from. If you find that your main pleasures come from just a couple of activities, perhaps you are focusing more on the results than on the processes. Most people don't enjoy housework or commuting, yet if you focus on the process of commuting instead of getting there, you'll enjoy the commute, and life, more.

■   When was the last time you were in love?

     For many people the answer is, when I met my husband, wife or partner, yet it doesn't have to be.

■   Be in love every day. Be in love with every new day.

     Easier said than done you immediately think, and you're right, except that we go back again in this book to the same basic, naive, childish notion that creative people just can't seem to shake. Why can't this world be a better world, why can't we be in love with each and every new day?

Some places and times are more conducive to the process of idea generation than others. One of those times is when you're in love. When you're in love, ideas just seem to flow.

Bonus to this reinforcement activity

Since you know where your pleasures are coming from, you can now check to see how they match up with what you really want. In an ideal world, where would you want your pleasures to come from? Again, distribute your ideal pleasures within the range of 100. If you do this exercise correctly, it will take some serious reflection.

Now compare your ideal distribution to the one you actually have. Where do the discrepancies lie? Those are the areas in life which frustrate you. Okay, now think what you need to do to make those areas more pleasurable. What would you have to sacrifice? Who around you would you need to communicate better with in order to help you attain more of your pleasures?

It would also be valuable if your husband, wife or partner did the exercise, since they will no doubt play a significant role in whether or not you succeed in achieving more of your fondest pleasures. You may also learn a lot about each other.

A new brainstorming model

Brainstorming is a highly familiar, proven but to some degree "tired tool" for gathering and developing new ideas. Every business uses brainstorming, whether internally in the conference room, or by bringing in consultants to help generate and evaluate ideas on specific problems. Everyone is convinced that they're doing something meaningful, when in fact brainstorming sessions are rarely as productive as they could or should be.

Edward de Bono, in his book *Lateral Thinking*, defines brainstorming

as a format setting for the use of lateral thinking. In itself it is not a special technique but a special setting which encourages the application of the principles and techniques of lateral thinking while providing a holiday from the rigidity of vertical thinking.

In recent years, the emphasis has been on teamwork, especially in business and the research sciences. It is questionable though whether original ideas can really come from teams. Original ideas are more apt to come not only from individuals but from individualistic individuals. Teamwork is most useful for expanding and applying an idea once it is raised. Given the emphasis on teamwork, it is natural that a lot of attention has been placed on the techniques for judging the ideas produced in brainstorming, rather than on the processes used to generate those ideas. Since one can only work with the best of the ideas which have been collected, the idea generation phase is as or more important than the selection phase.

It is assumed that brainstorming is a technique that everyone can use, when in fact the majority of the people who brainstorm bring severe handicaps to the process and cannot be expected to achieve anything more than mediocre results. Most brainstorming sessions fail to adhere to the theories of brainstorming which were laid out by de Bono and Alex Osborn, and are drastically scaled back to accommodate their participants.

Brainstorming: In theory

Alex Osborn called brainstorming

> a conference technique by which a group attempts to find a solution for a specific problem by amassing all the ideas spontaneously by its members.

By this definition it is:

- a process designed to obtain the maximum number of ideas relating to a problem or specific area of interest
- a technique that maximizes the ability to generate ideas.

De Bono has stated that the main features of a brainstorming session are:

- cross-stimulation
- suspended judgment
- the formality of the setting.

- *Cross-stimulation:* In a brainstorming session the provocation is furnished by the ideas thrown out by members of the group. An idea, which may appear silly, obvious or trivial to one person, can combine with other ideas in someone else's mind to produce something very original.
- *Suspended judgment:* The brainstorming session provides a formal opportunity for people to make suggestions that they would not otherwise dare to make for fear of being laughed at. In a brainstorming session anything goes. No idea is too ridiculous to be put forward. Wildness is encouraged. In order to accomplish this, none of the ideas are judged, evaluated or criticized until the session is over.
- *Formality of the setting:* Most people are so entrenched in vertical thinking habits that they have a very difficult time thinking laterally. They do not like being wrong or ridiculous even though they might accept it in theory. Brainstorming is a way then for people to get around their inhibitions. It is much easier to accept that "anything goes" as a way of thinking in a brainstorming session than as a way of thinking in general.

A fatal flaw

There are generally two kinds of brainstorming sessions. The first and simplest is conducted in a company setting using the employees and no external intervention. The second gets company employees out of their offices and puts them in relaxed environments under the supervision of consultants. Both types of sessions suffer from the same fatal flaw.

For brainstorming to work, participants must be able to put social rules and inhibitions aside for the time it takes to generate new ideas and solutions. The overwhelming majority of people cannot do this. They can't do it in personal settings and they certainly can't do it in business settings. Most people who brainstorm do want to come up with ideas but, more than anything else, they want those ideas to be applauded and accepted. They don't want to look foolish or stupid. These people have ideas that never come into their conscious awareness because fear of looking stupid automatically knocks them down. In brainstorming, you want those ideas. In brainstorming you need each and every idea, especially the really provocative ones.

People do come up with ideas when they brainstorm, lots of them. Not all are practical; many are silly, offbeat and bizarre. Because the ideas always lie within the realm of the person's accepted thinking, they aren't provocative. They're ideas which usually fail to challenge basic principles or premises. To come up with penetrating ideas, people need to be able to trespass social rules and shed their inhibitions and, without training, this is impossible.

In his book *Six Thinking Hats,* Edward de Bono stated that

> creative thinking is difficult because it is contrary to the natural habits of judgment and criticism. Most thinkers like to be secure. Creativity involves provocation, exploration and risk taking.

Although the purpose of brainstorming is to provoke new visions, the ideas that come out of most sessions are tame and domesticated. How can they be otherwise? All brainstorming sessions are bound by the same social rules and regulations that work to suppress our finest provocative thoughts and ideas. The notion that business executives will be able to brainstorm simply by getting them to relax is like thinking that they'll be able to handle the controls of a space shuttle on any given Sunday. The result will be the same. You'll go nowhere.

There are two ways to make brainstorming sessions work. Both are designed to help people put social rules and inhibitions aside. The first is the longer of the two, but it is also more comprehensive.

Creativity (and brainstorming) enhancement training

In order for brainstorming to succeed, its participants need to regain some of the creativity they had as children and the best way to do this is through creativity enhancement exercises and training. Most companies today are still highly reluctant to invest in any form of creativity training for their employees, even though creativity is something which can be effectively taught, given the right seminar-type format. What most companies want is something which can be qualified and measured.

You are creative if you are consistently able to see other perspectives and points of view. In business that one ability is invaluable for executives, a company's sales force, in customer service, the human resource department and the marketing department. To be able to see other perspectives, you need to eliminate boundaries and cast off previously held perceptions and limitations about how something looks, functions or should be. For most of us this means opening up, letting go. That's what brainstorming was designed to do, be a vehicle to allow people to open up and let go. The problem that besets most brainstorming sessions is that the structure isn't powerful enough to let that happen. Recent attempts to construct new brainstorming techniques have all focused on diminishing the effects of a person's ego in brainstorming, but something more is needed, the structure itself has to be strengthened.

Anonymous brainstorming

People have no trouble trespassing social rules when they're alone. It's the presence of others that inhibits them from coming up with penetrating ideas, yet the concept of cross-stimulation in brainstorming needs to be maintained. The obvious way of incorporating both is to structure brainstorming sessions in such a way that a person's contributions cannot be traced back to them. Only when brainstorming becomes anonymous do people finally feel free to open up and express everything. In theory this is what suspended judgment was supposed to achieve. People, however, know well that all the ideas generated in brainstorming will be evaluated later and that their bosses and colleagues will easily remember who came up with what. Suspended judgment doesn't mean "no judgment" but deferred judgment, and judgment is a powerful inhibiting factor.

Another inhibiting factor in traditional brainstorming is the fear that references to any provocative or delicate subject, and this includes almost anything to do with sex, will be misinterpreted, and the person who came up with them branded a social deviant.

Anonymous brainstorming can be used to help people overcome these fears and give them the confidence to release their most provocative, innermost thoughts, which is exactly what you want.

In *Lateral Thinking*, Edward de Bono stated:

> All groups exert a pressure toward uniformity on its members. For a brain-storming session to be effective, these pressures must be minimized.

- Anonymous brainstorming doesn't reduce group pressures, it eliminates them.
- Anonymous brainstorming doesn't diminish the problem of a person's ego in brainstorming; it eliminates it.

> It is amazing what you can accomplish if you do not care who gets the credit.
>
> *Harry Truman, former US president*

There are many ways to make brainstorming anonymous. A simple redesign of the room and the way participants are selected is one way, costumes and masks are another, a third is via the conference call, while yet a fourth is to hold it online.

Online brainstorming

How do you capture the energy of a brainstorming session and transfer it online? The answer to this question has long been, "you can't." The consensus has thus become that online brainstorming doesn't work. Yes, it does, if it's done anonymously.

The problem that has plagued online brainstorming is that people have tried to make it duplicate traditional brainstorming sessions instead of taking advantage of its natural built-in features.

It's true that an online session is slower and less dynamic than normal brainstorming, yet it has distinct advantages. The first is even greater anonymity, and therefore a deeper feeling of liberation. Many people feel that the written character is less apt to be traced and identified than someone's voice. Other advantages include cost, a wider and more selective range of participants, and the possibility of internationalizing your brainstorming sessions. Recent studies have shown that many of the best ideas come up shortly after the session, when no one is there to record them. If you're online, it's easier to have a record of everything that was said both during the session and for a certain period of time afterward.

It is important that everyone who participates in an anonymous brainstorming session, whether in person or online, feels secure that whatever they contribute cannot be traced back to them. External consultants, who fully explain the process and how that process ensures anonymity, should handle the sessions.

It is possible to structure brainstorming sessions in which social rules are truly suspended. It takes time and the people who participate need prior creativity training but the results can be spectacular. That kind of brainstorming session, however, is almost impossible to conduct today in normal business settings.

It is often said that creative ideas are only a part of what it takes to institute change, and that to implement an idea is more difficult than it is to generate or select it. It is also widely recognized that one of the fundamental problems is that every really new idea requires both management and the workforce to undergo significant change. The only way to overcome this is give everyone creativity theory training, so that they not only accept but begin to demand change. In brainstorming, it means giving all participants creativity training, then structuring your sessions so that no one knows the identity of the other participants and each participant is secure that there will be no judgment or censure attached to any of the ideas or fragments of ideas they contribute.

> Boundaryless behavior is our number one value. You must be open to an idea from anywhere, inside, outside, up, down. The only thing that counts is the quality of the idea, not the rank of the person originating it.
>
> *Jack Welch, former CEO of General Electric*

The only way to achieve boundaryless behavior is by creating an atmosphere where people feel free to say whatever they think, without fear of repercussions. That means horizontal communication. It's true that the only thing that counts is the quality of the idea. In order to get to that quality idea, however, one has to pass by many fragments of ideas, and those fragments of ideas need to be uttered without any fear of censure.

The entire world of the highly creative person revolves around expressing all their thoughts, fears, desires, ideas and feelings. That's what they've been trained to do.

Anonymous brainstorming achieves the following goals:

- It gives the average person the confidence to say whatever they think. It thus permits them to momentarily reach a higher level of creativity than traditional brainstorming methods would let them attain.
- It eliminates the tendency to only say what people believe will impress others.
- It removes the tendency to push for approval of one's own ideas in the follow-up phase.
- It takes away the influence of rank, authority, age, gender, race, friendship or animosity in the idea generation and evaluation phases.

The invisible nets that hold us are, for the moment, just too strong to be broken by the traditional brainstorming model, but all nets can be broken. Restructuring brainstorming sessions so that participants function anonymously is the best way of breaking some of those nets.

PART III

Letting Go

"Letting go means losing"

Creativity can be described as a letting go of certainties.
GAIL SHEEHY, AMERICAN JOURNALIST, WRITER

Invisible barrier nine is the fear that you'll lose something if you let down some of your defense shields. To become more creative, you must be willing to let down your shields and let go of the handrail, the shelter, the group, the comfortable way, and the secure way. The obstacles to creativity are almost always internal. In a person concerned with protecting his or her self, and that's the case with most people, practically all one's energy is spent monitoring and deflecting threats to the ego.

If you want to be creative, you cannot be concerned with how you look or what impression you're having on others. Instead, you must forget yourself long enough to look, see, combine, substitute, eliminate, magnify, simplify or reverse what appears before you. You have to let go of your image. You have to let go.

> The road back to creativity is a letting-go experience

Mihaly Csikszentmihalyi, University of Chicago psychologist, says this in his book *Creativity*:

> In everyday life, we are always monitoring how we appear to other people; we are on the alert to defend ourselves from potential slights and anxious to make a favorable impression. Typically this awareness of self is a burden.

Eternal vigilance is the burden all non-creative people must bear, eternal vigilance to the perceived attacks of others. That's why they maintain invisible defense shields, to monitor and ward off attacks to their egos. Becoming creative means letting down most of those defense shields, it means letting go and opening up, it means saying what you think and letting people see the real you. Why is that so hard to do? Why are we so afraid to let go?

Man wants to learn to swim and still keep one foot on the ground.
Marcel Proust, French writer

It can be argued that all life is a "letting-go" experience. The child has to let go of hands and furniture in order to take his first steps and walk, let go of his mother's side when it's time to go to school, let go of the edge and the bottom of the pool to learn to swim, let go of the family in order to get married, let go of his own children when they in turn grow up, and in the end, let go even of life itself.

Life is a letting-go experience. That experience means overcoming the fears and inhibitions which stop the all-important process of exploration. In terms of creativity, it means exploring the perspectives, paths, solutions, opportunities and ideas that others either can't or don't want to see. To do that one has to be capable of going where others don't go and dealing with things that others avoid.

Freedom is a feeling that scares most people. Because of this they shrink the world with which they have to deal to a size they feel they can cope with.

Nothing is more real, more potent and often more precious than our fears, yet so utterly meaningless when we're on death's door. Live as you would wish to have lived when you are dying, is a phrase that we objectively second, but subjectively reject. Occasionally something happens to us, which makes us stop and take stock of our lives, an accident or illness, or perhaps the death of a friend or relative. We pause, we reflect, we vow to change. We tell ourselves that from now on we're going to live our lives to the fullest, and sometimes we succeed in doing so, for a day, a week, maybe even sometimes a month before reverting back.

Given another shot at life, I would seize every minute, look at it and really see it, and never give it back.   *Erma Bombeck, American writer, on her deathbed*

The precious sacrifices, the daily worries, words and bodies under wraps, the slights, rancor, pride that were once so important seem so far away when you're close to death, but only when you're confronting death. Take away that confrontation and people revert back to their precious sacrifices and daily worries. There's a measure of defeat in every life. Some people just fail gradually, so they can say that they never had to face any real problems or crises. At some point they are forced to look back and realize that they never lived the kind of life they wanted to live. By the time they admit it, it's usually too late.

Life can only be understood backwards, but it must be lived forwards.
Søren Kierkegaard, Danish philosopher

Life is a letting-go experience. If only we'd let go earlier. If only we'd let go when there was still life ahead. If only.

Henry David Thoreau once said that "the mass of mankind lead lives of quiet desperation," while Helen Keller is often quoted as saying that "life is either a wonderful bold adventure or its nothing." Which statement is closer to your life? Most of us tend to live lives of quiet desperation, while hoping and pretending they are adventures.

It is not death that a man should fear, but he should fear never beginning to live.
Marcus Aurelius, Roman emperor

The letting-go process is similar to having huge weights lifted from your shoulders. The weights are your fears. The letting-go process is about letting go of your fears. It's fear which forces you to live behind invisible defense shields, and it's fear more than anything else which stops you from being creative. What you're taking off are weights that society says you should, but don't have to wear. You decide whether you want to wear them or not. You owe it to yourself to feel what it's like to take them off. Only then will you be able to see how heavy they were.

You gain strength, courage and confidence by every experience in which you really stop to look fear in the face. You must do the thing which you think you cannot do.
Eleanor Roosevelt, American stateswoman, former first lady of the USA

Everyone is afraid of something. The difference is that some of us can dominate our fears and others can't.

Boredom

Boredom occurs where we are obliged to pay attention to something we are not interested in. The result is a wandering of the mind, and a loss or distortion of whatever was being discussed. When was the last time you were bored? The greater part of the fatigue we suffer is of mental rather than physical origin. Boredom, resentment, a feeling of not being appreciated, the need to have to look busy, these are the things that exhaust the average worker. We get bored when we want to change or control a situation and can't. First comes a feeling of boredom, then a feeling of frustration. Non-creative people are better at coping with frustrations than highly creative adults and children are.

People who are easily bored are superficial. If you're bored, it's because you bore yourself. Sound familiar? It should, you've only heard these arguments over and over since you were a child. Getting bored easily is always looked upon as a negative character trait. It's associated with the idea that a person is bored because he bores him or herself, that the problem lies within the person, and not where they may be or what they may be doing.

What did you do most when you were a kid, besides sleep and play and study? The answer is, wait. You spent your childhood waiting, waiting for your parents to get up on Sunday morning, waiting for them to finish talking to your aunts and uncles, waiting for it to be your birthday, waiting for it to be Christmas. What did you feel while you were waiting? That's right, you felt bored. You spent a large part of your childhood being bored, didn't you? What about childlike adults, what happens to them? They naively want to rearrange the world to make it less boring, more meaningful and more compassionate.

There is a story told about the actor Laurence Olivier when he was performing *Richard III* in a London theatre. Olivier mumbles the play's opening soliloquy, then shouts the last three words of the next line:

Now is the winter of your discontent. Made Glorious summer by this SON OF YORK!

When asked why he chose to deliver the line that way, Olivier replied, "Why, to wake the fuckers up!"

> Wake the fuckers up!
> Wake the fucker up!

These are two similar but distinctly different things. The first is the mission of the highly creative person, the second the mission of the non-creative person.

Wake up world, the creative person screams, through his work. Wake up! Shake the cobwebs from your eyes! Take off your cozy earmuffs! React! Get together! Change! Do something about injustice!

Do something about violence! Do something about disease! Do something!

It's not easy to get people moving. It's not easy to get them to work together. It's not easy to make them aware of the perspectives and feelings of others. In order to do so, the creative person pushes, prods, upsets, disturbs, stuns and shocks people. Only by doing so does he or she get the public's attention. Only by doing so does he or she stir them from their comfortable routines and stupors.

> Dost thou think because thou art virtuous, there shall be no more cakes and ale?
> *Shakespeare, Twelfth Night*

The non-creative person tries to make the world a better place by conducting him or herself properly, by acting as a role model. Shakespeare adroitly points out that while this is well and good, it will not have much effect on the world unless everyone does it. The creative person's job is to motivate everyone else to do something. Most people believe this to be the job of the artist, but it is, in truth, the task of all creative people. It is their mission to observe and communicate, to make people see the things they would rather not see.

> No one must shut his eyes and regard as nonexistent the sufferings of which he spares himself of the sight. It's not enough to say, I'm earning enough to live and support my family. I do my work well. I'm a good father. I'm a good churchgoer. That's all very well. But you must do something more.
> *Albert Schweitzer, French medical missionary, philosopher*

What we cannot do is make the pain in the world our own. What we can do is have the strength to look at the situations which cause that pain and not flinch. What we refuse to be aware of does not go away. If anything it only becomes stronger.

A creative person expresses feelings, fears, ideas and desires that other people are terrified of expressing. As we've said in the opening pages, if you're creative it will permeate every aspect of your life. It won't leave you tranquil. The notion that you'll be able to dip your toe into creative waters from time to time is an idyllic one. The fact is that you won't even be able to wade in them. You'll have to plunge, and then you'll have to swim.

Waking people up

Waking people up is a formidable task, and the creative person must use all the weapons at his or her disposal, and this includes using disturbing sounds and images. In fact, it is only by using disturbing sounds and images that you will get someone's attention. The average person in an industrialized country today is exposed to over 2,000 advertisements, (that's including publicity) each and every day. How many of the more than 14,000 he sees each week do you think he remembers? How many have an influence on him? How many of the more than 800,000 ads you saw last year influenced you? If you want to wake someone up and get him or her to see something in a different and more meaningful light, you can't worry about disturbing or offending that person. We previously asked you to try to imagine what it would be like to be a tree. Now imagine what it would be like to be an alarm clock. Don't just assume you can do it. Actually try to imagine it. Go on! Then go further and imagine that you not only have to wake someone up but also make that person aware that today is different from all the other days of his or her life and that he or she is different from how they were yesterday or will be tomorrow.

> The role of the writer is not to say what we all can say, but what we are unable to say.   *Anais Nin, French writer*

That is not only the role of the writer, but the role of all creative people. There is a definite desire to want to better the status quo in all creative people. This desire makes them rebels, for people who are comfortable with their lives will not want to change anything. It has been said that Einstein explained why he spent so much time developing a new physics by saying that he could not understand the old physics.

The non-creative person's mission is to wake himself up. This is no easy task, because most people go to elaborate lengths to convince themselves that they are already alert. Man's two greatest talents are the ability to adapt to any circumstance and the ability to rationalize everything they do. The former talent helps you be creative. The latter does not.

Rationalizing is worse than reasoning because when we rationalize we try to defend our ideas, while when we reason we seek to understand those ideas. You are reasoning if your belief follows the evidence. You look at a subject with an open mind and then come to conclusions based on what you find. You are rationalizing if the evidence follows your belief, if you first decide then seek out arguments to bolster it.

In film:

> ## First rule of screenwriting — don't be boring

The most we expect from a film is that it changes our lives forever, the very least that it keeps us awake. If they made a film about your life, do you think it would keep people awake? Well, why couldn't it?

In life we kill time. In the cinema, time kills us. For a film to work, extreme vigorous emotion (not excitement, but emotion) must be integrated into every frame, every scene of every film.

In the theatre:

Never fear the audience, nor despise it. Coax it, charm it, interest it, stimulate it, shock it now and then if you must, make it laugh, make it cry, but above all, never, never, never, bore the living hell out of it. *Noel Coward, English playwright*

Creative people get bored easily. They accept it, while most non-creative people fight against it, telling themselves it's something they shouldn't be feeling.

> ## You will be more creative if you accept the fact that you get bored easily. Don't fight it. There's nothing wrong with it

The life of the creative man is led, directed and controlled by boredom. Avoiding boredom is one of our most important purposes.

Saul Steinberg, Romanian-born American artist

Everyone gets bored. It's a fact of life, something we learn we can't do anything about. We accept boredom the same way we put up with air pollution and inflation. Boredom is linked to the thought that there's really nothing I can do. Since creative people accept less than everyone else, they also don't accept that they can't change boring situations into non-boring ones.

In the case of a writer, how do you expect someone who just walked on Mars, who just rode into Vienna beside Napoleon, hell, who just made Napoleon ride into Vienna not to be bored at some routine meeting?

Ah you cry, but it's the same as when someone watches a film or reads a book, the escape is nothing more than a flickering, momentary respite from real life. Is it? For most people, yes, but the creative person is always working on his or her projects and ideas, even when they're at dinner with friends, or watching television. You're always working on your creations, thinking about them, shaping them and changing them. Since you never know what will trigger an idea, you're always looking, searching, exploring. The creative person wants to know about everything because he or she never knows when he or she might be able to use ideas and images to form a new idea.

When people are doing things they want to do, they don't get bored. They get bored when they have to do something that they really don't want to do but it's something they have to do.

I must create a system or be enslaved by another man's.

William Blake, English poet, painter

If you don't create your own structure, you have to deal with someone else's. Most people are relieved to learn they don't have to create their own structures in life. Creative people, however, desperately want to create their own structures. The fine and performing arts are often the vehicles they use to do this. The average person copes all day long with structures he or she did not create. It's called work. When it's over they go home and turn on the television to watch someone else's structure, someone else's creation. The creative person's need to build his or her own structure drives him or her to take up the virgin canvas, the fresh roll of film or a blank sheet of paper. It's a form of relaxation, but it's also a need, an overwhelming need to create one's own structure.

When I work I relax; doing nothing or entertaining visitors makes me tired.

Pablo Picasso, Spanish artist

When what is going on in a person's head is more interesting than what is going on around him, he or she gets bored.

While others believe they must always make the best of tedious situations, the creative person, like a child, is asking himself, "why must I? Why? If I can't change what's going on and make it interesting, at least let me leave!"

Creative people like to organize and control their situations. They are used to challenging everything they themselves didn't create. Hence they get bored faster when they're in someone else's situation. Creative people live with more emotion. While most people accept and even welcome that life is predictable and routine, the creative person's inner voice is screaming, no, no, no, it doesn't have to be!

Coping with "have to" is the most difficult thing they have to learn in life, the most difficult thing they have to do. Creative people are intrinsically motivated. They find their rewards in the activity itself, without waiting for external rewards or recognition.

Painting is no problem; the problem is what to do when you're not painting.
Jackson Pollack, American artist

We go back to the word "freedom," the freedom to choose, the freedom to decide, the freedom to do what one wants to do. It's important to realize that you have the capacity to shape your life the way you want to, that your problems as well as your successes are your own. It's too easy to blame failures on someone else or external situations. Part of "letting go" is coming to terms with the fact that you control your own destiny. The greatest tragedy in life is to let others assume control of it, to stop growing, to not exercise your own choices, to not try.

Creativity usually emanates from a sense of curiosity or from an inner drive for asking questions and solving problems differently. To do this, people must have freedom to express individuality of thought or action.
Pedro Cuatrecasas, president, pharmaceutical research, Parke-Davis in an essay in Ford and Gioia's Creative Action in Organizations

Obviously it's impossible to always do what one wants to do. We live in society, a society that is governed by laws and social conventions. That's why Picasso said he relaxed when he was working. When he was working, he did what he wanted, he chose, he decided. When he was creating, there were no situations when he felt he had to.

There is no must in art, because art is free.   *Wassily Kandinsky, Russian artist*

> **No must. Exactly. That's what creativity is all about. Freedom, that's what creativity is all about**

What man wants is simple independent choice, whatever it may cost and wherever it may lead.   *Fyodor Dostoevsky, Russian writer*

Minimize the situations when you feel you have to. Maximize the times when you do the things you really want to do.

To do all that one is able to do is to be a man; to do all that one would like to do is to be a god. *Napoleon Bonaparte, French emperor*

To do all that one is able to do is to be a human being; to do MORE of what one would like to do is to be a creative human being. That sounds like a pompous statement, but it's not. The reason most people don't do more of what they want to do is precisely because they're afraid of the reactions of other people if they do. They want so hard to please and to blend in. Fear stops people from being creative. If you want to be more creative, you have to let go, and to let go you have to stop being afraid.

Movement

God is really another artist. He invented the giraffe, the elephant and the cat. He has no real style. He just goes on trying other things. *Pablo Picasso*

How often do you try other things, not only new things, but other things? We all say we do. We all think we do. We all delude ourselves.

People are more creative when they are doing different things. Movement and change are vital for creativity. Repetition stifles it. The more often you do something in the same way, the more difficult it is to do it any other way.

I dreamed a thousand new paths. I awoke and walked my old one. *Chinese proverb*

People tend to do their best creative work when they step away from their day-to-day routines. The benefit of taking a vacation is not that it provides rest so that you're able to work harder when come back, but that the change it affords enables you to refresh your ideas and come up with new ideas.

The ability to shift opinions and perceptions is an important part of creativity. It includes the power to shift from foreground to background, think of things that are assumed to be negative as positive and vice versa and reverse assumptions.

The chains of habit are too weak to be felt until they are too strong to be broken. *Samuel Johnson, English writer*

The French artist Edgar Degas used to create a sense of movement and change by constantly moving the furniture and pictures around in his Paris apartment. Look around your house or apartment. When's the last time you moved the furniture around? Chances are that if you're like most people, you could walk through your house blindfolded without so much as bumping into a table. You know where every piece of furniture is simply because it's been there so long.

We know what a lot of you must be thinking. You don't move things because you like things the way they are. That smacks of another rationalization. People don't try different combinations of things to see what they like and they don't. They convince themselves that it would be a waste of time to try. If things are okay the way they are, they reason, there's no need for change. Chalk up yet another for the adequate.

John and Robin T. live in an affluent suburb of New York. He's worked for one company for twenty-three years; she's been with another firm for twenty-four. They've had the same house almost as long. Even though they go to different places on vacation, and try new restaurants, they're change resisters. Most people are. Most people feel no need to make significant changes in their lives. They're content with superficial changes.

It is said, often in jest, that a woman marries a man expecting he will change, but he doesn't, while a man marries a woman expecting that she won't change and she does. When it comes to resisting change, however, both sexes are equally at fault. Most people want to change, but spend their lives resisting it. People are suspicious of attempts to motivate them, to guide them in certain directions, to change them. The threat of change is nearly always disturbing. The healthier you are psychologically, the easier it is to accept change.

> **Change is essential to creativity. Movement is essential to creativity. Freedom is essential to creativity**

Movement and change are crucial to creativity. One needs to move, mentally and very often physically, in order to stop framing, get rid of the assumptions and change the perspective of a situation.

If you have a problem, don't sit down and try to solve it. Move mentally and physically. "If I do that I'll lose my concentration!" That's exactly what you want, to lose your concentration. You want to be able to assume a different perspective when you return, not the same tired, old one you had before you broke away.

> To be creative, move mentally. To do that, you may also have to move physically

Stare at an object for a little while. If you do, you'll find that the object tends to become fuzzy, or blurry, and that you need to blink or briefly look away and then back in order to make it sharp again.

What happens when you stare at something for too long is that the receptors in your eyes get tired and stop responding. The nerve cells in your sensory system then switch off. This process is called sensory adaptation. You become blind to what is right before your eyes. The same phenomenon explains why you can no longer smell a gas leak that you noticed when you first entered the kitchen.

When you don't use your imagination, it gets bored and switches off. You become blind to the opportunities right before your eyes, but you don't realize it until someone else points them out. Only then can you see what you had been looking at all along.

> Every now and then go away, have a little relaxation, for when you come back to your work your judgment will be surer since to remain constantly at work will cause you to lose power of judgment.   *Leonardo da Vinci, Italian artist*

Never rule out the blatantly obvious. It may just be the only solution possible. It also may be the best solution, but because it's so obvious we become suspicious of it. Never rule out the blatantly ridiculous either, it could also be the only reasonable conclusion.

When someone else sees something you were fully capable of seeing, but didn't, that person is labeled creative. Perhaps the person is, or perhaps he or she just happened to be on a different perspective at that moment in time, a perspective that you could have been on just as easily.

Ideas can come to you at any time, at any place. They rarely come to you when you call them directly, at least the good ones don't. An idea can come to you while you're talking on the phone, in the shower, playing a sport. We always tell our students, don't sit in the same seat every class and don't sit next to the same person. Change your perspective, move. Get up and change your seat halfway through the class. Moving changes your outlook on everything and helps to keep you from falling into predictable patterns.

> All truly great thoughts are conceived by walking.
>
>   *Friedrich Nietzsche, German philosopher*

The layout of most offices hinders creative thinking. If you work in a cubicle, or in an office without a window, your thinking will reflect that environment. There is a direct correlation between the kind of ideas that people have and the space they have in which to spawn them.

Have you ever had to write an essay for a test and not been able to organize your thoughts into one clear, crisp paragraph, let alone three or four? When you're sitting in one place, it's very difficult to come up with really new ideas and the ones you have you can't shake. Getting rid of ideas or thoughts that don't work is as important as coming up with new ones.

It's very difficult to write effectively if you have to sit in one place, if you can't move. Creative people, like children, can't sit still. They have to keep moving.

> **It's very difficult to be creative if you don't have the freedom to move**

Schools rarely encourage movement. In fact, they fight against it. In the lower grades students are routinely given assigned seats, something that helps the teacher but not the pupils. Even at university level, students have a tendency to sit in the same seats. Try getting up and walking about during an exam. Just try. One thought and one thought only will pop into the teacher's mind. You're trying to cheat.

Sit in your seat! Don't look anywhere! Don't move your eyes laterally. Look at your paper and only at your paper! That's fine if you're spitting back information, but if you're called upon to apply that information or write something where you need to organize your thoughts, a lack of movement is paralyzing.

Society today is becoming more and more visual. Today's child scans everything, from television to the Internet. Children who sit in front of a television with a remote control in hand are catching an image here, a phrase there. They catch the meaning of a program in a fraction of a second, get bored with it in a full second and surf on to the next channel.

The average American child spends more time watching television from kindergarten to twelfth grade than he spends in school. From the time he puts the television on till the time he shuts it off, the average American child surfs through the entire range of channels sixteen times. This programs a short attention span. Today's child learns visually, almost from birth.

Children are becoming adept at choosing among fast-multiplying options. The Internet is forcing them to process information at a far more rapid pace than ever before, and television and video games are forcing them to make rapid-fire, sequential decisions.

School systems, however, plod along using traditional, non-visual teaching methods. As our culture becomes more and more visual, the gap between student and teacher will widen and students will find it more and more difficult to learn.

> Do not confine your children to your own learnings, for they were born in another time.
>   *Hebrew proverb*

Concentrate, concentrate! That's the only way you'll get anywhere. Perhaps, but with creativity the more you concentrate, the more you go into the subject and the blinder you become. Short bursts of concentration work much better. Concentrate, look away, do something else, clear your mind, then come back. When you do, you'll see things differently.

The longer you work on a problem, the more accustomed you become to its details and the more difficult it is to see it differently. You may find yourself traveling the same mental route over and over. Solutions escape you because of your inability to mentally step away from the problem and see it differently.

A lot of creative people work on projects simultaneously. Whenever they encounter obstacles in one project, they shift to another. By having multiple projects, you're more likely to have a breakthrough somewhere. You're always moving. By shifting from project to project (or from one train of thought to another), you can bring elements and perspectives from one area that can help with another.

Change

First Principle of Design: Any change looks terrible at first

---

Most people are deathly afraid of change. One reason is a lack of confidence in their ability to adapt to an ambiguous or unpredictable environment. Change is disturbing. The natural tendency is to stay with what is known, to play it safe. Change can be frightening. It's the unknown and anything that we don't know we also fear. Our imagination rushes forward with dozens of apprehensions, all of which become more vibrant because they are indefinable and cannot be labeled.

Fear forces us to stick to what we know, to those patterns of behavior which have been successful in the past. If we never try anything new, however, we can't hope to grow. Growth means advancing to some place or some state that we have yet to experience. Incorporated into the fear of change are two others, "cenophobia," which is the fear of new things or ideas and "cacorraphiaphobia," the fear of failure. If you try something new, you don't know what your chances of failure are, and thus imagine them to be disproportionably high, but if you try something you've done before, you know your success/failure ratio.

Anytime you have change that challenges the traditional acceptance of a certain situation, you will have people who are worried that this is going to take us down the path to destruction. It's amazing to me how long that has been with us, probably since we evolved.   *Faye Waffleton, American feminist, activist*

There is a time for departure even when there's no place to go

That's a very scary statement for most people. Change is usually only acceptable if a better replacement or alternative is available.

Hitler's persecution of the Jews in Germany initially took the form of trying to get them to leave the country voluntarily. While they were allowed to go, they had to leave all their possessions behind. Many Jews astutely recognized that harsher measures would follow, and fled, while many others stayed behind. Survivors of the concentration camps who were asked why they had not fled before the war, when they'd had the opportunities, all gave the same answer: "I couldn't conceive of leaving my home and everything I'd worked for, and besides, I had no place to go." A condition of successful change has always been the acceptance of the uncertainty of the future.

Most people view change as something negative

They feel that changing is an admission of defeat, incompetence or inadequacy. It doesn't have to be. It really doesn't, but that's a difficult thing for most people to accept.

What is life, if not a process filled with adventure? Think about it. It's a trip, which has not yet ended. You didn't choose to go on this voyage of yours. You didn't have a say in the timing or the point of departure, nor did your choose the people who began the trip with you.

All trips force the people who take them to deal with change. The question then is not whether you must change or not, but whether you can harness the processes of change to work for rather than against you. If you accept that life is indeed a trip then there are several ways to look at it. You can use words such as "trek," "journey," "hike" or "odyssey." These words invoke visions of a grand and certainly laborious undertaking. In the 1960s, people came to call life a "trip," a trip filled with surprises and unexpected bumps in the road. Adults tend to regard life as a journey, while children and creative adults look upon it more as a sort of vacation. If you can think like a child, you'll find that you have an easier time accepting change.

The biggest job confronting most managers today is convincing the people who work for them that change doesn't mean loss. If we are resistant to change, we are resistant to discovery, invention, creativity and progress. Change is inevitable, yet we continue to be change resisters.

Everyone feels insecure to some extent. The important thing is to keep in mind that a good deal of insecurity is groundless. Most people are at least a little apprehensive about tackling a new assignment, trying to adjust to a new situation, and a lot of them aren't just apprehensive but downright scared. We usually go on, however, to meet the challenge successfully. The fears that accompany all new situations are enough to block our creativity.

> **To be creative, you must welcome rather than fear change**

Jake Winebaum, a former chairman of Walt Disney's Buena Vista Internet Group, reported in a recent issue of *Fast Company Magazine* that he found it difficult getting the people at Disney to fully embrace the Internet because it meant taking a chance. Change resisters at Disney protested that they didn't see the need for the transition to the new technology. He said:

> What they meant was that they were afraid of the new technology, afraid to venture into an arena where they couldn't be in control, and afraid of a situation in which their leadership would be questioned.

Being open to change doesn't mean embracing every new idea, for many new ideas lead nowhere. It does, however, mean being willing to suspend judgment long enough to give every new idea, no matter how bizarre or radical it may seem, a fair chance to prove itself.

If it works, it's obsolete.

Anonymous

Three things can be said about change:

- Change is inevitable.
- Everybody resists change.
- Without change there would be no progress.

The world we have made as a result of the level of thinking we have done thus far creates problems we cannot solve at the same level of thinking at which we created them.   *Albert Einstein, German-born US physicist, mathematician*

Change is an important part of leadership. No great leader leaves the world the way he or she found it. Changing something before anyone else does is both original and creative, yet it is not enough just to change something, or yourself, you must also make others aware that they too have the possibility of altering their lives.

How many times have you heard the following phrases?

- Don't rock the boat.
- Whatever you do, don't change a thing.
- Don't go looking for trouble.
- Kids need stability. It's unfair to move them to new schools and from their friends.
- What are you going to do if it doesn't work?

How many times have you heard these phrases? How many times have you uttered these phrases? How many times have you let your fears stop you from changing?

There is a certain relief in change, even though it be from bad to worse.

Washington Irving, American novelist

That's another scary statement. Creative people understand it though, because they are less afraid of change than other people.

Art Gogatz reveals:

When I tell a class that I change my watch a couple times a day, they find it amusingly odd. I don't just change my watch. I change all my clothes a couple of times each day when I can. I get bored wearing the same things. A change of clothes is like a splash of cold water, it changes my attitude and that changes the way I look at things.

How often do you change your "look"? The Beatles changed their look several times. They went from being a mop-haired, mod-clad combo to hippies and proponents of Zen before the rest of the music industry had time to adjust. By doing so they kept ahead of the pack, ahead of their competition. Madonna has done much the same thing. In the world of pop music she's managed to maintain her status for years. She went from virgin to material girl, to ambitious blond, to sex demon, to nudist, to mother. Like the Fab Four before her, she's always been ready for anything. That's the difference, the willingness to go anywhere and do anything. Yes, we said "anything," anything legal, of course. It shouldn't surprise you to learn that most people aren't ready for "anything," By the time most people decide to get up to dance the song is over.

You are not who you were yesterday

Of course you aren't. You're different. It's a new day, a new beginning, a new you in a new world. That's all easy to say. In reality, though, you know it's the same old you in the same old tedious world. Most adults don't feel different from one day to another, from one month to another and often from one year to another. Most adults don't want to have to deal with change.

Most businesses don't change until they have to. They wait until things are going badly before doing anything. People are the same. There is an often-repeated observation that you can't walk into the same river twice. While a river doesn't change from day to day, the water in it constantly does. In much the same way, no person is the same from one day to another. We're always a little older, always changing, always learning, always reacting to things happening around us.

Richard Farson, in his book *Management of the Absurd*, offers this:

Most often what gets organizations into trouble are faulty leadership styles, poor internal relationships and managerial blind spots. The delusional hope of a troubled organization is that it will be saved without having to make changes in these highly personal areas. The hope is that no members of the organization will have to make wrenching changes in the way they work together, or in their personal beliefs about themselves and the ways they make decisions. Thus, even when experts are called into troubled companies, the managers most often seek impersonal solutions, better ways to select new executives, a new formula for success, a new series of pep talks. They are seldom prepared for the intense self-examination that is so often necessary to reach the core of the problem.

People are the same. They're always looking for quick, painless solutions that are low risk and low cost. That's why they opt for short-term diets instead of examining their overall eating and exercise patterns and why they invest in lottery tickets, even though the chances of winning are astronomical. Yes, we want to lose weight and stop smoking and become firmer and healthier and smarter and richer, and we want all those things without having to change our basic ways of thinking and behaving.

There is considerable evidence to show that even though people know what they need to do to achieve their goals, they lack the willpower to do it. That's one of the reasons why we opened this book by talking about motivation. People know when things aren't right in their lives, yet most lack the willpower to effect real change. Instead they wait, hoping that time will spin some magic, yet knowing that time will only magnify the problem.

The best time to go to the dentist is before the tooth starts hurting. The best time to go to the doctor is before you get ill. In olden times in the Orient people paid the doctor when they were healthy and didn't pay him when they were ill. It was the doctor's job to keep them healthy. When someone got ill, it meant that the doctor wasn't doing his job properly. Therefore, the physician had no reason to get paid.

The best time to change is before you have to.

Risk

> When choosing between two evils, I always like to try the one I've never tried before.
> *Mae West, American actress*

It is often said in jest that you know you are middle-aged when you have two hot dates and you choose the one that gets you home earlier. That's the way most people live their lives. We want safe simulated adventure, amusement parks, theme parks, video games, not real adventure.

Remember what we said earlier about lateral thinking? We are all trained to think vertically, to go from one logical step to the next, moving all the time towards the one correct solution to a problem or issue. That's the way we tend to live our lives, moving from one logical step to the next, moving slowly forward, never backwards, never sideways, always forward, always logical.

We study in order to get jobs. Once we have the job we want, the only logical reason to leave it is for a better one, better meaning better benefits or security, better opportunity for advancement, the promise of on-the-job training, and of course the big one, more money. There's progress inherent in this line of thinking, there's a sense of advancement. Someone who takes a second mortgage on their house in order to finance their own business is taking a risk, yet there's logic here. One is taking a financial risk for a greater financial return. People can understand that. What throws them is when you do something illogical.

In the 1980s Art Gogatz and his wife decided to move to Europe:

> At the time I was vice-president of an advertising agency in New York and my wife was working on her graduate degree in philosophy. What we were doing made no sense to other people. We weren't going to Europe for better jobs, or any jobs, for that matter. We weren't going because we had scholarships. We were going simply because we wanted to. Friends and family flipped. They told us over and over again that we were crazy. They screamed even louder when I refused my advertising agency's offer to double my salary if I stayed. What we were doing made no sense to anyone, except to us.

When you live your life by doing only things that makes sense, you are listening to your head. When you live your life by doing what you truly and deeply want, you are listening to your heart.

Art recalls

> When I came home and told my wife that they'd double my salary if I stayed, she asked me a very good question: "If we stay will you be twice as happy?" The answer was, of course, no, and so we set out for Europe, and ended up living there thirteen years."

*   *   *

> It is the heart always that sees, before the head can see.
>
> *Thomas Carlyle, Scottish writer*

If you follow your heart, how do you justify your actions to other people? In effect, you can't. Creative people accept that you can't always justify things and go ahead, while non-creative people exhaust themselves attempting to justify everything they do to everyone and, in the end, bowing to reason and doubt.

> The heart has reasons which reason knows nothing of.
>
> *Blaise Pascal, French philosopher*

Intuition

> The only real valuable thing is intuition.   *Albert Einstein*

The capacity for making intuitive decisions is a basic ingredient of creativity. Intuition means relinquishing control of the thinking mind and trusting the vision of the unconscious. Because it can't be rationally justified, more often than not it too is opposed.

One definition of intuition: *The direct knowing or learning of something without the conscious use of reasoning.*

When we trust our intuition, we are really turning to the wisdom of the unconscious. The unconscious mind is far more suited to creative insight than the conscious mind, for there are no self-censoring judgments in the unconscious. The unconscious mind is free from the rationality that channels conscious ideas into a linear, vertical mode. Hence, ideas that would be rejected by the rational mind have a chance to be born. The question is: Do we trust them, or do we reject them? Most people reject them.

Viola Spolin, the renowned drama teacher, has this to say about intuition:

> Intuition emerges in the right half of the brain, in the metaphoric mind, the X-area, the area of knowledge, which is beyond the restrictions of culture, race, education, psychology and age. It is deeper than the survival dress of mannerisms, prejudices, intellectualism and borrowings most of us wear to live our daily lives.

Most people simply don't trust their intuition. If you make a decision intuitively, how do you explain it to your family, your boss or your directors? How do you defend yourself if it goes wrong? Better not take a chance. Stay with reason. Stay with logic. No one can question that.

> First feelings are always the most natural.   *Louis XIV, French king*

Children growing up are rarely taught to trust their intuition. In fact, it's quite the opposite. You also still hear people talk of intuition as women's intuition, as if it were something strange or marginal that men don't dare possess.

Trusting your intuition means listening to your heart

Knowledge is the distilled essence of your intuitions, corroborated by experience.
Elbert Hubbard, American editor, educator

Intuition is becoming increasingly more important today, simply because there is so much data to process. How do we go through it all? What's important and what's not? How do we know when we have enough? Do we keep looking, or go with what we have?

Matz's maxim: A conclusion is the place where you got tired of thinking

Ted Turner, of Turner Broadcasting, was once asked how he could have known that a market for a cable news services existed, before the launch of CNN. The question was an important one because it involved a major investment at an early stage in the evolution of his business empire. Turner sat back and thought for a minute, then calmly replied: "I just knew it."

How to break through invisible barrier nine

This barrier is one of the more difficult ones to break through because we are all afraid to really let go. We're afraid to be out of control even for a few minutes. When you learn to swim, you're out of control as soon as you let go of the edge or the bottom of the pool. When you learn to ski, most people are first taught to snowplow, which is, in effect, a way to brake. That works fine as long as the ground is level or the slope is an easy one, but as soon as the slopes gets steeper, it doesn't work. To really ski, you've got to keep the skis parallel and brake by turning across the slope. What's difficult is to get an adult beginner to point their skis straight down the slope for a few seconds before they turn. For those few seconds you are out of control, and you have to learn to accept it, or you won't ski.

ACTIVITIES

1. Think about how security-oriented you are. Just thinking about these things can help you to realize patterns and trends of which you may be unaware. What kind of insurance do you have? What kind of retirement benefits? How much do you worry about getting sick? How much do you worry about retirement?

    How much do you travel? Do you have places and countries that you would love to visit but have put off mainly because you're afraid that if you go, you'll have to deal with another language, another culture, and a set of new and destabilizing circumstances which will take you out of your area of security and control? Make a list of the countries you visited in the last five years, countries which you visited on your own, without the help of a group or a tour, countries where you didn't speak the native language? For most people, three countries would be lot.

2. When was the last time you changed your look? Dig out some photo albums and look at the pictures which were taken over the last five years. Except for looking older, what changes do you see?

"I'm not afraid of other people"

In order to be creative we have to relinquish control and overcome fear. Real creativity is life-altering. It threatens the status-quo; it makes us see things differently. It brings about change and we are terrified of change.

MADELEINE L'ENGLE, AMERICAN AUTHOR

On a scale of 1 to 10, with 1 being not at all afraid and 10 terrified, rate your fear of the following:

- Death
- Snakes
- Ridicule
- Illness
- Failure
- High places
- Other people
- Mice or rats
- The unknown
- Darkness.

If you're like most people, you will say that you are most afraid of death and illness and least afraid of darkness and other people.

> If you're not afraid of other people then why do you dread having to stand up before a group of complete strangers and talk, sing, act or play music?

It's true. Most people are terrified to stand before a group and make a presentation. Hundreds of thousands of jobs require making presentations, addressing groups both up and down the chain of command, running committee meetings, heading up teams, representing the company in different venues, and explaining to prospective clients why your product is better than a competitors. Public speaking is a common source of stress, but it doesn't have to be.

One of the exercises we asked you to do at the end of barrier number one was to write down three things you would love to do but are too embarrassed to do. If you didn't do the exercise, take a few minutes and do it now. The things can be anything you want. There are no correct answers. The only stipulation is that they should be legal things.

The most common answers are:

- Speak, sing, act, dance or play music in public
- Open, honest communication. Tell people what I think (tell them off, or, conversely, how much I care for them)
- Dress the way I want, or at times undress, be nude, or partially nude, in public.

All three things are easy to do when we're alone. When no one is around, even the shyest person can belt out a song or deliver a moving discourse, yet put us in front of an audience and we immediately freeze. Saying what we think is never a problem if we're alone, neither is a lack of clothes. Bring in the neighbors, however, and boy do we have a problem.

Fear of rejection, ridicule and failure also come from a fear of other people. Whether you realize it or not, this fear controls much of your thinking and behavior. Fear of other people is a powerful force that keeps a businessman or sales professional from prospecting, cold calling, calling higher in an organization, asking for the order, going for the close, or asking the customer for information so they can offer real solutions. It keeps all of us from asking for raises, asking people out on dates, asking for promotions, asking for what we want.

Let's face it. The biggest fear for most people is OTHER PEOPLE. Fear of other people keeps countless talented candidates from landing the jobs they want. Your résumé serves one purpose, to get you an interview. Once you get one the real work begins, yet job interviews are another common cause of stress.

What's the best way to approach a job interview? As with many things in life, you'll do much better if you embrace the process, rather than focusing on the result, which is the job. To attain significant results in anything from losing weight to speaking a second language, you need to love the process. When you don't have a passion for what you're doing, you don't do it well.

Look at it this way. What is a job interview? It's a chance to talk about you, and people pay psychiatrists big money for that privilege. In a job interview you're getting someone to listen for free. If you adopt that kind of mindset, the job interview becomes something you look forward to, not something you loathe. People who enjoy something radiate self-confidence and that attracts rather than repels.

How can you come to love something you're afraid of? By first understanding that you don't like it because you're afraid. If you conquer your fear, it will become easier to warm to the process.

We promise according to our hopes and perform according to our fears.
François, duc de La Rochefoucauld, French writer

What is the worst thing that can happen to you if you have to speak or sing in public and do it badly, that you'll *look* foolish, stupid, and ridiculous to others? No, the worst thing is that you'll *feel* yourself foolish, stupid and ridiculous.

We all want to sing well, perform well, play well, but it's not always possible. If you sing in public, and you make a fool of yourself, can you say, "so *what*?" These are two little words, but two very important ones. So what? If you can say them, and mean them, you can start to overcome your fear of performing in public.

The problem is not one of singing. Even if you have a horrible voice, you probably sing occasionally when you're alone. The problem is not you but other people. You want to maintain a certain image in front of other people.

Obviously, though, the problem is you. You're concerned about your image. You weren't as a child. Children are not as afraid of appearing ridiculous. For non-creative people, not appearing to be silly, stupid or ridiculous is one of their major preoccupations. For creative people it's not a major preoccupation, and for highly creative people it's not a preoccupation at all.

So I sang. So I made a fool of myself. So what? I'm still here. I'm still the same. Nothing's changed. The sun will come up tomorrow. The same people will love me. The world will still go round. Spring will come again. So I sang, so what? No harm done. Better to have made a fool of myself than to have sat on my hands and done nothing. That's right, better to have made a fool of myself than to have done nothing. Creative people actually believe that.

Looking back, I imagine I was always writing. Twaddle it was, but better to write twaddle or anything, anything than nothing at all.

Katherine Mansfield, American author

Better to have made a fool of myself than to have sat on my hands and done nothing. Better to write garbage than nothing at all. Better to do something, even if it doesn't work, than to do nothing. Do you believe that? Could you believe that?

Now, we've been talking worst-case scenario that you make a fool of yourself. Perhaps you won't. In fact, you probably won't. You just can't worry about whether you will or not, because if you do, the anxiety will prevent you from doing anything. Most people actually want to be the one performing, it's just that the fear of performing vastly outweighs the desire. The result is frustration at not being able to perform, relief sure, for not having to get up there, but frustration quickly follows any sense of relief that you may have.

Creative people want to sing, want to act and want to perform. When they do, they may experience uneasiness, but nothing to rival the stomach turmoil, which non-creative people feel. In class, when you ask for volunteers for an exercise, books fly open and eyes find things on the floor to focus upon. Students are relieved not to be chosen and the unlucky ones who are picked do what they have to do as rapidly as possible and scurry back to their chairs.

The feeling that highly creative people have (and this feeling outweighs any natural feelings of uneasiness the person may have) is, why should I let someone else make the speech when I can do it! Why should I let some other person perform when it can be me up there? Why should I let someone else be the fool, when I can be the fool, when I can be a better fool! Why should I sit here and listen to that guy sing? I want to sing. You have to want the attention, you have to need the attention, you have to crave the attention.

It's better to be looked over than overlooked.   *Mae West, American actress*

Can you go up to people you don't know and talk to them? Can you walk into a room of people you don't know and feel comfortable with them? If you can't, you're going to have a hard time delivering a presentation, for a presentation doesn't mean simply knowing your subject, it means establishing an emotional bond with your audience, and that starts with them feeling that you feel comfortable.

Any time you give a speech or make a presentation, there is an element of trust, a special bond that has to develop between you and the audience. That bond does not depend on what you say but upon what the audience senses about you. Insecurity is something people quickly pick up on, so is sincerity.

If you ever feel inclined to be timid as you are going up to someone, just remind yourself, "why should I be frightened, he's just a person who is obviously more frightened of me than I am of him, or he would have approached me first."

If everyone suddenly disappeared, and you were given one wish, that wish would be to bring everyone back. People cannot and do not want to live unrelated to other people. If you cannot live without them, then why should you fear them?

Art Gogatz relates the following from his childhood:

When I was twelve years old and in junior high school in the Bronx in New York City, I went shopping with my mother one day for shoes. For some strange, inexplicable reason the store had a pair of red suede shoes. I say strange because at the time red suede shoes for men or boys was something that was unheard of. Back then, men's clothing was very conservative; it actually still is, but back then it was worse. Anyway, I told my mother that I wanted the red shoes. She looked at me and said, "if you wear those to school, the other kids will make fun of you no end and then you won't wear them, and I'm not going to buy you two pairs of shoes." "I don't care," I answered. "I want them." "Okay, I'll buy them for you," she said, "but you're going to have to wear them every day, no matter how much the other kids laugh." "Deal," I answered, and went home with the shoes. The next day at school it was just as my mother had predicted. The kids were beside themselves, laughing and hooting like banshees. It bothered me, but not that much. Same thing happened the next day and the next. By the second week, it had all blown over. The shoes were no longer a topic of interest or comment at school. I'm glad my mother had the courage to let me decide whether to buy them or not, a lot of other parents wouldn't have done that.

Creative people want to control their own lives and hence fight, not only against the limits and boundaries which society imposes, but also against the psychological barriers.

Acting is a razor's edge between the sublime and the terribly silly.

John Hurt, British actor

Actors, models and all those who perform before the public are able to do what you're not able to, which is overcome their embarrassment and their inhibitions. Do they look natural on camera? Do they radiate confidence? Of course, they do. When the camera lights come on, they are able to turn on the charm. Is it easy to do? Well, most people need to be slightly drunk to get rid of their inhibitions. Creative people can do it without alcohol. They know that everyone else is too scared to appear silly, and they'd rather be silly than scared. If you think back you will find that anything you've ever done that ultimately was worthwhile, probably initially scared you half to death.

> **If you want to be creative, you can't worry about looking silly, not in person and not through your work**

Have you ever considered that if you don't make waves, nobody, including yourself, will know that you are alive?

Theodore Isaac Rubin, American psychiatrist, author

Remember we said that everyone sings in the shower. People find it easier to sing before a group of friends than they do in front of a group of strangers. Actually it should be the opposite. Strangers are people you'll never see again. They're like people sitting in the back of the balcony. You don't know them, they don't know you, and you'll have no contact with them once the performance is over.

Sing for your friends and they'll remind you of it for years to come. Yet the average person would still rather sing for their friends. They'd rather sing for their friends because they feel at ease, whereas they feel uncomfortable with strangers.

No one can make you feel inferior without your consent.   *Eleanor Roosevelt*

> **No one can make you feel foolish without your consent either**

That's right. You yourself sit squarely at the controls of your very own problem. Imagine what it would be like to feel comfortable before any audience, before any public? We come back to a word we've used over and over in this book. That word is **Freedom**!

Feel comfortable with and before anyone, anytime, anyplace? Easier said than done, you're thinking. I'll never be able to do that! In fact, no one can! All right, consider this: People who produce art, no matter the media, must learn to deal with vulnerability, rejection and criticism through their work. It is easier to deal with personal criticism if you've already experienced it via your work. That's why we said at the beginning of this book that the highest form of creativity is a blend of intellectual and artistic creativity.

A Zen master, talking to a group, asserted that he could heal ailments by the use of words alone. One of the men questioned the master: "You mean mental ailments, don't you? Words can affect the mind, but not the body." The Zen master looked at the man very sternly and said: "That was a very stupid remark." At that the man's body tensed, his face turned red and he was about to protest, when the master continued: "If those words can have such an effect on your body, surely other words can have other effects."

No one wants his or her remarks to be called stupid. No one wants his or her work to be called stupid. No one wants to be called stupid. However:

If you want to be creative, you can't worry about what people think of your creations. If you do, you'll stop creating
If you want to be creative, you can't worry about what people think of you. If you do, you'll stop creating

---

If you want to feel comfortable in any situation, you've got to throw yourself into it. Go in the direction of your fear. Facing fear costs you no money and takes no special talent. What it does take is commitment and motivation. Speak, sing, act! TRY! Most people do a fraction of what they would like to do. Most people never try. Only when you try and succeed do you realize how far you can go.

> Life's but a walking shadow, a poor player
> That struts and frets his hour upon the stage
> And then is heard of no more   *William Shakespeare*, Macbeth

How long do you want to be on stage in life? Seconds, minutes, hours? What about weeks or months or years? How long do you want to be in the spotlight?

Art Gogatz reveals:

All my students who perform exercises before the group, whether it be speaking, singing or acting, find the exercises to be "letting-go" experiences. They discover they weren't as hard as their anxiety led them to believe they would be. They gain confidence. Of course they don't immediately overcome their fears of being before the public. That takes time and more practice, but they do get there. So can you.

When was the last time you were absurd in front of other people? Was it when you were a child? Was it when you were drunk? You can't separate creativity from risk taking. The best ideas are so crazy, so ahead of their time that people are going to laugh at them and at you for coming up with them.

Overcoming the fear of other people means summoning the courage to let go of your image and just be yourself. Most of us spend our entire adult lives trying to be someone else, someone cool, someone knowledgeable, someone in control, someone perfect. People don't want you to be perfect. They want you to be just like them, only without their fears. That's right, without their fears.

> It's a miserable state of mind to have few things to desire and many things to fear.
>
> *Francis Bacon, Irish painter*

If your present situation doesn't give you the opportunity to overcome your fear of public speaking, register for a class. Ask more questions at work, at meetings. Ask more questions. Ask lots of them. What kind of questions?

Dumb questions

Dumb questions refocus our attention on issues that are being taken for granted. They bring us back to basics. They make us look at issues and problems from the beginning. They focus on the whole rather than on the parts. They are childlike. Children ask dumb questions. You used to ask dumb questions.

Remember the children's story, The Emperor's New Clothes? That was the story in which two tailors wove clothes for an emperor with magical thread that would be invisible to any incompetent person. Of course no one could see the clothes for the thread didn't exist. No one in the land, the emperor included, dared to admit they couldn't see the new garments. On the day the emperor wore the clothes in public, it fell to a child to say: "But he isn't wearing anything!"

> Children and creative adults say the things that everyone else just thinks

Don't be ashamed to say what you are not ashamed to think.
Michel de Montaigne, French essayist

Saying what they think often gets children and creative adults into trouble. Children are excused because they don't know any better. Creative people know better, but they just can't help themselves. They can't keep it in. They can't swallow it. They can't *just think* it. So they say it, and it often does get them into trouble. Creative people use many ways to say it, directly is one, but also via their poems, stories, photographs and music.

A person usually has two reasons for doing something: a good reason and the real reason.   *John Pierpoint Morgan, American financier*

The creative person tells you the real reason, and that often embarrasses the listener. "Why do we have to go to Aunt Rose's?" Dumb question! "Because we have to!" "Why do we need a meeting?" Dumb question! Why? It's a dumb question because no one ever asks it. Everyone just assumes that meetings are important. Some are, but others just aren't. The average business executive in North America spends more time in meetings than in anything else. The average meeting is too long. The average meeting includes people who don't have to be there. Think back to the last meeting you attended. You were happy to go, weren't you? Why? Because important things happen at meetings and only important people get to go.

Men love war because it allows them to look serious.
John Fowles, American novelist

They love meetings for the same reason. So do women. Let's go back to your last meeting. In retrospect, was the meeting too long? Were you bored? Was a lot of the time spent on tangents and detail? Did you leave the meeting with the same enthusiasm with which you went in?

Corning Glass, Equitable Life, Johnson & Johnson and Westinghouse are just some of the firms that have tried to cut down the time their people spend in meetings by experimenting with "stand up" meetings.

> It does work, no question about it. People don't b.s. They get right to the point because they hate to stand.   *Frank Anthony, vice-president, Corning Glass*

The only way to take leaps when using lateral thinking is by a provocative or dumb question. Provocative questions, however, are not always socially acceptable. Neither are dumb questions. Questions should be intelligent. Questions should reflect not only our understanding of the subject under discussion but also our intelligence. They should impress people. At all costs, avoid dumb questions. Why? Dumb question! Because you don't want to appear stupid, do you? Ah!

Reuben Mondejar has taught seminars all over the world. At each, he encourages the audience to ask questions and many people do. At the close of a session, however, there are always people who come up to him with additional questions, to which he replies: "It's a shame you didn't ask the question during the session. I'm sure others could have benefited from the answer." Of course, Reuben knows why they didn't ask the question during the session. They were afraid their questions wouldn't sound intelligent enough.

> He who asks is a fool for five minutes, but he who does not ask remains a fool forever.   *Chinese proverb*

The only dumb question is the question you don't ask

Launegayer's Observation: Asking dumb questions is easier than correcting dumb mistakes

---

A lot of people at meetings are afraid to ask questions. They're afraid their questions will appear stupid and that the questions will make them look bad.

The ordinary person puts up a struggle against all that is not himself, whereas it is against himself (his work and his creations), in a limited but all essential field, that the creative person has to battle. It's a totally different battle. That's what most people don't realize. *It's a totally different battle.*

The formulation of a problem is often more essential than its solution, which may be merely a matter of mathematical or experimental skill.

Albert Einstein, German-born US physicist, mathematician

My greatest strength as a consultant is to be ignorant and ask a few questions.

Peter Drucker, American management consultant.

In his book, *Innovation and Entrepreneurship* Peter Drucker goes on to state:

An innovation, to be effective, has to be simple. It should do only one thing, otherwise it confuses. All effective innovations are breathtakingly simple. Indeed, the greatest praise an innovation can receive is for people to say: "This is obvious. Why didn't I think of it?"

The consultant's principal role is to make a company aware of the processes that may be limiting its growth. The organization is usually aware of the problems, but is in the denial stage. Most people also define a problem as something outside themselves. You often hear them say, "the problem is 'those people.'" The desire for advice usually does not include a person's, or a client's, own way of thinking and acting.

> Advice is what we ask for when we know the answer but wish we didn't

Rationalizations are what we search for when we know what we should do but don't have the courage to do. The consultant's role, like the artist's, is to make others poignantly aware of what they already know but don't have the courage to act on. The firm, after all, has an interest in maintaining the status quo, including commitments to people and programs that may no longer be advantageous. A good consultant must be able to move a firm out of this tendency. A good consultant mustn't be afraid to ask dumb questions.

Dumb questions help you to simplify things. They help you to break out of your traditional ways of looking at things. They are at the birth of anything really new. It has been said that knowledge is a process of amassing facts, but that wisdom lies in their simplification.

Dumb questions are efficient questions. They force you to see things in a simpler and therefore clearer manner. They force you to look at old things in a new way, and that's what creativity is all about.

Boundaries

Rules are prisons.   *William Bernbach, American co-founder of Doyle,*
Dane Bernbach, advertising agency

Creativity cannot exist with hard boundaries and strict rules. In fact, creativity tears down boundaries and opens doors. Creative people fight against the confines of boundaries, limits and details, which in our culture are very clearly set forth. Rules, regulations and beliefs reflect these tight, linear boundaries.

Convictions are also prisons. They don't let you see far enough. They blind you, even to the obvious.

> **Creatively speaking, boundaries inhibit and limit what may or may not be done, not what can or cannot be done**

Boundaries are like assumptions; when no boundaries exist, people tend to create them. Boundaries, assumptions and restrictive thoughts are all things that prevent you from being as creative as you should be. Most people limit themselves to what may or may not be done. Highly creative people concern themselves only with what can or cannot be done. They don't break laws or commit crimes in their search for creativity, but they do break social rules, they do break the invisible nets that stop everyone else. In terms of creativity, who has the advantage and who has a disadvantage? The playing field isn't level. In fact, it's not even the same playing field.

When you think of limits, you create them. You can be trapped by not letting go of your beliefs, opinions, worries and anxieties. We've talked about creativity as being a "letting-go" experience. Boundaries serve as protections, but they are also used for the purpose of control. They restrict the very people they are protecting.

Writing has laws of perspectives, of light and shade just as painting does or music. If you are born knowing them, fine. If not, learn them. Then rearrange the rules to suit yourself.   *Truman Capote, American novelist*

That is true not only for writers, but for all creative people. Anyone who crosses boundaries can expect to find critics. Therefore, to cross boundaries, you must be willing to take risks.

Daring to dare

To dare is to lose one's footing momentarily. To not dare is to lose oneself.
Søren Kierkegaard, Danish philosopher

The only really sure way to avoid making mistakes is to have no new ideas. No new ideas, no provocative ideas, no daring ideas, no radical ideas, that's the philosophy to which most of us adhere . If we only come up with ideas which make no waves, then we end up not using any of our ideas but only the warmed-up ideas of others. It's sad not to have any new ideas, but it's sadder yet to have ideas and be afraid of them.

The reality of a situation is almost never as bad as fear makes it seem. Once people are caught up in an event, they cease to be afraid. It is the unknown which frightens people.

Studies show that experts in sports such as parachute or bungee jumping, hang gliding or white water rafting display little or no anxiety prior to the jump, flight or run. Beginners, on the contrary, are plagued with anxiety for hours, days and even weeks before. The anticipation of what they are about to do fills them with stress. Beginners play out everything in their minds before the jump or the flight. What they imagine is that the parachute fails to open or the boat hits the rocks. The anxiety that accompanies risk taking stems from the fear of failure.

Human beings are the only creatures who are allowed to fail. If an animal in the wild fails, it will probably die. People, however, are allowed to learn from their mistakes and failures.

I've missed more than 9,000 shots in my career. I've lost almost 300 games. Twenty-six times I've been trusted to take the same winning shot and missed. I've failed over and over and over again in my life and that is why I've succeeded.   *Michael Jordan, pro basketball player in a TV commercial for Nike*

Fear of failure is what keeps many of us from turning our innovative ideas into action, from following our dreams. The fear cycle starts with the imagination running wild. You imagine everything to be worse than it is, and you magnify the consequences of the anticipated failure until you give it catastrophic proportions.

Nothing in life is to be feared. It is only to be understood.
Marie Curie, French chemist

"Do that which you fear to do, and the fear will die" is a phrase that many famous people have uttered. It is true, but perhaps not right away. Perhaps the phrase should be: "Do that which you fear to do and the fear will *begin* to die."

> We pay a heavy price for our fear of failure. It is a powerful obstacle to growth. It assures the progressive narrowing of the personality and prevents exploration and experimentation. There is no learning without some difficulty and fumbling. If you want to keep on learning, you must keep on risking failure, all your life.
>
> *John Gardner, American poet, author, educator*

One of the most common responses to the fear is to back up, shy away and procrastinate. The inevitable phone call, the unpleasant decision is put off while you immerse yourself in "busy work", detailed work which you tell yourself is important. For most people time is a scarce commodity. There's never enough. Being busy, however, is often the blanket that hides our fears. By keeping busy with what we know we can do, we avoid having to face the possibility of failure.

Whenever we're afraid, it's because we don't have enough confidence in our abilities to cope with a certain situation. Usually it's because the situation's a new one, or perhaps it's an old situation with new people involved. Fear beats us down more than anything else because when we're afraid we find excuses not to try, and without an attempt, there's no hope of success.

> An essential aspect of creativity is not being afraid to fail.
>
> *Dr. Edwin Land, inventor of the Polaroid land camera*

A man who is afraid of doing badly in a job interview fails to get the job. The failure then reinforces his fears, for he has the evidence to prove how bad he does in interviews. What's sad is that when you are afraid, you don't do your best. Confidence alone will not always get you through every situation, but if you're confident, at least you won't handicap yourself. You'll give every situation your best shot.

It should be remembered that Babe Ruth, perhaps the most famous and celebrated player in the history of baseball, struck out 1,330 times in his career. Not everything we do can be successful, yet if we don't do something out of fear that we may not succeed, we won't really do very much with our lives. Every time you don't try, you've already failed.

Most people believe that you're finished if you go bankrupt. They equate bankruptcy with having to beg coins on the street, yet statistics tell us that the average millionaire entrepreneur in the US has gone bankrupt 2.8 times before he or she made a million dollars. Most of us never give ourselves a chance to go bankrupt. Risk, we constantly tell ourselves, must be avoided.

If you don't expose yourself to risk, you can't learn anything. If you're sure of the outcome of something, what do you learn from doing it? Creative people take risks. Most times they don't consider the risks as being risky. It must be noted that the risks rarely involve physical adventure (parachute jumping or mountain climbing), but tend to be emotional, such as leaving a comfortable job or lifestyle, or intellectual, (approaching someone you do not know, discussing intimacies, breaking social taboos). They are risks that put the person into conflict with society. What one is doing is breaking social rules to attain complete freedom. Emotional risk taking, as distinguished from physical risk taking, and creativity go hand in hand.

Creative people don't consider breaking social rules as something risky, while other people do. The only risk for creative people is to acquiesce, follow everyone else, and let society dictate how they should act and feel. If you are willing to do something I won't, I'll regard your action as risky. You may well not consider it risky, but from my perspective, I certainly will.

Creativity:

Take the obvious, add a cupful of brains, a generous pinch of imagination, a bucketful of courage and daring, stir well and bring to a boil.

Bernard Baruch, American educator

You will note that the largest ingredient is courage and daring. Our brains are designed to set up patterns and condemn anything that does not fit them. Creative thinking is different from this normal, step-by-step way of working. Most people want security and feel very uncomfortable with the provocations and explorations that creativity involves.

Peter Drucker, management consultant, in his book *Innovation and Entrepreneurship*, makes this observation:

The popular picture of innovators, half pop-psychology, half Hollywood, makes them look like a cross between Superman and The Knights of the Round Table. Alas, most of them in real life are unromantic figures, and much more likely to spend hours on a cash flow projection than to dash off looking for risks.

That's quite true. The majority of creative people are not reckless. They don't take risks too often. The difference between them and regular people is that creative people are *capable* of taking risks when they need to, while non-creative people are not. All growth is a leap in the dark. You may have an inkling of what you'll find at the bottom of that leap, but you can never be sure. You've got to be willing to take that risk.

How many times have you heard the phrase, "that idea's crazy," or simply, "that's crazy?" Labeling an idea as crazy is a sure way of killing it. No one wants to have crazy ideas, what we all want are practical, workable ideas. We must remember, however, that all the great, far-reaching ideas were so far ahead of their time that they seemed crazy when they were first introduced. What we need to do is nurture our crazy ideas. That's what we do after all when we brainstorm, we collect ideas and the crazier the better. Next time you're tempted to call an idea crazy, look at it from a different angle. Don't say, "it's crazy," and then forget it, instead, say "is it crazy enough?"

The idea that is not dangerous is unworthy of being called an idea at all.
Elbert Hubbard, American educator

When's the last time you had an idea that someone thought was crazy? If you can remember it's because your crazy ideas are too few and far between or because you don't have the confidence to express them. Try. There's nothing wrong with having crazy ideas.

How to break through invisible barrier ten

This barrier is another tough one. Just admitting that you are afraid of other people is important, because the vast majority of people don't like to think they are.

The best way to get start to get rid of this barrier is by doing anything that gets you in front of an audience, and that includes acting, performing, public speaking or teaching. It's the best way. In fact, it's really the only way.

It should be noted that it is natural to be afraid of other people to some degree. It should also be noted that there are some very self-centered people who have little or no fear of others. Their need to pursue their own interests pushes them to use everyone around them. Those people are never very creative.

This invisible barrier is such a pesky one that we'll continue to deal with it in the next chapter.

ACTIVITIES

Make a list of the people you know who you're afraid of. It could be anyone, a colleague, a relative, a neighbor.

If you're like most people, your list will not contain more than three names. What percentage is that of the people you know? It's a very small percentage, right? Okay, then who are you afraid of? You're afraid of people you don't know. Your task then is to agree to drop your defense shields and get to know as many people as you possibly can.

"Everyone has inhibitions"

The creative person always walks two steps into the darkness.
Everybody can see what's in the light. Darkness is important
and the risk that goes along with it.
BENNY GOLSON, AMERICAN JAZZ MUSICIAN

On a scale of 1 to 10, with 1 being no embarrassment at all, and 10 dying of embarrassment, rate how you'd feel in the following instances:

- Suppose you slipped and fell in a crowded public place, spilling a bag of groceries
- Suppose you were a guest at an elegant dinner, and the person seated next to you spilled his plate into his lap while eating
- Suppose you were the one who spilled the plate
- Suppose you discovered you were the only person at a particular social occasion who was dressed casually while everyone else was dressed formally
- Suppose you entered an apparently empty office, turned on the lights and surprised two colleagues who were making love
- Suppose it was you who was making love, when a colleague of the same sex entered
- Suppose it was you who was making love, when a colleague of the opposite sex entered
- Suppose your mother had come to visit you when you were in the university and accompanied you to all your classes for a week
- Suppose you were completely naked in the bathroom and the best friend of your husband or wife were to walk in
- Suppose a friend of yours confessed that they were in love with you, but you didn't have the same feelings.

The minimum score is 10, while the maximum is 100. How close did you come to 10? Remember that we said that no one can make you feel foolish without your consent? Well, what happens when you feel foolish, you get embarrassed, right? Therefore, no situation can embarrass you without your consent. You agree to be embarrassed.

> You cannot embarrass me. It's unbelievable. I've been like this my whole life.
> *Cameron Diaz, American actress*

To be fully creative you have to:

Minimize your embarrassment and minimize your inhibitions

"Why? Why can't I feel embarrassment and still be creative? Why can't I have a few inhibitions and still be creative? Everyone feels embarrassed once in a while. Everyone has inhibitions."

One definition of embarrass: *to cause to feel self-conscious, confused, ill at ease.* One definition of inhibition: *a mental or psychological process that restrains or suppresses an action, emotion or thought.*

Embarrassment and inhibitions prevent you from being creative by blocking all ideas that do not conform to those you already accept. They scream "no," and refuse to let you even consider "what if."

> The great majority of patients experience themselves as stifled and inhibited by the excessive and rigid limits insisted on by their parents. One of their reasons for coming to therapy in the first place is this conviction that all of this needs to be thrown over-board. People must recover the lost aspects of their personalities, lost under a pile of inhibitions, if they are to become integrated in any effective sense.
> *Rollo May, American psychologist*

Embarrassment and inhibitions restrain and suppress your actions, emotions and thoughts
---

You want to express rather than suppress your emotions and thoughts. That's why you have to fight against your inhibitions. Embarrassment and inhibitions cause stress and studies have shown that when people are under stress, their thought processes narrow. This narrowing prevents divergent thinking, which is the ability to see connections between distantly related ideas and contexts. Stress compromises one of the fundamental skills of creativity and innovation.

All living souls welcome whatsoever they are ready to cope with, all else they ignore, or pronounce to be monstrous and wrong, or deny to be possible.

George Santayana, Spanish philosopher

Since creative people view the world from multi-perspectives, they consider things that others categorically reject. They deem fewer things monstrous and wrong. They're more open. They have to be.

The creative person is curious about everything. She wants to know about all kinds of things because she never knows when these ideas might come together to form a new idea. It may happen thirty minutes later or thirty months later, but she has faith that it will happen. You need to be curious. Curiosity will conquer fear even more than bravery will.

What are you curious about? What are you not curious about? If you had to make two lists to answer these questions, which list would be longer? If you're creative, the first list would be impossible to complete, because you'd need to list everything in the world, while the second list would have nothing written on it. The highly creative person, like the child, is curious about everything.

Don't listen to what they say. Go see.   *Chinese proverb*

To release your curiosity, however, you'll need to get rid of your embarrassment and inhibitions. One of the important steps toward a more creative life is the cultivation of curiosity. Embarrassment and inhibitions suppress your natural curiosity. You have to overcome those things and let your curiosity flow.

Everyone has talent. What is rare is the courage to follow the talent to the dark place where it leads.   *Erica Jong, American writer, feminist*

At the end of invisible barrier one, we asked you to list three things you would never ever do, under any circumstance. The only stipulation was that they should be legal things. If you haven't done the exercise, take a few minutes and do it now.

Some typical answers include:

- parachute or bungee jump
- pierce anything other than my earlobes
- commit suicide
- cheat on boyfriend, girlfriend, husband or wife
- be naked in public

- group sex or sex in public
- homosexual relationship
- hunt
- live in a certain place or country in the world.

In terms of creativity there is a danger in saying that you will never ever do something. When you do that, you permit your thinking to become rigid. By locking onto a preset way of looking at the world, you're rejecting other possibilities, other perspectives and other points of view. Minds, like beds, are useless if they're always made up. When you build fences, you create boundaries and those boundaries serve to limit as well as protect you.

To be creative you don't have to do anything and everything, but you should be willing to consider doing anything and everything and you should also be able to imagine a situation where you could conceivably have no other choice but to do what you swore you'd never ever do.

> One of the greatest obstacles to creativity is the fixed idea

Never parachute or bungee jump

For the people who swear they'd never parachute jump for fun, we answer, okay, what happens if you fall in love with someone whose passionate hobby is parachuting? He or she does it every weekend with their friends while you just sit on the sidelines. "Please try it, just once!", the love of your life begs you over and over, "Please, you might like it!" And so you might. What are the alternatives? Give up a person you love? Spend your weekends apart, year after year? Make someone you love give up a sport and friends they love?

I'll never fall in love with someone who jumps out of planes, you maintain. Really? How can you tell whom you'll fall in love with? It could be anyone, absolutely anyone!

Never commit suicide

Many people say they'd never commit suicide, but what would you do if you had a terminal illness accompanied by mind-wrenching pain, and drugs that made you feel nauseous all the time? Art Gogatz had a good friend some years ago who was diagnosed with a brain tumor. Art remembers toward the end his friend said, "I can't take it anymore. You know how hard I've struggled these last five years, but the pain is too much. The medication doesn't help anymore. I can't go on. All I want is for the pain to stop. I want to die."

Never cheat on my partner
The wedding ceremony includes a pledge of mutual fidelity, yet divorce rates in many western countries are at their highest levels. Many marriages manage to survive extramarital affairs. Conservative estimates for extramarital affairs in many western countries are upwards of seventy percent. None of those people on their wedding days ever thought there would come a day when they'd want to be in the arms of another.

Never hunt?
Your plane goes down in the wilderness of Alaska with winter approaching. Your child is with you and also your faithful dog. All survive. You've no provisions. You try to exist on berries and plants, but what do you feed your dog? Would you watch your dog starve to death, or would you kill an animal for food? Could you watch your child starve to death? Could you hunt at that point? Yes!

Ah, foul, you cry! Those are extraordinary circumstances. What you meant is that you would never jump out of a plane, cheat on your husband or wife or hunt under normal circumstances.

> The creative person readily imagines circumstances that are both normal and abnormal, while the non-creative people stay locked into what is normal

That is a difference and it is a *huge difference.*

Read the following statements. For those that you judge to be always true, circle T. For those that you judge to be not always true, circle F.

1. Donkeys are stubborn   T   F
2. Pigs are dirty   T   F
3. God is everywhere   T   F
4. University graduates earn more than non-grads   T   F
5. Animals have legs   T   F
6. Ice is cold   T   F
7. "Fuck" is a bad word   T   F

8.	Seeing is believing	T	F
9.	Iron is solid	T	F
10.	The sky is blue	T	F
11.	Needles are pointed	T	F
12.	What goes up must come down	T	F
13.	Doctors are intelligent	T	F
14.	A person who kills another is a murderer	T	F
15.	Cotton is soft	T	F
16.	Balls are round	T	F
17.	The sun rises in the east and sets in the west	T	F
18.	Plants grow in earth	T	F
19.	Water is wet	T	F
20.	Good men do not cheat	T	F
21.	Cats have four legs	T	F
22.	Time is money	T	F
23.	Birds fly	T	F
24.	The rich can buy whatever they want	T	F
25.	Yes means yes	T	F
26.	Leaves are green	T	F
27.	No one wants to die	T	F
28.	Snow is white	T	F
29.	Cement is heavy	T	F
30.	Running is faster than walking	T	F

Now count and see how many you have of each. The average is about ten true and twenty false.

Do you remember what we said a few pages back? One of the greatest obstacles to creativity is the fixed idea. All right. Then you shouldn't be surprised to learn that all thirty statements are false.

In case you don't believe us, let's look at some of the answers.

1. Donkeys are stubborn. Generally yes, but not all donkeys. You can say, most donkeys, but not every single donkey
3. If you believe in God, yes. If you don't, God won't be everywhere

4. Bill Gates of Microsoft never graduated from a university and he earns more than anyone else
5. Not all animals have legs
6. Dry ice doesn't feel cold. In fact it feels hot
7. Some people yell, oh fuck, when they win something, like the lottery.
9. Liquid iron
11. Needles with their tips cut off
14. The person who pulls the switch for the electric chair is an execu- tioner, not a murderer
15. Frozen cotton
16. Rugby balls, American footballs
17. At the north and south poles
19. Ice
23. Penguins
29. Not if you take a small piece of cement
30. Depends who's walking and who's running. Olympic walkers go pretty fast

Remember, one of the greatest obstacles to creativity is the fixed idea or the fixed way of looking at things.

> But I'm coming to believe that all of us are ghosts. It's not just what we inherit from our mothers and fathers. It's also the shadows of dead ideas and opinions and convictions. They're no longer alive, but they grip us all the same, and hold on to us against our will.   *Henrik Ibsen, Norwegian playwright, in* Ghosts

Let's return to the question we talked about in invisible barrier ten. What else would you love to do but are too embarrassed to do? Other common answers, besides speak, sing, act, dance or play music in public, include:

■ dye hair or change style (look), have something pierced
■ approach someone you don't know and tell them you like them
■ talk about intimate subjects with certain people (for example with parents)
■ go nude in public (for example: at the beach)
■ perform a striptease, or pose for nude photos.

We've said that to be creative you have to see differently, and to do that you have to be capable of being different. Creative people don't look different. They're capable of looking different, that's all. Most people aren't capable unless it's Halloween or they're drunk. As a matter of fact, creative people actually enjoy looking different from time to time. They like it because they know it sets them apart.

Creativity involves a willingness to break away from established patterns and try new things, but it doesn't mean being different for the sake of being different.

> Creative people must be able to deal openly and frankly with any subject, because if you exclude certain subjects in the generation of ideas (lateral thinking), you limit your thinking

Art Gogatz sometimes does an exercise with his adult students, in which they ask each other questions that have no restrictions. Art explains:

"The questions can be about anything, absolutely anything. Since the students are often apprehensive, I let them first ask me questions about anything and everything, as personal and intimate as they want. The only stipulation in the exercise is that you must answer all questions posed as honestly and candidly as you can. Of course it's possible to cheat, but that defeats the purpose of the exercise. After the initial session the students then ask each other questions. They all take turns asking and answering. It's a bit like therapy and the purpose of the exercise is to demonstrate that no subject is taboo, that there is nothing that can't be honestly talked about, dealt with and coped with.

                    *   *   *

All art is a kind of confession, more or less oblique. All artists, if they are to survive, are forced to tell the whole story, to vomit the anguish up.

                                              James Baldwin, American writer

All creativity requires some kind of confession. All creative people are forced to tell the whole story, the whole true story. The idea of this exercise is to get students to push out their boundaries, have them cope with things they normally avoid and show them that they never need to be embarrassed. Students come out of this exercise with a sense of confidence and buoyancy and often remark: "It wasn't as difficult as I thought it would be," to which Art replies:

No, being honest and open isn't difficult. You did when you were a child. What you've learned since is how to avoid, cover up, blush, restrain, and suppress. Those are not natural tendencies.

Psychologists know that patients find relief just by talking about their problems and anxieties. When we talk about something, we often gain better insight into it. We see the issue in a new way, with a new perspective.

People who are able to say everything become able to do everything.
Napoleon Bonaparte, French emperor

With whom are you really, truly honest? What secrets do you have that you've never told anyone? Why do you keep them? Most people keep things hidden because they're ashamed and worry that if they were to tell someone, that person would think less of them. It all comes back to image. We want to project a favorable image and hide everything which might hurt or weaken that image. Creative people, however, want to know everything, reveal everything, say everything and see everything. They're curious about everything. They want nothing hidden, no secrets. They want everything out in the open. Walt Whitman once said that he never gave lectures. "When I give, I give myself," he revealed. People in the fine and performing arts also learn not to hold back, in life and in their work. They give themselves, for better or worse.

When I work, I'm too open. I reveal everything. *Nicole Kidman, Australian actress*

How many people have you let into your life?

If you're like most people, the answer is between five and twenty. Who are they? They're your parents, your brothers and sisters, your husband or your wife, your lovers, your children, maybe a therapist or family doctor, and perhaps one or two lifelong friends. These are the only people who you allow to see you the way you really are, with all your talents and all your faults. The rest of the world you keep at arm's length, no, you keep them even further away, much further away. You don't even let them get to know you at all. You don't let them penetrate your invisible defense shields.

The more I traveled the more I realized that fear makes strangers of people who should be friends. *Shirley Maclaine, American actress*

One of the main differences between creative and non-creative people is that creative people have accepted to let more people into their lives, both through their work and also personally. If you want to be creative, you have to let down your defense shields.

How much are you willing to give up to be happy? This question is at the heart of psychological therapy. To attain something you want, you have to be ready to give up something in return. We may then go on to ask: How much are you willing to give up to be thin? How much time, how much energy, how much of the food you love? How much are you willing to give up to be successful? How much are you willing to give up to be in good physical shape? How much are you willing to give up to be highly creative? In the case of overcoming the fear of other people, it is the willingness to sacrifice security, control and comfort. It means accepting vulnerability.

> If you ask me what I came to do in this world, I, an artist, I will answer you, I am here to live out loud.   *Émile Zola, French writer, critic*

Creative people are always naked

Creative people are here to live out loud. They're always naked, always naked and vulnerable via their work. The acceptance of vulnerability is something which separates creative from non-creative people.

You cannot tell the truth about your character if you're an actor, about your subjects, if you're a photographer, about your characters, if you're a writer, if you're not truthful with yourself.

Art Gogatz tells the following story:

> Years ago, when I was living in France, I was watching one of the talk-show type programs on French television, which is not as censored as similar programs are in the USA. They were interviewing Serge Gainsbourg, a popular French singer, poet, actor and avant-garde philosopher. He and the host chatted for a while, in French, about a variety of topics. Then they brought out the next guest, American singer, Whitney Houston. The host talked to Whitney in English, then translated her comments into French for the studio and television audiences. Finally the host turned to Serge Gainsbourg and said, in English.

> "She's pretty, isn't she?"

> Gainsbourg, who handled English pretty well, replied, "Yeah. I'd like to fuck her."

> Houston's eyes grew wide in disbelief. "What'd he say?" she stammered.

"Don't pay any attention to him, he's drunk," the host soothed the ruffled Houston.

"No, I'm not," Gainsbourg immediately told the audience, in French. "What I said was that I'd like to fuck her, and I bet there are a lot of the guys in the audience who would too. I just said what I happened to be thinking."

The host did not translate Gainsbourg's last comments to Houston, and instead brought up the subject of Houston's upcoming concert. The three went on to talk normally and nothing else was said about Gainsbourg's comment.

*   *   *

I've looked on a lot of women with lust. I've committed adultery in my heart many times.   *Jimmy Carter, former US president*

Carter revealed what a lot of people refuse to accept or admit. People who are frightened by their thoughts repress them, so they are not aware they exist. Freud called this internalized and very powerful censor the "superego."

A patient says, "Doctor, last night I made a Freudian slip. I was having dinner with my mother-in-law and wanted to say: could you please pass the butter? But instead, I said, you silly cow, you have completely ruined my life."

Why can't we be more direct and honest? That's another naive, childish, creative adult notion, yet it's too easy to dismiss it all by saying, "we can't." The bulk of criticism of Clinton's behavior in the Monica Lewinsky affair centered more on the fact that he initially failed to tell the truth and not that he'd had oral sex with a White House intern.

Clinton lied. A man might forget where he parks, or where he lives, but he never forgets oral sex, no matter how bad it is.
                                    Barbara Bush, former first lady of the USA

Richard Nixon suffered a similar fate years earlier when he lied to cover up the Watergate break-in. Ted Kennedy's Chappaquiddick cover-up dashed whatever hopes he had for the presidency. California Congressman Gary Conduit initially denied having an affair with Chandra Levy.

Politicians aren't the only ones given to covering up. *USA Today* ran an article in July 2001 revealing that the American actor Jason Priestly had completed a three-month alcohol-counseling program after pleading no contest to drunken driving. He wrecked his car in a December 1999 accident in which a passenger was injured. The newspaper reported that Priestly had first pleaded innocent, saying he swerved to avoid a deer.

People get indignant when they learn that others, especially elected officials, lie. Yet lying seems to be a common, if not universal action. If it is, shouldn't it be recognized as such, and the indignation dropped? If not, shouldn't more people be taught to express their thoughts openly and honestly?

> Truth has no special time of its own. Its hour is now – always.
>   *Albert Schweitzer, French medical missionary, philospher*

Why do we have to lie? Why can't we be more open and direct? The answer is fear. We are afraid to admit the things we do, afraid of public opinion, afraid of what people will say, afraid again of other people.

Is it really possible to say everything you think?

Richard Farson, in his book *Management of the Absurd*, relates the following story:

> The provost at a university was committed to a participate approach. All matters that needed deciding were brought before the students and faculty. The entering freshmen were impressed that they could express themselves so freely, that they could challenge the provost, even use obscenities with him and get away with it. It was so exhilarating to the young people that they neglected to appreciate the debilitating effect on the provost. Each incoming class would go through somewhat the same ritual, testing and abusing the leader. The provost resigned his post in the third year.

The provost in this story had the right idea. It's too bad he didn't have the capacity to see that idea through. If he'd had creativity training he might have. Creative people want brutally honest communication and they don't care what words they or someone else uses in the process. It's sad to note how few people are capable of sustaining open, direct dialogue. Students, like employees, should have access to those in power, and should be able to challenge any rules, procedures or decisions, using all the words that are available. It's an indictment on our system when a student cannot say what he or she wants to a provost, or any other adult. It's sad that one can't express everything one thinks. So many problems in this world are caused and aggravated by the lack of communication.

From *Alice in Wonderland:*

> There was a table set out under a tree and the Hatter and March Hare were having tea at it. Alice took a seat next to the March Hare.
>
> "Your hair needs cutting."
>
> The Hatter had been staring at Alice for a few minutes and these were his first words.
>
> "You should learn not to make personal remarks," Alice replied. "It isn't very civil."
>
> "It wasn't very civil of you to sit down without being asked," said the Hatter.

Is it possible to say everything you think? Even if it is possible, it's not advisable. We all have to live in society, and our interaction dictates that we adhere to social rules and that implies learning a certain degree of civility, diplomacy and tact. The only exceptions occasionally granted are to children, who we say are too young to know better, senile people, who we say are too old to remember how they're supposed to act, extremely wealthy people, who we sometimes fondly call eccentrics, drunks, people who are mad, and highly creative people.

> The instinct of nearly all societies is to lock up anybody who is truly free. First, society begins by trying to beat you up. If this fails, they try to poison you. If this fails too, they finish by loading honors on your head.
>
> *Jean Cocteau, French writer, art critic*

Is it *really* possible to say everything you think? No, but creative people always try their best. It has been said that the average person thinks fifty thousand thoughts a day. How many of them get expressed? The answer is precious few.

If you had to choose between too much communication and too little, which would you choose? Before you answer, remember that neurosis is characterized by a lack of communicativeness, an inability to participate in the feelings and thoughts of others or to share oneself with others.

> A creative person's entire world revolves around expressing their thoughts and ideas, while the non-creative person's entire world revolves around not expressing their thoughts and ideas

Vincent Ruggiero offers this on the expression of ideas in his book *The Art Of Thinking*:

Every new idea we think separates us from others, and expressing the idea increases the separation tenfold. Such separation is frightening, especially to those who draw their strength from association with others and who depend on others for their identity. Such people are not likely to feel comfortable entertaining, let alone expressing new ideas. They fear rejection too much.

Have you ever said something which you belatedly realize may be offensive? "Only kidding," you throw out, to soothe things over. Humor often lets us treat subjects that would be taboo in serious discussions.

If you're going to tell people the truth, be funny, or they'll kill you.

Billy Wilder, American film director

Think for a minute about jokes. Most of our jokes deal with one of the taboos. The routines of most stand-up comics are laced with barbs on sex, politics or social issues. They poke fun at things and people we hold sacred, and we not only permit but also relish it, simply because it's not treated seriously.

A dirty joke is not a serious attack upon morality, but it is a sort of mental rebellion, a momentary wish that things were otherwise.

George Orwell, English writer

Throughout history the fool or jester was used to open up people's thinking. In fact it was the court jester's job to jolt the king and the yes men who surrounded the monarch out of their thought patterns. The jester's parodies were valuable because they often forced the king to re-examine his assumptions.

> It is the purpose of all creative people to make us aware of precisely the things that we don't want to be made aware of, to express what people are not ashamed to think but are ashamed to say

If that means having to play the fool, so be it. The creative person must use whatever means are available to jolt people, for the average person maintains an elaborate system of anti-jolt defense shields. To be able to constantly say what people are not ashamed to think but are ashamed to say requires courage, a lot of courage. It will also entail not being ashamed or embarrassed about anything. That too requires courage.

'Tisn't life that matters. 'Tis the courage you bring to it.

Sir Hugh Walpole, first British prime minister

How do you meet people?

Most people cannot go up and talk to someone they find attractive but don't know. Only rarely can they tell an acquaintance, associate, friend or even a loved one how they feel about them. If they could, Hallmark would be in deep trouble. Instead of communicating your emotions, too often you leave them to be "implied" and understood. Sometimes, those feelings are not understood, at other times misunderstood. In the case of someone you'll never see again, it's no communication at all.

We all have expectations about the nature of our relationships and their outcomes. Since we rarely ever discuss these expectations with the other person, our hopes are rarely ever fulfilled, and this leaves us disappointed and disillusioned. We are also never taught how to effectively deal with all those disappointments.

Richard Farson, in his book *Management of the Absurd*, offers this insight about relationships:

> Managers think the people with whom they work want them to exhibit consistency, assertiveness, and self-control, and they do. But occasionally, they also want just the opposite. They want a moment with us when we are genuinely ourselves without façade or pretense or defensiveness, when we are revealed as human beings, when we are vulnerable. This is not just in leadership but in every human situation. It's what wives want from husbands, what children want from parents, what we all want from each other. It's what most arguments and conflicts are unconsciously designed to produce: to get us to reveal that the other has had an impact on us.

Statistically, most people meet their husband or wife through their business relations or contacts. How do people meet people? You happen to be in the same class. You happen to work for the same company. You happen to be at the same party. You happen to know someone who has a friend who has a friend. You happen to be in the same elevator.

Do you see a pattern here? There's one word that keeps coming up again and again. That word is *happen*. How do you meet people? You meet people by *chance*!

What would you do if the next time you walked into an elevator, you found yourself face to face (or side by side) with someone you found intensely attractive? If you're like most people, the answer is, nothing, unless the elevator happened to get stuck. What do you think the chances would be of that happening? Okay then, what else could you do? That's right; you could talk to him or her. What? You can't? Why not? "Because I don't know what to say. I'll probably say something stupid and look like the world's biggest idiot. I'll get rejected and probably insulted!"

Face it. You failed to meet the guy or the girl you were most attracted to in life because you were afraid. Yes you were, you were afraid of them, afraid of their reaction. Ah, but it's normal, you rush to point out. Everyone is afraid in those situations. No, they're not. True, most people are. Maybe even ninety-eight per cent of people are, but some people aren't, for the restraint here is self-imposed. It's just another invisible net, and it can be cast off as easily as it was donned.

Let's go back to our situation. You see a girl or a guy that you just think is absolutely, but absolutely fabulous. You pass hundreds, even thousands of people each day in the street, but this time, this one is special. This one makes you queasy. This one leaves you pale and breathless. What do you do? If you keep walking, you'll never see them again in your life. What can you do?

We've all seen this kind of situation on television sitcoms. If you do manage to go up to them, what do you say? Well, one thing you shouldn't say is a line you heard on a sitcom. In fact, don't use a line at all. A line is a flippant statement that's supposed to make you appear bright and witty, but really makes you look like a superficial flirt. We are all so accustomed to sitcoms that we unconsciously slip into their jargon. Listen to the communication in any American office. Most of it is sitcom banter. We've come to feel that we can't end a conversation without upping the other person with some dazzling one-liner. The US could be renamed "sitcomville."

Okay, if you don't use a line, then what do you say? How about what you feel, how about the truth? Just tell them the truth that you don't know why but you find them attractive, and although you'll probably never see them again, you wanted to tell them. Nothing may come of it, but nothing will surely come of it if you don't talk to them. Even if nothing comes of it in terms of a relationship, look at the progress you've made in terms of your self-confidence and self-confidence is a vital part of creativity.

You still think that you'll look foolish, but remember that no one can make you feel foolish without your consent. If you think of it in those terms, you can't look foolish. If you believe what're you're saying, it'll be natural. There are three important things to remember. First, you are not doing this to pick up someone. It is reserved for those extremely rare instances when you see a person who overwhelms you, who totally devastates you from the first moment you lay eyes on them. Second, this has nothing to do with sex, and it should not be thought of in those terms. Third, you don't have to go around approaching people in the street, but you should be capable of doing it. If you needed to do it, could you? The fact that most people can't doesn't matter. It only matters that you can do it.

Of all forms of caution, caution in love is perhaps the most fatal to true happiness.
Bertrand Russell, English philosopher

The strongest fear in the situation we've been talking about is that of rejection. If you're successful, everything comes out Hollywood, but you know the world isn't Hollywood, you know it's Realitywood, and in Realitywood you get rejected. Okay, if you do, so what? You won't have lost anything.

Attraction is more often than not a two-way street. Anyone you are truly, and we stress the word "truly", attracted to may very well be attracted to you. Of course, the person you're attracted to may be involved with someone else, or just not emotionally available, or they may not find you attractive, but then again they just may. Statistics show that people suffer most in their lives from failed interpersonal relationships and rejections, or from the lack of relationships, isolation and alienation. The best way to happiness may well be to improve relationships, and that means giving chance encounters some well-needed assistance. People often first decide it's time to get serious and then go about choosing from among the relatively small group of suitors available. Even when you're in love, it doesn't necessarily mean that the person who you adore is the love of your life, only that he or she is the best person you've met up to that moment. Real success at anything entails a thorough understanding of the subject. If you're going to study psychology, you're not going to limit yourself to just reading a few books. No, you're going to read as many as you can. It's the same with relationships. If you drop your defense shield, you'll be able to expand the number of relationships you have and multiply the chances of finding the right person.

I married the first man I ever kissed. When I tell this to my children, they just about throw up. *Barbara Bush, former first lady of the USA*

Let's go back to your objections to going up and talking to people you're attracted to. What was the last of the objections you initially voiced? Oh, yes, that you'll get insulted. Maybe you will, but sincerity is something which can be sensed. If you are truly sincere, the other person will realize you are and won't insult you. Our experience has been that if you are sincere, the other person takes what you say for what it is, a truly rare compliment. If you're a woman, chances are the man in the elevator won't find your comments offensive. What? You thought we were only talking to men? Hardly. If you're a woman, why can't you tell a man you find him attractive?

> "Because, it's not done! Men are the ones who are supposed to make the first move! Because if I tell him I'm attracted to him, he'll think I'm some kind of a whore!"

Well, if you never see him again, what do you care what he thinks of you, and if your overture does work, he'll soon find out you're not. The only way you lose is if you say nothing, yet that's exactly what everyone does.

Perhaps you're afraid of approaching other people because you think you'll get sued. There's not much chance of that if you're sincere. We're not telling you to harass or annoy anyone. All we're saying is that if you sincerely think that someone is superbly attractive, express that feeling, politely, and as eloquently as you can. If you're still worried about getting sued, then simply avoid doing it in the USA. The States is the only country in the world that's lawsuit happy. Don't forget there's a big, big world out there.

How, you may ask, is going up to people on the street and talking to people in elevators going to make me more creative?

First of all you should treat this for what it is, an exercise. We're not telling you to do this frequently, not at all. You should do it only when you really feel something intense for someone. The purpose of the exercise is to free you up, to make you experience a sensation of letting go. Who says you can't go up to someone you find attractive and tell them? Other people say you can't, just because they're afraid. Society, convention, custom, habit, says you can't. Aha! You can! You really can!

What you are doing in this exercise is eliminating boundaries, previously held perceptions and limitations about how something looks, functions or should be, and embracing for one short, brief, flickering, but profound instant *complete freedom*.

Since creative people question and challenge everything they themselves did not create, they look upon conventions, customs and habits not as things to be meekly accepted but as things to be challenged.

Security is mostly a superstition. It does not exist in nature. Life is either a daring adventure or nothing. *Helen Keller, American essayist*

We can all stop people on the street if it's an emergency, or when we're lost, because at those times we don't care about social implications or restrictions. Most people would "die of embarrassment" if their father-in-law or mother-in-law were to happen to walk into the bathroom and catch them in the shower. If, however, the shower door were to shatter and you were standing there bleeding, with fragments of jagged glass all around, you would welcome someone's help and your lack of clothes wouldn't be a problem. The emergency would cancel the social restrictions. Creative people don't adhere to the same number of social restrictions as other people do. They don't need to wait for extraordinary circumstances. They can imagine that any situation is an emergency situation. It's yet another difference, another huge difference.

Lives which function around problems

> Not taking risks is in itself a great risk

"Sure that's easy to say. Take risks. Most people who say that are rich and successful. They can afford to fail. I can't. I have a family and financial obligations. If I take a risk and fail, it's not just me who's going to suffer."

Sound familiar? We've all told ourselves something similar. We all worry about not making it, about failing. Some of us worry about getting ill, some of us about losing our jobs, or about being rejected. We spend time thinking about what we'd do if we lost our job, or what we'd do if our husband or wife died. What we're doing is worrying about a situation that isn't real. A realist may point out that it's planning, and perhaps it is, but it's worrying all the same. It's worrying not only about problems that you have but also those that you might have.

Many people approach life as a series of problems to solve. Their lives are inextricably tied to their problems, both real and anticipated. They plan their lives to be as problem-free as possible. Most of us walk around with an unspoken question in our minds, that question is, what's going to go wrong today? We live our lives by avoiding pain rather than seeking happiness. Our happiness thus becomes the avoidance of pain.

> When I look back on all these worries, I remember the story of the old man who said on his deathbed that he had a lot of trouble in his life, most of which had never happened.   *Sir Winston Churchill, British statesman, orator, writer*

We come back to the question of what it is we really want. Most of us avoid that question and concentrate instead on what we don't want. We end up spending most of our lives trying to avoid everything we don't want, instead of trying for what we do want.

Most people don't deviate from their paths because they've convinced themselves that should they dare, more bad things will happen than good things. You must also keep in mind that in terms of creativity, we are not advocating that the risks you take be financial or that they turn your lives or the lives of those around you upside down. The risks we've been talking about are ones which make you challenge habit and convention, risks which help you stop and question the things which others accept and take for granted, risks which help you to become aware that other perspectives, paths and solutions do indeed exist.

What's the most outrageous thing you've ever done?

What's the last risk that you remember taking? We don't mean a physical risk, or a risk which involved breaking the law, but an emotional risk, a risk which took you beyond society's invisible nets? What's the most outrageous thing you've ever done? What was the last outrageous thing you did? How can you have outrageous ideas if you've never done anything outrageous, if you won't do anything outrageous? One of the points we've been making in this book is that you don't need to do outrageous things; you just need to be *capable* of doing them. A professional golfer who needs to be capable of regularly hitting a seven iron over water to a well-bunkered green practices that shot. It's the same thing with creativity. Yes, you only need to be capable of doing something outrageous, but in order to do that you too need to practice.

> Be prepared to give up every preconceived notion, follow whatever and to whatever abyss nature leads, or you shall learn nothing.
>
> *Thomas Huxley, English biologist*

The purpose of life is to live it, to taste experience to the utmost, to reach out eagerly and without fear for newer and richer experience.

Eleanor Roosevelt, stateswoman, former first lady of the USA

If you always do what you've always done, you'll always get what you've always got. You'll always do what you've always done if you always think the way you've always thought.

Try removing the word "problem" from your vocabulary for a while and replacing it with "challenge," or better still replace it with the word "opportunity." A stumbling block, after all, can also be a stepping-stone to other things. Remember that you can't think and worry at the same time.

The future has many names. For the weak it means the unattainable. For the fearful, it means the unknown. For the courageous, it means opportunity.

Victor Hugo, French writer

Brilliant opportunities unfortunately often come disguised as insolvable problems.

Albert Einstein's three rules of work were:

1. Out of clutter, find simplicity
2. From discord, find harmony
3. In the middle of difficulty, lies opportunity.

Propose anything, and step back. In industrialized countries, countries that are dominated by a complex system of laws, rules and regulations, the majority of people will immediately look for all the problems connected with implementing the idea.

A pessimist sees the difficulty in every opportunity, an optimist sees the opportunity in every difficulty. *Winston Churchill*

Let's go to the beach or the ball game! Problem? The traffic. The crowds.

Let's play tennis! Problem? My backs hurts a bit today, and anyway didn't they say it might rain.

Honey, I've been offered a great job overseas. Problem? We can't change the kids of school. It'll be too traumatic. They'll never adjust. And our friends, what about our friends?

Nothing is miserable unless you think it so.   *Boethius, Roman philosopher*

The same can be said for many of the things we do each day. Things either inspire you and fill you with imagination or give you a headache. What looks like a bump in the road to one person will look like a boulder to someone else. It depends on your perspective, on the way you want to see something. Everyone is capable of seeing stars just as everyone is capable of seeing mud. Some people see more mud and others more stars. You'll see more stars when you're in the process of doing something you want to do than when you're doing something you have to do. If you really want to go to the beach and it starts to rain, you'll say, "maybe it's only a shower," while if you weren't that keen on going, you're reaction will be, "looks like it's going to rain all day."

Today is the tomorrow you worried about yesterday

If you look for problems, you'll find them and they'll give you enough reasons not to take action. You'll stay with what you know, stay with what you have. If you risk nothing, you'll do nothing, you'll have nothing and you'll be nothing. You may avoid problems and suffering, but you won't learn, change, grow or live. Most people think that opening up, getting rid of embarrassment and inhibitions, and expressing your deepest thoughts ideas and emotions is risky, but creative people know that the risk is in not letting go. If you are creative, the hard part isn't to express yourself but the opposite; the hard part is to keep it in, to keep it under wraps, to hide it, to squirrel it away until the conditions are ripe and right. The conditions are always right.

How to break through invisible barrier eleven

What inhibits you? That's a tough question. We usually think of inhibitions as reasons to go into therapy. Thus we like to think of ourselves as uninhibited, but the truth is that we all have inhibitions.

How do you get rid of your inhibitions? Good question. Psychologists tell us, and rightly so, that it takes years and years of therapy and even then your progress may only be temporary. That's true, but psychologists usually don't treat normal people, they treat severely inhibited people. Our experience is that most people would love to get rid of some of their inhibitions and are secretly hope that a situation and/or person will come along and assist them.

ACTIVITIES

What questions would you not want to be asked? What questions, in fact, would you refuse to answer? Don't worry about when, where and by whom the questions would be asked. Assume that they could be asked anytime, anyplace, by anyone, on the record or off it.

Okay, list the questions you'd refuse to answer. Those are some of the topics you are inhibited about.

"I can't make a difference"

The freer an individual, the healthier he is.
Because when you have prejudices, when you are bound by
taboos, it's going toward a constriction of the personality and a
constriction of your outside world.
PHYLLIS KRONHAUSEN, DANISH PSYCHOLOGIST, AUTHOR

When you constrict your personality and your outside world, you lose your natural creativity, for being creative means being able to look everywhere and consider everything.

This barrier is at the root of creativity. It's the desire, the naive desire, the childlike desire to want to make the world a better place. It is not just a desire to turn your private wishes into reality but a desire to see many of the injustices in the world eliminated. It has been said that the creative person forces you to enter his or her personal world, a world of images and symbolism where daydreams are disguised, and when you enter that world you will find a childlike soul shocked by the lack of tenderness in the world.

Freedom

What creative people cherish above all else is freedom. Freedom is the right to be different, the right to choose your own values and beliefs. There is a responsibility in making a decision by yourself. Creative people don't passively accept society's judgment on what is acceptable and what is not. They make their own decisions. They may, in fact agree, but they may also disagree.

> Nothing is more difficult, and therefore more precious, than to be able to decide. *Napoleon Bonaparte, French emperor*

Many of the things that were considered scandalous years ago are accepted today. What is immoral today may very well be accepted tomorrow. People who hold fewer things to be immoral may not be as perverted as a lot of people think; they may just be ahead of their time.

Police closed Amedeo Modigliani's sole Parisian exhibition the day it opened. A subsequent exhibition in Toulouse was closed when mobs threw rocks through the gallery window. This was France in 1918. The reason was that the nudes in his paintings showed pubic hair, the depiction of which at the time was considered scandalous.

It took another forty-eight years for pubic hair to appear in a major motion picture. The film was Michelangelo Antonioni's *Blow-up* (nominated for two Academy Awards) and the flash of pubic hair was so fast that most people didn't even notice it.

In France in 1918 no respectable woman would be seen in public without a hat. While many people smoked, only men could do so in public. The bathing suits sported by both women and men alike are absurd compared to what can be seen today on the world's beaches. Times change, and with them also go fashions, customs and values.

> What is morality in any given time or place? It is what the majority then and there happen to like, and immorality is what they dislike.
>
> *Alfred North Whitehead, English philosopher*

By the time we become adults most of us are too heavily influenced by society to challenge accepted practices and beliefs.

Vincent Ruggiero talks about "acculturation" in his book *The Art of Thinking*:

> The process of being exposed to society, home, neighborhood, church and school is what sociologists call acculturation. It means settling into our cultures. That process is influenced by our families, economic status, religions and political orientations. Acculturation can occur subtly, creating the illusion that our values, attitudes and ideas were formed independently of other people and circumstances.
>
> Say to yourself, my mind is full of other people's influences and attitudes, which I received and accepted. Many of those ideas and attitudes are not hardened into principles and convictions. Yet some of them are surely erroneous and unworthy. Decide as objectively as you can which ideas deserve your endorsement.

Creative people seek to understand all the practices and beliefs that surround them. That process leads them to challenge many things. They try to get others to look at the word with a free, open, virginal spirit. It means getting people to see the point of view of their neighbor and also of their enemy. It means getting people to expand and to accept rather than to limit and condemn.

> I have striven not to laugh at human actions, not to weep at them, nor to hate them, but to understand them.   *Benedict Spinoza, Dutch philosopher*

Being creative means not setting particular boundaries, or embracing particular theories. Rather, it means constantly learning, and that learning means learning to remember that other viewpoints and perspectives do indeed exist, learning to delay the "automatic no" which we use to shield us from the outside world, learning to say "what if," learning to be honest with ourselves first, and then with others to the extent that it's humanly possible, learning to look at each new day with the freshness of a child, learning something each and every day. All that's not easy, until you actually try to do it. Once you do, you'll find it the easiest and most natural thing you've ever had to do.

To confront the challenges in our rapidly changing world requires courage, the courage to challenge convention. Why be creative? Why challenge the rules? Why run the risk of failing and looking foolish? The world is changing rapidly. It's no longer possible to solve today's problems with yesterday's solutions.

Obscenity, violence and censorship

One dictionary definition of obscene: *Offensive to one's feelings, or to prevailing notions of decency, disgusting, repulsive.*

> Anything can be obscene. Nothing has to be obscene

To what extent do you agree or disagree with that statement? Think about it for a few minutes, then rate the following film sequences on a scale of 1 to 10, with 10 being totally obscene and 1 being not the least obscene. Please note carefully the above definition, before rating the film sequences. The sequences all come from actual films (European, Hollywood, underground and so on):

1. Woman wearing a traditional one-piece bathing suit
2. Man and young girl naked (no physical contact)
3. Graphic film of a man and a woman having sexual intercourse
4. Young man being transformed into a monster
5. Emaciated victims of Nazi concentration camps
6. Young woman being buried alive
7. Graphic film of a man and a woman having anal sex
8. Two men having anal sex
9. Young boy forced to watch his mother brutally killed
10. The eye of a Hiroshima bomb victim being forced open to reveal the damage
11. Young woman being forced into slavery
12. Woman masturbating with a religious artifact
13. Man with two penises having sex with two women
14. Gun being placed in a man's mouth and fired
15. Man having a sexual relationship with a sheep

Many people find the majority of these film sequences offensive.

These are the composite answers from six upper level undergraduate business classes at a university in South America in 1996–98:

1.	Woman in a one-piece bathing suit	1.0
2.	Young man transformed into a monster	1.5
3.	Man and young girl naked (no physical contact)	1.8
4.	Sexual intercourse between man and woman	2.7
5.	Young woman forced into slavery	3.5
6.	Young woman being buried alive	4.3
7.	Man and a woman having anal sex	4.5
8.	Emaciated victims of Nazi concentration camps	4.7
9.	Young boy forced to watch his mother killed	5.3
10.	The eye of a Hiroshima bomb victim being forced open to reveal the damage	5.5
11.	Gun being placed in a man's mouth and fired	5.6
12.	Two men having anal sex	6.5
13.	Woman masturbating with a religious artifact	6.8
14.	Man with two penises having sex with two women	7.0
15.	Man having a sexual relationship with a sheep	7.6

Note that the "most obscene" film sequences all refer to sex, rather than to violence. Being buried alive is perhaps the most horrible form of death, yet there are nine other sequences which are rated more obscene.

The horrors of the Nazi concentration camps were unimaginable, as was the immense horrors of Hiroshima, yet neither was rated as obscene as a man having a sexual relationship with a sheep.

This attitude is a byproduct of modern society, which in North and South America regards sex as a far greater evil than violence. Television and films bear this out. Put on the television any night in the USA and count the instances of violence. If you don't see it in films or on any of the cop shows, you get it graphically thrown at you on the news, for news channels also have to compete for ratings.

On the battle of Albuera in 1811:

> How horrible it is to have so many people killed, and what a blessing that one cares for none of them.   *Jane Austen, English writer*

This seldom-expressed attitude is unfortunately very prevalent. The fact that millions of people half a world away may be dying of a disease is horrible to someone in Paris or New York only because of the threat that the disease may eventually reach France or the USA. If an epidemic is devastating Nigeria, one would become more emotionally involved if one knew Nigerians, or if one had visited the country. Our defense shields keep us from becoming emotionally involved in almost all of what we see on the late news and read in the newspapers.

> Happiness can be purchased only at the price of repressing and denying too many of the facts of life.   *Rollo May, American psychologist*

The American culture maintains that sex and violence are equally bad, yet, in fact, violence can and is routinely shown on television and in Hollywood, while nudity and sex are not shown.

> These days to get (a film) an R rating, you need to show something really outrageous, like a naked woman. The system is still Puritanical in matters of sex, adult romance and flesh.   Time *magazine, July 29, 2002*

> The classic court attitude towards nudity is perhaps best represented by a 1960s New York State censorship decision, which instructed its staff as follows: "In the scene in which the girl is tortured while hanging by her hands, eliminate all views of her with breasts exposed." This instruction clearly considers nudity to be more dangerous than violence, or as comic Lenny Bruce once observed, Americans cannot stand the sight of naked bodies unless they're mutilated.
>   *Amos Vogel.* Film As A Subversive Art

How many people have you seen killed on television alone in the last year, in the last month, in the last week? How about last night?

One recent news article on teenage violence reported that by the time they are sixteen years old, American children have passively witnessed over thirty thousand murders on television and in the movies.

Violence shapes and obsesses our society, and if we do not stop being violent, we have no future.   *Edward Bond, British playwright*

Many Hollywood films today tend to be graphic portrayals of the "roadrunner principle", namely that death and violence are not always serious or fatal.

Are you sure the hero killed that horrible villain? Just because they shot him twelve times and he fell off the Golden Gate Bridge doesn't mean he's dead. How do you know the fiend isn't lurking in the shadows, waiting for you? How do you know he won't be in the back of your car when you get in?

Advances in cinematography and special effects now permit Hollywood to show violence in a stronger and hence more believable manner than ever before. The audience now actually begins to feel what it's like to be there in the battle, right in the thick of the blood and gore.

These are the results of the same exercise given to similar groups of students at a French university during the period 1996–98:

1.	Woman in a one-piece bathing suit	1.2
2.	Young man transformed into a monster	2.0
3.	Man and young girl naked (no physical contact)	2.2
4.	Sexual intercourse between a man and a woman	2.7
5.	Man and a woman having anal sex	4.2
6.	Man with two penises having sex with two women	5.0
7.	Gun being placed in the mouth and trigger pulled	6.1
8.	Young girl forced into slavery	6.2
9.	Two men having anal sex	6.6
10.	Woman masturbating with a religious artifact	6.7
11.	Man having sexual relationship with a sheep	7.1
12.	The eye of a Hiroshima bomb victim being forced open to reveal the damage	7.7
13.	Young woman being buried alive	8.0
14.	Emaciated victims of a Nazi concentration camp	8.1
15.	Young boy forced to watch his mother brutally killed	8.3

You will note that the four most obscene film sequences now are ones which pertain to violence, whereas on the other side of the Atlantic the four most obscene all dealt with sex.

> War is pornographic. War is one of the most pornographic human activities that exist. *Luciano Benetton, Italian clothes designer*

> I've always found it very difficult to understand the laws as far as nudity in America, how some things are pornographic and some things are not. It's against the law to go topless on the beach, but you can go buy a gun. That just seems so absurd to me. *Ellie MacPherson, Australian model*

When people see the actual film sequences, their opinions always change dramatically.

- Young man transformed into a monster is actually taken from Disney's *Beauty and the Beast*.

In the film, a young man answers his door one cold, stormy night to find a horribly wet, dirty, old woman seeking shelter from a storm. What would you do, if it were to happen to you tonight? Would you let her into your house, or would you shut the door, with the words, "Go to a motel"?

In Disney's tale, the old woman was a witch, who turned the callous young man into a monster, a beast. And then what happened? She didn't stop there. She turned the poor, innocent people who worked for the man into teapots, candlesticks and clocks, for all eternity! How would you like to be turned into a clock for all eternity just because your boss didn't help some street beggar?

- A young woman buried alive is from Disney's classic, *Snow White*:

> "And now, a special sort of death for one so fair," the wicked witch cackled. "What shall it be? A poisoned apple! One taste and Snow White's eyes will close forever! The dwarfs will think she's dead and bury her!"

- Young girl forced into slavery is Disney's *Cinderella*.
- Young boy forced to watch his mother brutally killed is from *Bambi*.
- Man having a sexual relationship with a sheep comes from Woody Allen's 1972 comedy, *Everything You Always Wanted To Know About Sex But Were Afraid To Ask*.

Obscenity is in the mind of a person.

In this exercise, one group judged Woody Allen to be more obscene than Hiroshima and the other considered *Bambi* a greater evil than Hitler's extermination camps. Eight out of ten deemed *Snow White* obscene.

Conclusion:

Anything can be obscene

Most people find nothing obscene about the first clip we mentioned, a woman in a one-piece bathing suit, yet in parts of our world, it most certainly is. In many Arab countries, the sight of a woman's bare forearm, or even her wrist, is obscene.

When the World Cup Soccer Tournament was held in the USA in 1994, the government of Iran had a problem. Football is popular in Iran. They wanted to televise the matches yet also wanted to avoid showing scenes of female spectators in shorts, T-shirts and halter-tops. They got around this by running the tournaments on a eight second delay which gave them time to splice in crowd footage from the Winter Olympics.

Anything can be obscene. *Snow White* can be obscene. *Bambi* can be obscene.

Nothing has to be obscene

The greatest danger of obscenity is censorship. People have a difficult time saying, "all right, I find it offensive, but perhaps others won't." The normal path is, "I find it offensive, therefore others must as well, therefore it must be offensive and therefore it must be limited."

To limit the press is to insult a nation. To prohibit reading of certain books is to declare the inhabitants to be either fools or slaves.
Claude Adrien Helvétius, French philosopher

The books that the world calls immoral are the books that show the world in its own shame. *Oscar Wilde, Irish writer*

It is censorship which creative people challenge, because censorship says "you can't see that, you can't say that, you can't do that."

In December of 1998, the Shv Sena movement in India violently attacked several theaters in that country, which were showing *Fire*, a film about lesbianism. Jai Bhagwan Goyal, a member of the Hindu movement commented in an interview in the *New York Times*:

> Even if we assume lesbianism does happen, what is the point of showing it to people? Everyone knows what goes on between a husband and wife, but they do not do it in the middle of a road. It is unfair to show such things. It can corrupt people.

The rationale here, and it is classic, is don't show scenes of lesbian love to women because it will entice them to try it. If that is true, why then do we allow scenes of murder and violence to be shown?

An Associated Press story on movie violence published in many American newspapers in the wake of the Colorado high school shootings included this comment from a twenty-two-year-old college student from Las Vegas: "Movie violence doesn't bother me, because it's all fake, but young people should be kept away from movies with sex, because they see how to do it." There's strange logic at work here. Let's keep young people in the dark about sex, but let's show them how to kill.

> Censorship is the tool of those who have the need to hide actualities from themselves and others. Their fear is only their inability to face what is real. Somewhere in their upbringing they were shielded against the total facts of our experience. They were only taught to look one way when many ways exist.
>
> *Charles Buikowski, American author*

In its broadest sense, the word censorship refers to suppression of information, ideas or artistic expression by anyone, whether government, church, private group or individuals. Censorship has the effect of limiting the diversity that would otherwise be available and the root motivation for it is a fear that the expression, if allowed, would do harm to individuals in its audience or society as a whole. It is fear, real or imagined, that drives the censorial impulse.

The following are examples taken from a long list of books, which have been banned or challenged at some time in their printed lives:

Ulysses, James Joyce
Brave New World, Aldous Huxley
Catch 22, Joseph Heller
Lord of the Flies, William Golding
The Sun Also Rises, Ernest Hemingway
From Here to Eternity, James Jones

The Catcher in the Rye, J.D. Salinger
Go Tell It To The Mountain, James Baldwin
Women in Love, D.H. Lawrence
1984, George Orwell
The Naked and the Dead, Norman Mailer

Where they have burned books, they will end in burning human beings.

Heinrich Heine, German poet

The illogical part of the censorship of sex in the USA today is that it's aimed almost entirely at the visual, as if the sole danger was in seeing. The audio tracks of many American films are now laced with sexually explicit words, while the visual images remain as pure as freshly fallen snow.

A film such as the acclaimed *Good Will Hunting*, contained no nudity, but was loaded with words like "fuck," "shit," "bitch" and "asshole." There was even a lengthy joke in the film about fellatio. The policy on television and in Hollywood is "say it but don't show it."

The FCC received hundreds of complaints about the October 2003 Golden Globe Awards when Bono, lead singer of the rock group U2, said "This is really, really fuckin' brilliant." The FCC later decided that Bono's comment was not obscene because he did not use the word to describe a sexual act.

Quick! Don't think of a blue cat!

What's the first thing that came to your mind? A blue cat! Even if you make a conscious effort not to think of it, your third or fourth thought, however fleeting, will be of the cat. If we hear a word, we form an ever so brief mental picture of what we hear. If we hear the word "fuck," we think about it, be it only for a flickering second, but we do think about it. What's the difference between forming a mental picture and actually seeing an image on a screen? For one thing, what races through our minds is very often far more vivid than what we actually might see.

Our point is that it is absurd to censor the video without censoring the audio. Creative people will point out that it is a shame to censor anything at all, and they're right. From the point of view of creativity, they are perfectly right.

Society says that words such as "fuck" and "shit" are bad, dirty words that should never be used. All our dirty words have sexual connotations, although many simply deal with natural body functions.

Violate, murder, massacre, slaughter, slay, butcher, torture, strangle, decapitate, mangle, flog, impale! These aren't bad words.

The next time something goes wrong, the next time your car gets a flat tire, instead of muttering, "oh fuck," try, "oh massacre!" You'll sound stupid, right? But think for a minute what you're doing when you say, "oh fuck." You're associating something bad (flat tire) with sex. To say that fuck is a bad word says that fucking is bad or dirty. That comes from the historical idea that all things sexual were bad and unclean.

Where does that leave us on violence?

The more truly violent species all appear to have exterminated themselves, a lesson we should not overlook.

Desmond Morris, British zoologist, anthropologist

On the Falklands War of 1982:

The Falklands thing was a fight between two bald men over a comb.

Jorge Luis Borges, Argentine writer

All wars are fights between bald men over combs. In the final analysis, they're all senseless. It doesn't matter what the fight was over. Afterward, people don't even know, or care. War settles nothing. To win a war is as disastrous as to lose one. In war, there are no winners, only losers, yet this too is a naive, childlike notion. If, however, we believe it's impossible to curb man's lust for violence, we will never give ourselves a chance to change.

So long as there are men there will be wars.

Albert Einstein, German-born US physicist, mathematician

Creative adults spend their entire lives fighting for ideas that regular adults think are impossible. Regular adults accept the world the way it is and always try for attainable changes. Creative adults try for large-scale, exhaustive changes. Conventional thinking says that war is impossible to stop, it can only be contained and many people feel that it serves a specific purpose. Unconventional thinking says that:

War is not an adventure. It is like typhus.

Antoine de Saint-Exupéry, French novelist, aviator

War and violence are not adventures. They are diseases and should be treated as such.

Taboos

Nature knows no indecencies; man invents them.   *Mark Twain, American writer*

When a person feels embarrassed, they close up and contract. To be fully creative you have to open up and let go. Creative thinking requires a state of mind that allows you to look for new ideas. You use crazy, wild, impractical ideas, or just as often fragments of ideas as ways of getting to practical new ideas. You challenge convention, and search for ideas everywhere, under, over, inside, outside, on top of and behind, not only things and people but also emotions, fears, desires and ideas. You turn things over and inside out. You search everywhere. You don't limit your search to what you like or what's easy to gain access to, you search everywhere, including and especially in places that everyone avoids, the taboos.

> ## For creative people, no subject is taboo

Remember your list of everything you did in the course of a day from invisible barrier one? It probably failed to mention anything you did on the toilet and, if you're a woman, anything to do with your period. Even thought these subjects exist, they're taboos and by definition, untouchable and therefore not suitable for your list.

A dictionary definition of taboo: *to prohibit or forbid because of tradition, convention.*

Since creative people challenge everything they themselves did not create, they treat taboos not as things to be left alone, but as subjects to be examined and challenged.

Are you going to let society tell you what's good and bad, right and wrong, nice and not nice? Are you going to let society tell you what you can and cannot say, even what subjects you can and can't cover? Don't worry. Everyone does. Life is easier that way. It's all done for you. It's simpler. Creative people, like adolescents, have a difficult time with that. Creative people may in the end agree with what society tells them. That's fine, as long as they can make the decisions for themselves. What they hate is to be handed something and be told, here believe this, accept this. Don't question it. We've already done your thinking for you. We've already decided what's good for you and what's not.

Critical to creativity is not accepting things without questioning them. Good examples of things we fail to question are superstitions. When we learn the origins of superstitions, we usually see that we neither need to fear nor abide by them.

Two of the more popular superstitions are those of a black cat and walking under a ladder. Many superstitions have their origins in religion and these two are no exceptions.

The origin of the black cat dates back to the witchcraft persecutions in 14th and 15th century Europe. It was widely believed that when witches made pacts with Satan, they were given small animals called "familiars." These animals served as links between the witch and the Devil. One of the most common of household animals was the cat and black has long been associated with evil. Hence, when a black cat crosses your path it was deemed as a sign of impending misfortune.

Many people avoid walking under ladders, yet few know the origins of this widely held superstition. The space that a ladder forms when it inclines against a building or structure is that of a triangle. It is that triangular space that poses the problem, for when you walk through it you were thought to be violating the Trinity, Father, Son and Holy Spirit.

Knowing the origins helps you decide whether or not you want to abide by the superstition. Understanding the origins of taboos helps you accept the stigma attached to them.

The foundation of creativity is freedom. Freedom is choice, independent choice, nothing handed to you as a doctrine, nothing imposed, nothing that can't be challenged. That is why creative people find it almost impossible to live under dictatorships. It is the loss of freedom which they find unbearable.

> The spirit of truth and the spirit of freedom, they are the pillars of society.
> Henrik Ibsen, Norwegian playwright

They are also the pillars of creativity.

A dictionary definition of freedom is: *Exemption or liberation from the control of some other person or power. The absence of hindrance, restraint, confinement or repression.*

Dostoevsky has said that what people want most is free, independent choice, and that they are willing to bear the responsibility which comes with it.

Most people want security in this world, not freedom.

H. L. Mencken, American journalist, editor

Dostoevsky and Mencken offer opposing views, and both points of view are valid. The fact of the matter is that in practice many people have consented to give up their freedom in a lot of what they do. Creative people, like adolescents, don't want to give in to custom and convention. That is one of the fundamental differences between creative and non-creative people.

Children will often point at a dwarf or handicapped person while their parents wish they'd ignore the person the way adults have learned to do. Creative adults have this childlike quality of being able to treat areas that others would rather avoid. Sometimes just pointing out what's going on, or not going on, is sometimes enough.

In any society the artist has a responsibility. His effectiveness is certainly limited and a painter or writer cannot change the world. But they can keep an essential margin of non-conformity alive. Thanks to them, the powerful can never affirm that everyone agrees with their acts. That small difference is very important.

Luis Buñuel, Spanish filmmaker

There is a tension that exists between society and the creative person. In each instance, however, the creative person goes further than society wants him to. The whole point of creativity is to make others around you uncomfortable.

Inventiveness is essentially a rebellious act

Taste is the enemy of creativeness.   *Pablo Picasso, Spanish artist*

Who determines what is and what is not good taste? Society does, the people, the masses. Something which is in good taste must please the majority of the people. If you try to write a story, paint a picture or make a film that pleases everyone, that story, painting or film will reflect good taste, but it won't wake up a living soul!

It is difficult enough to produce a meaningful creative work without handicapping yourself with the notion that the work needs to be tasteful. If you're worried about offending, you'll never get anywhere. Your work or your ideas must be capable of offending. Your work, or your ideas, must be capable of disturbing people enough to wake them up, enough to make them start to become more aware of things they routinely see but still don't see.

This is the problem that prevents the vast majority of people from becoming creative.

> **You must be willing to at least consider everything, no matter how radical, outrageous or disgusting**

The unnatural, that too is natural.   *Johann Wolfgang von Goethe, German writer*

The more you can open up life for yourself, whatever it might be, even the unpleasant aspects of it, means going in a safer and healthier direction.
Phyllis Kronhausen

For the creative person, there are no taboos.

Do you remember an earlier quote from Marcel Proust which said that man wants to learn to swim while keeping one foot on the ground? Well, that same man also wants to create without offending anyone. Both notions are impossible.

In art, all who have done something other than their predecessors have merited the epithet of revolutionary. Art is either plagiarism or revolution.
Paul Gauguin, French artist

So is creativity. The idea of the virginal artist or creative person is absurd. The idea of the dignified creative person is also absurd.

Dignity, hell! There is no dignity in creativity, just as there is no dignity in war. It's whatever it takes to conceive the idea and then get it expressed in a way which makes an impact, wakes people up. You can't care what people may think of you when you dare to trespass the social rules that they are afraid to approach. There is no dignity in the regular baring of your soul, no dignity or privacy in the transparent world in which you live. One is never dignified when one is alone. When you're alone you can do all the things you wouldn't do in public.

The difference between creative and non-creative people, is that creative people, like children, are not afraid to say and do in public everything they think and do in private, in part because they view those things as natural and in part because they know it will set them apart and that they'll command your attention. They don't worry about having to be dignified. There is no dignified death, just as there was no dignified birth.

One exits the same way one came into this world, kicking and screaming, if not loudly and physically, then quietly but kicking and screaming nonetheless. What's not natural is to try so hard to live the years in between birth and death with such a supreme measure of dignity that we should shudder at the thought of unwrapping our thoughts and our bodies. Dignity? There is no dignity for the highly creative person!

> Creativity comes from accepting that you're not safe, from being absolutely aware, and from letting go of control. It's a matter of seeing everything, even when you want to shut your eyes. *Madeleine L' Engle, American writer*

Creative people have fewer inhibitions than non-creative people. They must. You never know where your ideas will come from. One idea may lead to another and another and it's from the twentieth idea or the hundred and twentieth that the breakthrough comes. In order to get ideas, you must be willing to explore all paths, willing to open all doors, both real and psychological. You have to be curious about *everything*.

Curiosity

Like children, creative people are curious about everything. Alice (from *Alice in Wonderland*) is the classic example:

> Alice started to her feet, for it flashed across her mind that she had never before seen a rabbit with either a waistcoat pocket, or a watch to take out of it, and burning with curiosity, she ran after it, and saw it pop down a large rabbit-hole under the hedge. In another moment down went Alice after it, never once considering how in the world she was to get out again.

We said earlier that in order to think creatively, we must be able to look afresh at what we normally take for granted, that in order to be creative, you must look at things from multi-perspectives. Take the time to see what something looks like from the top, the bottom, the back, the sides, inside out, outside in. You have to be curious about everything. You have to want to know.

> Curiosity is the key to creativity. *Akio Morita, former chairman, Sony Electronics*

Aren't you curious to know what other people look like without their clothes? Children are. Are you? Of course, when we say, other people, we mean all other people, young, old, male, female, everyone! Since a "yes" plunges you into the waters of more than one taboo, the normal answer is, "no!"

There's nothing wrong with being curious, about everything and everyone. We're all curious. Creative people are no more curious than everyone else. The difference is that normal people suppress their curiosity, while creative people don't. It's another difference, another big difference.

Curiosity is a small and fragile plant that requires above all, freedom.
Albert Einstein

The suppression of curiosity begins in childhood and continues thereafter. Most people suppress their curiosity as adults and thus lose the ability to raise meaningful questions about things. To limit yourself to your first idea is a disaster for your imagination. The best way to get a good idea is to get as many ideas as you can. Always remember that any particular way of looking at things is just one of many other possible ways. Inhibitions hold you back. If you have them, you're like a soccer player playing on a restricted field, while your opponents use the entire field.

Nudity

Man is the sole animal whose nudities offend his own companions, and the only one who, in his natural actions, withdraws and hides himself from his own kind.
Michel de Montaigne, French moralist, writer

Students in art school have nude models to draw, paint and sculpt, often from the day they begin their training. This is done not merely to learn how to draw the human body (if you can draw, you can draw anything), but to accustom the students to nudity. It is difficult to be creative if you are inhibited by anything and nudity is one of society's strongest inhibitions.

Nudity is a subject we have been conditioned to avoid. It's a door that society tells us to close and keep closed. We all live with closed doors. To return to creativity means flinging open those doors, one after another! The more doors you can open, the freer and more creative you will be.

We are taught to be shameless is the worst thing, but it isn't until one loses one's shame, that one is really free.   *Bette Davis, American actress*

> Nudity and the exposure of sex organs cause neither shame nor surprise in primitive society, nor among children. It requires special education to produce that apparently spontaneous horror which Western people experience when they see the naked body.   *Rene Guyon.* The Ethics of Sexual Acts

A creative person may or may not choose to be nude, but if he or she happened to be, or happened to be with others who were, it would not embarrass them.

Children are not born with any shame about nudity. They learn to be ashamed of their own nudity. Shame, with respect to nudity, is relative to individual situations and customs. It is not absolute. An Arab woman, for example, if encountered in a state of undress, will cover her face. In pre-revolutionary China it was shameful for a woman to show her foot, and in Japan, the back of her neck. In 18th century France, while deep décolletage was accepted, it was improper to expose the point of a woman's shoulder.

> What spirit is so empty and blind, that it cannot recognize the fact that the foot is nobler than the shoe, and skin more beautiful than the garment with which it is clothed?   *Michelangelo*

If I become a nudist, will I be more creative? No, but if nudity inhibits you, you will be less creative. Any inhibition will handicap your creativity. We're not saying that you should become a nudist, only that you shouldn't mind being nude, that you shouldn't let it become an obstacle.

Are you capable of being nude with a group, or in front of a group? If others are nude, or even partially nude, do you feel embarrassed? Do you get all silly and red? Do you look away? Do you change your behavior? If you're like most people, you do. What's to be gained if you don't? Liberty, confidence, freedom!

There are many things in life which could be pretty scary if you really thought about them. Think about all the things which could go wrong when you get behind the wheel of your car for example, things like accidents, breakdowns and getting stopped by the police for doing something you're not supposed to. We're able to function because we don't think about all that could go wrong. For certain things, though, we tend to have unrealistic fears. Fear of flying is an unrealistic fear. Flying is by far the safest form of transportation in the world, yet there are a lot of people who dread having to fly. Fear of nudity is another unrealistic fear.

Standards for nudity, like clothing, are, if anything, universally inconsistent. A bikini is accepted on the beach but is restricted elsewhere.

Underwear on the beach is a no-no, though it covers the same amount of flesh as a bikini, and perhaps even more. Few groups agree as to which parts of our bodies should be covered and which parts should be openly displayed. Many people find it difficult to understand the logic behind any other form of clothing and adornment other than their own. The thought of viewing parts of the body that they generally keep covered so disgusts them that they pass laws to protect themselves from it.

Saudi Arabia is one of the world's strictest Islamic states, where unrelated men and women are kept separate in schools, workplaces, restaurants, banks and government buildings. In public Saudi women must wear loose-fitting head-to-toe black cloaks. Because the salespeople in stores are almost exclusively male, women's clothing stores are not permitted to have fitting rooms. The religious police circulate freely, scolding women for displaying the slightest hint of skin or wayward strand of hair on their heads. By western standards this is extreme.

By western standards, nudity is extreme, yet children are not born with any shame about nudity. They learn to be ashamed.

> **Olum's Observation: If God had intended us to go around naked, He would have made us that way**

Most people walk around in suits of invisible armor, which serve to keep everyone else from getting to get too close. They're afraid that someone might hear their precious thoughts, or catch a glimpse of their precious bodies. Clothing is a type of armor. As such, it's more symbolic than practical, but it's armor nonetheless. We expect clothing to protect us against a variety of threats. Some of them, like cold, the sun and insects, are physical threats, but some are psychological and those are the ones which are more imagined that real.

> Clothing separates us from our own bodies as well as from the bodies of others. The more society muffles the human body in clothes, camouflages pregnancy, and hides breastfeeding, the more individual and bizarre will be the child's attempts to understand, to piece together a very imperfect knowledge of the life-cycle of the two sexes and an understanding of the particular state of maturity of his or her body.   *Margaret Mead, US anthropologist*

It has often been said that sex is hardly ever just about sex. Well, nudity is hardly ever about nudity either. It's a social taboo and thus, for the creative person, stands there to be challenged.

One must remember that clothing itself, or the lack of it, is neither moral nor immoral. It is the breaking of tradition which causes the problem.

There are two kinds of nudity, group and individual (individual meaning one person nude while others are not). Of the two, group nudity is easier because everyone is in it together. Responsibility and guilt are therefore both shared.

> Emperors, kings, artisans, peasants, big people, little people, at bottom, we are all alike and all the same; all just alike on the inside and when our clothes are off nobody can tell which of us is which.　　　　　　　　　　*Mark Twain*

Creative people don't mind, and in fact often prefer, being the only one nude. Why? The answer is the audience. An important dimension to creativity is the audience. There is a crucial social dimension to the creative act.

Who wants to walk around naked if you're alone? Think about it. When you're alone, you're always naked, or conversely never naked. Let's take it one step further, if you're alone, what does it matter whether you're naked or not.

Speak in front of an audience, sing in front of an audience, play music in front of an audience, act in front of an audience, be nude in front of an audience. You either feel vulnerable in front of the audience or you don't. You either love to be in front of an audience or you don't. The highly creative person has to be in front of an audience, if not physically, at least through their work, through their screenplays, their music, their sculptures, their creations, their ideas.

There's openness, frankness, transparency connected with creativity. When you create anything you are putting yourself at risk. You're showing yourself to the world via your work or your ideas. There's vulnerability. There's candor. There's honesty. There's nudity. Creative people are used to showing everything, their innermost secrets, their thoughts and their emotions. After baring your soul, baring your body is easy. People who won't bare their bodies rarely succeed in baring anything else. Creative people are far more public than non-creative people. They're more open. They have to be. Remember that the road back to creativity is a letting-go experience.

When Pope Paul IV complained about the nudity in Michelangelo's Sistine Chapel frescos, the artist reportedly replied:

> "Tell the Pope that this is a small matter and it can easily be made suitable; let him make the world a suitable place and the painting will soon follow suit."

There are people who will tell you:

> Nudity doesn't inhibit me. I've no problem with it. I just don't ever feel like being nude in front of others.
>
> Why?
>
> Well, I don't think I look very good. I'm twenty pounds overweight, I have cellulite. I wouldn't have minded when I was younger, but now, I just can't.
>
> Do you still go to the beach? Do you still put on a bathing suit?
>
> Of course.
>
> Do you wear shorts? Do you wear T-shirts? Leotards?
>
> Yes.
>
> Then it's not about looking fat and ugly. It's about guilt. It's about sex.

What bothers people about nudity is its connection with sex. Except for medical and, at times, artistic purposes, no other purpose for nudity is recognized except for sex. Nudity is about the exposure of sexual organs. If you're not comfortable with sex, you won't be comfortable with nudity.

Sex

Rene Guyon, in his classic, *The Ethics of Sexual Acts*, points out the link between nudity and sex.

> The mere fact that certain organs are related to certain functions affords no ground for excommunicating them. It is only through the prohibition of sex that special value comes to be placed upon the exhibition of sexual organs.

Same sex nudity is widely accepted, where cross-sex nudity is not (for example locker rooms, steam rooms, saunas, bathrooms). In some European countries you find unisex bathrooms and there are far more co-ed saunas and steam rooms in Europe than there are in the Americas, yet it's normal throughout the world to separate males and females as soon as they take off their clothes. Traditional thinking says that male–female nudity inevitably leads to sex, and sex is something to be ashamed of. That's the underlying idea. Back in the 1960s the idea of having co-ed dormitories in American universities and colleges was a radical one. Conventional wisdom said that if you put young men and women together in the same building, all they'd do is have non-stop sex. Today co-ed dorms are the norm. They work. You take them for granted. In fact, today you have a hard time imagining what all the fears and objections were back then.

> To exterminate the passions and desires merely in order to do away with their folly and its unpleasant consequences, this itself seems an acute form of folly. We no longer admire dentists who pull out teeth to stop them hurting.
>
> *Friedrich Nietzsche, German philosopher*

Man's sexual inhibitions have a long history and religion is more often than not involved. From its early days Christianity was a sex-negative religion. Sexuality was, according to early Christian teaching, given to people solely for the purposes of reproduction. All sex outside marriage was a sin and inside marriage it was meant to be only for procreation. It was not until the 16th century that the idea of sex purely for pleasure was advanced.

Jeffrey Richards, in his book *Sex, Dissidence and Damnation,* described the prevailing attitude toward sex in the medieval and renaissance eras:

> The only permitted form of sexual intercourse was the missionary position. All other variations were penalized. There was three years penance for the woman on top, which was deemed as contrary to nature that prescribed that the man should hold the dominant position. Three years was also the penance for oral and for rear-entry heterosexual intercourse, deemed to reduce man to the level of the beast because that is the way animals mated. Couples were urged to have sex only at night and then only partially unclothed.

Many people today do not accept oral, anal and homosexual acts as variations, but continue to view them as aberrations and refuse to remove the idea of guilt.

> Homosexuality is assuredly no advantage, but it is nothing to be ashamed of, no vice, no degradation, it cannot be classified as an illness. It is a great injustice to persecute homosexuality as a crime, and cruelty too.
>
> *Sigmund Freud, Austria founder of psychoanalysis*

Again, we are not saying that to be creative you need to embrace all aspects of sex, just that you should be able to deal with them, talk about them and accept them as sources of inspiration and ideas.

Sex education

Fear stems from ignorance, and awareness begins with education. Although sex education varies greatly from country to country, there is often a great reluctance to talk to children about sex. Many parents dread having to talk to their kids about sex and put it off until they're sure the child picked it all up elsewhere.

In its "there are some things money can't buy, for everything else there's MasterCard" campaign, MasterCard ran a print advertisement recently which showed a young woman looking directly at the camera. The copy of the one page magazine ad read:

- a video explaining human sexuality: $19.99 online
- a book on how to talk to your kids about the "S" word: $23 online
- getting up your courage to do the face-to-face: priceless

What's sad here is that parents too often do need to get up the courage to talk not only to their children but also to each other. In an earlier chapter we talked about people not asking themselves and their partners what they really want. In a recent creativity seminar that Art Gogatz taught in France, two out of thirty-five students answered the anonymous, written exercise of three things you would love to do but are too embarrassed to do by stating: "Tell my parents I love them."

Five graduate students in a group of twenty-one in Hong Kong said the same thing in a similar exercise. That's sad. Communication is a two-way street. For every child who can't communicate with his or her own parent, there is a parent who can't communicate with his or her child.

People often say that they wished their parents had talked to them more about sex. Because of a devastating AIDS epidemic, people in South Africa are now being forced to confront sex and sexual values on a much more open level. Sadly, it takes an epidemic, an emergency to get people to confront their taboos. Too many people still look at AIDS, HIV and sex as forbidden things that can't be discussed.

You often hear parents, even highly educated professionals, who believe: "Why do children need to know about sex? My daughter is four-teen. In my eyes she's still a little girl. I would rather she remained igno-rant about sex for the time being."

People and especially parents need to be more open, yet it's difficult to discuss sex with your children when you can't even bring yourself to confront it. Since many parents cannot talk to their children about sex, they rely on the schools. In the US, however, a typical course in sex education is just one or two classes of a more general high school or junior high school health education course.

> American teens have the worst of all worlds. Our children are bombarded and confronted with sexual messages, sexual exploitation, and all manner of sexual criticism. But our society is by and large sexually illiterate.
>
> *Faye Wattleton, American feminist, activist*

A recent study conducted by the Henry J. Kaiser Foundation, a US health research organization, found that many parents want teenagers to receive comprehensive information about sex, delivered without value judgments. The report polled 1,501 sets of parents and students, as well as teachers and principals. Nearly two-thirds of parents said sex education should last half a semester or more but just over half still maintained that classes should not be mixed.

The report found growing broad support for sex education, yet if you look at the above stats, not wanting the classes to be mixed shows an existing or perceived embarrassment factor when it comes to discussing sexual themes in the presence of the opposite sex.

"Our teacher talked about it in a very dry way, and many of the boys used it as a way to tease the girls. Most of the class didn't really understand it." This is a common observation of students in sex education classes.

> Community and religious leaders wrongly believe that sex education promotes promiscuity. We must summon the courage to talk frankly and constructively about sex.   *Pascal Mocumbi, prime minister of Mozambique*

Can you imagine what it would be like if you felt no embarrassment when it came to sex? Can you imagine what it would be like if nothing embarrassed you? Can you imagine what you'd feel? Freedom, you'd feel a sense of freedom, and you'd be on the way back to regaining your creativity.

The links between sex and creativity

There links between creativity and sex are numerous. The creative person seeks to wake others up, and to that end the topic of sex is useful for getting attention. A second link is formed because creative people feel that we should be able to treat all subjects (taboos) without embarrassment or shame. They thus challenge conventional thinking on them. These are two important links between creativity and sex. There is also a third.

Silvano Arieti, in his book *Creativity: the Magic Synthesis*, asserts:

> The concept of sublimation or diversion of sexual energy from the original aim plays an important role in Freud's concept of creativity. Thus when sexual energy is not spent in the proper sexual activity, it is displaced and invested in pursuits, like the creative, which seem unrelated to sex. The creative person is a frustrated individual who cannot find fulfillment in sexual gratification or other aspects of life and who therefore attempts to find it in creativity. In contrast, the biographies of many gifted people who also had a rich sexual life seem to contradict such assumptions.

Are highly creative people frustrated? In a manner of speaking, yes indeed they are. If they weren't, they wouldn't have such strong desires to wake everyone up and get them moving. Are they also sexually frustrated? Perhaps too the answer here is yes, but not in the way Mr. Arieti means, not in the way that they cannot achieve normal sexual fulfillment, or to the point where creativity becomes a substitute for sex. Creative people expect more fulfillment from sex than most people do, just as they expect more out of life. Most people are sexually frustrated to the extent that their sex lives aren't what they would ideally like them to be (neither are most people's lives). The non-creative person rationalizes and accepts this, while the creative person does not.

> Sex is admittedly the most important subject in life. It is the thing which causes the most shipwrecks in the happiness of men and women.
>
> *John B. Watson, American psychologist*

It has been said that tensions which stem from other difficulties in relationships would be ignored by many couples if the sexual relationship were more satisfactory.

That brings us to another point. Freud maintained that: "unsatisfied wishes are the driving power behind fantasies. Every separate fantasy contains the fulfillment of a wish, and improves unsatisfactory reality." According to Freud, the creative person's desire to know the unknown can be traced back to curiosity about sexual matters. Only unsatisfied people (and here we are not talking about unhappy people, but people who desire and believe they can achieve more and more) have fantasies or daydreams in play.

Just as the child finds fantasy an improvement over reality, the child-like adult creates a work in which he or she can satisfy both his or her daydream wishes and desire to change a certain slice of the world.

How to break through invisible barrier twelve

The way to break through this barrier is to realize that everything you do has an influence on others, has an influence on the world in some way and that you can make a difference. It is well to remember the words of Albert Schweitzer, words which we quoted earlier: "no one must shut his eyes and regard as nonexistent the sufferings of which he spares himself the sight. We must do something more." If you can embrace that thought, you can overcome this barrier.

ACTIVITIES

Let's say you found a bottle with a genie, and were given three wishes. What would those wishes be? Note: You cannot wish for more wishes. You have three and only three.

What did you wish for?

Most people wish for some sequence of health, money and power, for them-selves, of course. Some wish for the same things for their families and some for a cure to a loved one's disease. The wishes are always personal. Rarely do people wish for something which would benefit all mankind, or the planet.

Accepting vulnerability

Our lives are censored, for the most part self-censored. We fear emotionality, intimacy, sensitivity and vulnerability. We rarely say what we really feel, rarely let down our defenses. We censor ourselves, and then demand that others censor themselves as well.

Creative people are less afraid to show that they're vulnerable. They're less afraid to let people see them the way they really are, which is with abundant and unique talents but also with many weaknesses. If you're embarrassed by your weaknesses, and therefore hide them, you don't work to overcome them. In order to correct them, you first have to admit that they exist.

Today in the USA, women-owned businesses are growing at twice the rate of those run by men, according to the Center for Women's Business Research. Women-owned businesses in the USA also exceed the average revenue growth rate for all American businesses. Why are women-owned businesses doing so well? One reason is that women are willing to ask for help and direction, while men hate to ask. There's a degree of vulnerability in asking for help. Creative people, like children, are less concerned with having to impress, less concerned with their image and much more ready to admit their fragility.

Self-confidence

It is a vulgar and barbarous drama which would not be tolerated by the vilest populace of France or Italy. One would imagine this piece to be the work of a drunken savage.

Can you guess the play which is being reviewed here? It's Voltaire reviewing Shakespeare's *Hamlet*.

Creative people develop high degrees of self-confidence because they have to. They need to be self-confident to survive. There are people who will praise the things you create or the ideas you come up with, others will be indifferent, while others may criticize or even ridicule them. You have to be able to deal with all those reactions. You have to be able to accept criticism. Your work, especially in the beginning, probably won't be very good. You've got to keep going, keep learning, keep creating. You can't quit. Even when your work improves, it may still be roundly criticized. Most famous artists had their work blasted at some point, even work that was later judged to be masterpieces. Picasso, Van Gogh, Soutine, Gauguin, Modigliani, Manet, Renoir, all were criticized and criticized heavily.

Creative people are self-confident because they have to be, and because their training lets them. When you stop being embarrassed (and while that does not happen overnight, there is a "eureka" element to it), your priorities change, for you no longer have to be on guard. You no longer worry about the same things as everyone else.

Make a list of the things you would love to do but are too embarrassed to do, and then after you have them listed, actually go out and do them. Overcoming embarrassment builds confidence, and without confidence you won't be very creative.

An artist is a creature driven by demons. He doesn't know why they chose him and he's usually too busy to wonder why.   *F. Scott Fitzgerald, American writer*

Creative people actually like their demons, they're friends with them, and they're not afraid of them. Who are these demons? They are the urges which everyone else suppresses; ideas, desires, wishes and wants, which go beyond the norms of accepted belief; ideas which get you into trouble.

Creative people have such enormous self-confidence that they have a sense of higher self. They often believe that nothing is impossible, almost to the point of having control over their environment. They believe that by just being present they can control their environment and their circumstances.

Circumstances? I make circumstances!   *Napoleon Bonaparte, French emperor*

As a writer you create people, settings and circumstances. You let some characters die and others live, you make some fall in love, while you cruelly break the hearts of others.

If you would have me weep, you must first of all feel grief yourself.

Horace, Roman poet

Ask an actor or actress to cry and they will think of something so sad that in a few minutes they actually begin to shed tears. When a writer creates a tragic scene, he or she must first experience and feel that sense of tragedy inside in order to allow others to feel it on paper or the screen.

It is said that soon after Walt Disney finished the film *Bambi*, he showed it to his family and friends at a private screening. That night when Disney went to say goodnight to his young daughter, he found her in tears.

"What's the matter?" he asked.

"Bambi's mother," the little girl sobbed. "She didn't have to die!"

"But it's only a story, only a film," Disney soothed.

"Yes, but you could have saved her!" his daughter came back. "It would have been so easy for you to let her live!"

In writing, you must kill all your darlings.   *William Faulkner, American writer*

Disney did, and created a timeless classic. In creativity, you can't play it conservatively. You've got to take risks. You've got to go for the heart. You've got to go for the emotion.

Emotion

One ought to write only when one leaves a piece of one's flesh in the inkpot each time one dips one's pen.

Leo Tolstoy, Russian novelist

That's a hell of a statement! Normal people only experience that kind of emotion by being personally involved in some highly charged situation, by reading a book or seeing a photograph or a film. It is the task of the creative person to build vigorous emotion, first in himself, then transfer it to others via his work or his ideas. If you don't feel emotion as a creator, others surely won't.

A work of art which did not begin in emotion is not art.

Paul Cézanne, French artist

> **You can't create anything if you don't feel the emotion that goes with it**

People don't go to the cinema so they can see the characters on the screen laugh, cry, get frightened or get excited. They go to have those experiences themselves. They read a novel for the same reasons.

The cinema, literature and television all provide opportunities to experience emotion. Within the safety and isolation of a darkened theatre, your own home or your own mind, it is possible to leave the world behind and let yourself be engulfed by surging thoughts, feelings and emotions. All filmmakers, like all writers, have a single goal, to provoke emotion in their audience. When a film or novel creates emotion, it is successful and when it doesn't, it fails.

> The cinema makes it possible to experience without danger all the excitement, passion and desire which must be repressed in a humanitarian ordering of life.
> *Carl Jung, Swiss psychologist*

Creative people will create, no matter the results, no matter if they're being paid or not, no matter the hour, the weather, the place. They just have to create. It's what they enjoy most.

Creative people don't need to have heightened emotions, but they do need to express the emotions they feel. Most people suppress their emotions. Most people can't tell other people what they feel, while creative people have a difficult time not doing that. They can do it themselves and they can do it for their characters through their films, their novels and their work.

Most people are frightened by too many emotions. We are taught (men especially) that emotions are our enemies and if we show them we'll get into trouble. Creative people, on the other hand, are frightened by a lack of emotions. We are taught to prefer reason to emotionality and to believe that we can see something better when we have no emotional involvement. A person, however, sees better when his emotions are aroused. In fact, we don't really see something unless we have some emotional involvement with it. Teachers see this in the classroom, advertisers see it in the marketplace, speakers see it in the faces of their audiences.

Americans have a reputation in the world as being open, friendly and easy to talk to. They talk to one another, in airports and stores, on trains and in waiting rooms. What they say to each other though is not very personal. Even if you're introduced to someone at a dinner or a party, most of the conversation centers on books the people have read, restaurants they've been to, films they've seen or things in the news. It's all about issues and it's impersonal as hell. Emotions and feelings are hidden behind invisible but super-solid defense shields. Many Americans and indeed people worldwide have the habit of distancing themselves from the process of interpersonal communication instead of jumping in. They overuse their defense shields.

In a June 2000 telephone poll taken by *Time* and CNN, 1,218 people in the USA were asked what they would let a reality-based TV show film. These were some of the replies:

● Thirty-one percent answered they would let the show film them in their pajamas. Wow, thirty-one percent would let people see them in their pajamas, in baggy, non-revealing, rumpled pajamas. Only thirty-one percent. A full sixty-nine percent said, "no way."

● Twenty-six percent said they'd let the show film them crying, seventy-four percent didn't want to be filmed showing that or any kind of emotion.

● Only eight percent said that they'd be willing to appear naked, even though the television censor clouds up the genital areas when the program is aired, so that nothing is actually revealed.

Small wonder that only two percent of adults are judged to be highly creative. How can you bare your soul if you won't bare your body? How can you create if you won't bare your soul? How can you create anything if you don't feel the emotion that goes with it? You can't. You just plain can't.

To be fully creative, it isn't necessary to be nude, or a fool, or even to take risks. What we're saying is that you merely need to be *capable* of:

■ Open, honest expression
■ Accepting change
■ Challenging the accepted
■ Looking foolish and/or different
■ Dealing with any subject
■ Taking emotional risks.

Masculinity and femininity

One word that characterizes creative people is "complex." They tolerate apparent contradictions because they themselves have contradictory traits. Traditionally, men are brought up to repress those aspects of their personality which are considered as feminine, while women are expected to do the opposite.

Scratch an actor and you'll get an actress.   *Dorothy Parker, American writer, poet*

Creative women, however, tend to test out as more dominant and "masculine" than do other women, while creative men are more sensitive and less aggressive. This tendency toward androgyny is sometimes confused with homosexuality, but in fact it comes from the ability to balance the masculine and feminine parts of their personalities.

In his book *The Path of Least Resistance* Robert Fritz has this to say about creative people:

> Creators are an enigma to many people, because creators seem to tolerate apparent contradictions quite easily. To creators, however, these are not contradictions but opposites that need to be balanced continually. Creators live simultaneously in many universes. Each universe has its own set of governing principles. When a creator performs a creative act, many separate and distinct universes suddenly converge in perfect alignment.

*   *   *

I'm not afraid to show my feminine side, it's part of what makes me a man.
Gerard Depardieu, French actor

People are afraid to show both their masculine and feminine sides. They're afraid to be thought of as homosexual should they do so. People don't want to express their most secret emotions, ideas or desires for the same reason that they don't want to be nude. It's because they think they'll be vulnerable without their clothes or without a positive image. That takes us back to the idea of needing protection. Protection against whom or what is the question we must ask. It's not against bears or bugs that we feel we need to defend ourselves but against other people.

Everyone is a moon and has a dark side which he never shows to anybody.
Mark Twain, American novelist

Art Gogatz relates the following incident:

Last year when I was in France, I entered a perfume store to buy cologne. The saleswoman showed me to the men's section and asked if I was looking for anything particular. I answered that I wanted to change scents and that I was looking for something with a hint of vanilla or cinnamon. She showed me three, none of which I liked, then started to show me other fragrances. When I insisted that I really wanted something with vanilla or cinnamon, she replied, "we don't have any others. Sorry." Instead of leaving or accepting a different fragrance, I looked across to the vast women's section. "What about in the women's section," I asked. "Oh, there are lots of colognes with those fragrances over there," she answered. "Well, why can't I look at them?" I pressed on. The question stunned her. She looked at me, then at the women's section, then again at me. "I guess you could," she finally conceded.

Why can't men use women's colognes and perfumes? What's the difference between a cologne for a man and one for a woman anyway? Do you know? Does anyone? It wasn't long ago that society sent men to barber shops and women to beauty parlors. Now they go to the same hair styling salons. Why can't it be the same with other things? If you're highly creative, you find yourself saying, "why can't it be" a lot.

If you had to go back into the past, and could be anyone but yourself, who would you be? Art Gogatz says that:

seventy-five percent of the students in my classes pick someone famous. Twenty-five percent opt for someone who is representational of a time. An example of this would be a knight in the middle ages, an artist of the Renaissance, or a hippie of the 1960s. Every time I ask this question, I get one or two female students who choose to be men. Rarely do I ever, ever get a man who chooses, even hypothetically, to be a woman.

If you accept reincarnation, then it is quite probable that in a former life you were someone of the opposite sex. It is also possible that you were an animal or even a tree. Most people prefer not to think about that, however.

What is most beautiful in virile men is something feminine; what is most beautiful in feminine women is something masculine. *Susan Sontag, American novelist*

Sensitivity is an important part of creativity. Without sensitivity, which is a heightened state of awareness of what is going on around you, you do not have the raw material needed to create. The more sensitive you are to your surroundings, the more creative you will be. You cannot be sensitive to your surroundings if you are constantly thinking about yourself, if you are constantly worrying about what you look like and what others think of you or your work.

Women: The ones in control

In most societies in the world, but especially in the industrial societies, women function as the catalysts when it comes to dealing with the taboos. While attitudes toward dating and sex changed greatly in the second half of the twentieth century, a double standard still exists in relation to sexual activity, with reputation affecting only young women in a negative way.

Many women today still feel that they are not supposed to show the same amount of interest in nudity and sex that men do. Girls are as curious about sex as boys are, but young women learn that if they don't suppress most of that curiosity, they run the risk of being labeled promiscuous, something which young men don't have to worry about.

Heterosexual men enjoy looking at pictures of nude women and many will admit to liking pornography, while fewer women admit to liking the same things. "Pornography is made by men, and it treats us as objects", women often complain. "We don't relate to pornography because it's sex without feeling, without love," they also assert. It is true that a lot of women don't like pornography, but a lot of women (and also a lot of men) don't like pornography, or many aspects of sex, because society tells them they shouldn't.

> Pornography is sexual reality. If a person cannot deal with pornography, he cannot deal with the reality of sex. *Camile Paglia, American writer, feminist*

We are not saying you should like pornography, or that it's sexual reality, or that it's men's sexual reality, only that you should not let yourself be inhibited by it. Society still tells boys that they shouldn't cry or be sensitive or sentimental, or show excessive emotion. Society makes us play lots of games and adopt many roles. It has traditionally said that man is the sexual aggressor; he's the one who must ask the woman out, he's the one who must make the first move. It falls to the woman to encourage or and cool his advances. In fact she's the one in control, the one with the power to step on the gas or the brake, the one who determines which way the relationship moves.

Women worldwide still need to come to grips with the notion that they can have and can express the same interest in sex as men. Men also need to come to grips that woman can. As a creative person you can't worry about what other people think of you, you can't worry about being labeled a homosexual if you're a man or promiscuous if you're a woman, if you do, you won't be able to shock people enough to wake them up; and you won't be able to create. You are what you are, a person, who is curious about everything.

The USA is a sexually charged, yet largely sexually unfulfilled country. Because of that we are obsessed with sex. Roman society was the only other culture that was as preoccupied with sex as we are. Sex fills American advertising, literature, music, films and television, yet these media are all subject to censorship. Even though sex surrounds us, it's a difficult urge to satisfy, for society is also there reminding us that sex is naughty and bad. The result is a sexually charged yet sexually unfulfilled society.

Earlier we discussed Benetton advertising. Benetton took a huge risk when it began its shocking ad campaign. Benetton was an international company, and its huge customer base was at risk. At the time Benetton's customers were women, most of them in the twenty to thirty-five age bracket. That's exactly the target audience that conventional wisdom thought would be highly offended by the ad campaign. If the audience had been male, it would have been easier to do, advertising experts thought, but you can't show those kinds of provocative ads to women. If you do, they'll stay away in droves. What did we learn from Benetton's revolutionary ad campaign? We learned that women aren't as easily shocked as we thought they would be, that innocence and demureness are only roles that society forces them to play.

The July/August 1999 issue of *Working Woman* magazine contained an article on sex in advertising.

> "According to a recent study, women are a lot more accepting about sexual ads, even more than men are," says Kim Barnes, senior partner at ad agency Bozell Worldwide. "Only a quarter of women surveyed were turned off by steamy advertising, while nearly half of men polled were."

Finding the time to create

A lot of people maintain: "I'd love to do something creative, paint or take up photography, or maybe play the piano, but I just don't have the time." If you want to do something badly enough, you'll do it and if you don't, you'll find lots of reasons why you shouldn't. It takes more creativity to get rid of the excuses we put in the way than it does to come up with an idea in the first place.

It's similar to dieting and exercise. Most people know they should exercise; they just keep putting it off, telling themselves they don't have the time. The fact is they don't want to do it. Not having time is a very good excuse. It says, "see I want to. Gee, I wish I could, but what I'm doing is really so important (making money) and I'm really so important, that I can't." Good tactic. Not only do you get to tell people how important you are, you even get them to feel sorry for you. They should feel sorry for you. The only person you're deceiving is yourself.

Losing weight is one of the most difficult things a person has to do. America is overweight, vastly overweight. In fact, over fifty percent of Americans are overweight and twenty-three percent of the country is now obese. Most people find it easier to remain fat than to lose weight. They accept being fat. If you accept being overweight, you will be. To lose weight the desire to be thin must outweigh the desire to eat, for eating is indeed a pleasure, comparable only to sex, and a pleasure that is far easier to satisfy.

Statistics vary, but conservatively speaking, seventy percent of Americans who are more than fifteen pounds overweight started some sort of diet last year. Diets don't work. They are designed to make you lose weight in a short period of time by drastically altering your eating habits. You either crack and give up, because the diet is too severe, or go back to the way you normally eat when the diet is over and put the weight back on. To lose weight, you have to want it, *badly want it*. To be creative, you also have to want it.

Not having enough time is an excuse. If you want something badly enough, you'll make time, you'll borrow, beg or steal it, but you'll find it. Time is never the problem. Many people think, "I'll make money now and do all the things I really want to do later, when I retire." The majority of people don't do more when they retire, they do less, and less and less. Time, they find, wasn't the problem after all.

There are two valuable commodities in the world, time and money. Time is the real currency of life. While money can be earned, spent and earned again, time cannot be earned again. It will eventually run out. Life will end. We worry more about money than time, often because it's the easiest thing to concern ourselves about. Deluding ourselves that there's always time, we push the thing we want to do off into the future, wasting the precious currency of time in the form of boredom and postponements.

Half our life is spent trying to find something to do with the time we have rushed through life trying to save. *Will Rogers, American comic*

When they retire, most people don't know what to do with their time. They're coming from lives that were made up of two things, work and leisure. Take away the work and all you have left is leisure, but after they retire people are afraid to travel, afraid they won't be able to communicate in foreign countries, afraid of all new things. Worries about having to live an additional twenty-five or thirty years on fixed incomes prevent them from spending their savings, new aches and pains keep them from playing all the sports they thought they would. They slow down, mentally and physically. They do less and less. They stick to what they know. Their worlds start to shrink.

> Iron rusts from disuse, water loses its purity from stagnation; even so does inaction sap the vigors of the mind.
> *Leonardo da Vinci, Italian artist*

It happens to all of us occasionally, but it hits retirees hard. When they get there, retirement isn't what they expected. Anyone who's waiting for retirement is waiting for something to stop. That something is the pain associated with work, for work is, after all, work and should be dull, tedious, and boring.

Creative people, however, don't consider what they do to be dull, tedious or uninteresting. If you love what you do, it's not work. Creative people don't want to stop, don't want to retire.

It has been said that old age is like a masquerade party, when the masks are dropped. For most of their lives, people wear masks, masks, which hide their innermost selves from the world. Why hide? Why protect? Why cover up? Why suppress? What was I so worried about all my life? These are questions that we ask ourselves at some point late in life. If only we'd have asked them earlier. We did, when we were children.

It is also said that older people grow more and more childlike. It's true that older people often do find fewer things shocking. Enjoyment too is not measured now by achievement, but reverts, as it was when they were children, to the process.

> Perhaps one has to be very old before one learns how to be amused rather than shocked.
> *Pearl S. Buck, American novelist*

Perhaps one has to be very old, or very young.

When someone reaches the age of retirement, he or she usually hopes to stretch out an enjoyable old age by taking it easy. If that person does, however, manage to fulfill his or her dream of taking it easy, he or she will not lengthen his or her life, but shorten it.

The older you get, the more physical and mental exercise you need. Unfortunately today this is the exception rather than the norm. Physical afflictions turn people away from exercise and into the arms of doctors.

Before they realize it, they become professional patients, trooping from one doctor and one pharmacy to another. Their interests vacillate from the news in the newspapers to the news on CNN to their illnesses and back again. Capabilities fade. They fade for all of us. Exercise slows the fading process. A creative attitude slows the fading process.

To retire is the beginning of death.   *Pablo Casals, Spanish cellist, conductor*

Let me give a word of advice to you young fellows who have been looking forward to retirement: have nothing to do with it. Listen, it's like this. Have you ever been out for a late autumn walk in the closing part of the afternoon and suddenly looked up to realize that the leaves have practically all gone? And the sun has set and the day gone before you knew it, and with that a cold wind blows across the landscape? That's retirement.

Stephen Leacock, Canadian economist, humorist

We'd like to add something to that description of retirement. And the sun has set and the day gone before you knew it, and with that a cold wind blows across the landscape, *and you're all alone, for everyone is busy somewhere else doing other things.* That's retirement.

People let themselves grow old by discarding their dreams and ideals. Years dry and wrinkle the skin but lack of enthusiasm for someone or something wrinkles the soul.

Creative people don't have that dilemma. They don't retire, because what they're doing is what they most want to do. Hence they don't have to adjust to different lifestyles. Their theater season never ends. The audience keeps changing, but the plays keep running.

Keeping the ideas flowing

How do you begin to create? How do you go about having ideas? Do you wait patiently for inspiration to hit you?

How does one go about having good ideas? You have a lot of ideas and throw the bad ones away.

Dr. Linus Pauling, Nobel Prize, Chemistry, 1954, Peace Prize, 1962

Having ideas, like anything else, is all about practice. The more golf, tennis or basketball shots you try, the better you'll play. The more hours you devote to piano, the better you'll play. It's the same with creativity.

Creative people always seem to have a lot of ideas, a lot of things to work on, a lot of projects. They actually seem to have too many things to do. For them the problem is not having ideas but not being able to execute them all. Don't stop at your first idea, even though you think it's great, go on and on, to the second, to the third. You can always come back to your fourth idea after you've looked at forty or fifty.

"You mean I have to come up with forty or fifty ideas? Are you crazy?"

Most people stop as soon as they get their first adequate idea. The best way to get a good idea is to get as many ideas as you can. When you move from one idea to another, the new idea may not be any better than the one you just left. What you have gained, though, is a better appreciation of the value of the old idea, which is now no longer held simply because you had never considered any alternative but because it is better than the other alternatives.

How do people get their ideas?

- They generate them via lateral thinking
- They don't let themselves be seduced by the adequate, but strive for something better, and better and better
- They express their ideas, however radical or crazy, rather than swallow them for fear of what others will say. An idea which is expressed will often be vastly different from one which is in your head
- They use ideas as stepping-stones to get to other ideas
- They embrace new things. They say "what if" instead of immediately, "no"
- They look for ideas in places that others avoid
- They observe and listen. They have heightened degrees of sensitivity and observation.

In photography, the smallest thing can become a subject, an insignificant human detail can become an inspiration. What is more fleeting than the expression on a face?   *Henri Cartier-Bresson, French photojournalist*

Everywhere you look you find inspiration. If a creative person were to live in a shack in the middle of nowhere, he or she would still find plenty of inspiration. We all have plenty of ideas, the problem facing most people is how to transfer those ideas to action. The solution is to start, right now, today, now! Don't wait, and don't worry if your initial results are horrible. They will be. You've got to keep going, keep working. Enjoy the process and screw the results.

> Don't think. Thinking it is the enemy of creativity. It's self-conscious and anything self-conscious is lousy. You can't try to do things, you simply must do them.
>
> *Ray Bradbury, American author, creator of* Star Trek

Most people put being creative off, until the moment is right, until they buy all the materials, a new camera, a new computer, until they have room, until they redo the den, until they clear out the garage, until they build a darkroom, until they're not so busy at work, until they're in the mood. "Mood" is a funny word, and a devastating one for creativity. Most people believe that in order to create one must be in the mood, that you must be inspired, and that this inspiration will hit you like some kind of moonbeam. Well, you don't and it won't.

It is often said that a too-hectic environment, one that fails to provide quiet time for reflection and introspection, hampers creativity. That's not true. Creative people work everyday, everywhere, whether they're in the mood or not, whether the lights are on or off, whether there's noise or dead silence. Actually highly creative people are almost always in the mood. There's nothing they'd rather do.

> I once asked John Steinbeck how I could best learn to write. He answered one simple word. Write! *Lew Hunter, American screenwriter*

What's the best way to learn to play golf? Play golf! What's the best way to learn to play guitar? Play guitar!

In effect, those are classic answers, and we don't fully agree. If you write every day you will improve, but there's a possibility that your writing will become mechanical. We believe that the best way to learn to write, or paint, or sculpt, or any of the other media, is to develop a love for the process of creating. How do you do that? You do that by making it easy, by pushing out your boundaries, by opening up, by trying new things, by getting rid of your inhibitions, by developing your own values, and by taking risks. In short, by doing all the things we've been talking about. If you do, you'll want to create, you'll have to create, you'll love to create, and it will become easy!

> I sometimes feel that I have nothing to say and I want to communicate this.
>
> *Damien Hurst, British artist*

That's typical of creative people. Even though you may not have anything specific to say, you still have an urge to communicate, while non-creative people fear the communication process and therefore fail to express all the ideas and thoughts they do have.

Louis Catron, in his book *The Elements of Playwriting*, sums up the problems that writers face. The problems the writer faces, it must be remembered, are not particular to writing. They are the same for all highly creative people:

> The empty computer screen or blank sheet of paper is every writer's antagonist, creating barriers to the writer's goals. This writer's nemesis is an opponent you must combat vigorously and earnestly, arm-wrestling it to defeat, prepared to struggle every day if necessary until you win. On its side are all the old enemies, such as procrastination, self induced doubts, or a desire to achieve perfection.

Creating something shouldn't be that difficult. It shouldn't be a struggle. A struggle is tiresome. A struggle is laborious. There should be no self-doubt. There should be no fear, and without fear there will be no procrastination.

Richard Walter, in his book *Screenwriting*, takes Louis Catron's comments one step further:

> All writers hate to write. To sit alone in a room, hour after hour, attempting to fill blank paper with story, character and dialogue worthy of an audience is not fun. To be sure, writers love having written, but all writers hate to write. Writing, like banging your head against the wall, feels terrific when you stop.

These are some of the problems:

- *Self-doubt:* Is this good enough? Is it meaningful, or is it just a bunch of junk? Am I kidding myself? Do I really have any talent?
- *Fear:* Of what? Of not being able to say what I want to say, no that's not it, of having nothing to say, that's it. I'm afraid of having nothing to express.
- *Procrastination* is a result of fear and self-doubt. You can't get started because of fear of failure.
- *A desire to achieve perfection* is a form of procrastination. I won't begin until I know I can do it perfectly. If you wait for something to be perfect, you'll never do it. You'll become so frozen with fear and judgment that you'll eventually give up the entire process.

When inspiration does not come to me, I go halfway to meet it.
Sigmund Freud, Austrian founder of psychoanalysis

Richard Walter continues:

A writer who truly wants to start writing must first of all shed the naive need to enjoy himself. Enjoyment is for audiences. Enjoyment is for later. Fun is for after writing.

That's like saying that the best part of skiing is sitting around the lodge afterwards. It is for people who are afraid of breaking something. Is the best part of tennis the shower afterward? Not for those who don't worry about how they're going to play! Take away the fear and creating becomes easier. Since it becomes easier, it will also become fun and the result is that you'll be better at it.

Children don't have as difficult a time beginning something because they're not as concerned with the results, as adults are. Ask a child where the fun is in art. They'll answer it's in the doing, not in the after art.

Mama exhorted her children at every opportunity to jump at the sun. We might not land on the sun, but at least we get off the ground.
Zora Neale Hurston, American writer

Blocking in any creative media has to do with fear. Take away the fear and you take away the blockage. Take away the fear and you get off the ground. Most of this book has been devoted to how you go about eliminating those fears. Remember something we said early on. The answer to who is creative is, you are, if not now then as soon as you'll let yourself be.

No one is holding you back but yourself. Nothing is holding you back but your fears.

In modern society all citizens should be potential inventors. Why then do so few of them indulge in active creativity, while the others are satisfied to enjoy their inventions second-hand, such as watching them on television?
Desmond Morris, British zoologist, anthropologist

Why indeed? Anyone can do it. You can do it. You can!
One could say that I became creative when:

- I stopped worrying about what others thought of me

- I began to push out my boundaries and became aware of other points of view
- I stopped regarding change as negative
- I began to listen to my heart instead of my head
- I stopped being embarrassed
- I became more self-confident
- I began to let down my defense shields
- I stopped being afraid.

Staying fresh/staying young

> I roamed the countryside searching for answers to things I did not understand. Why shells existed on the tops of mountains. How the various circles of water form around the spot, which has been struck by a stone and why a bird sustains itself in the air. These questions and other strange phenomena engaged my thoughts throughout my life.
>
> *Leonardo da Vinci*

How would you describe a tree to a blind person? In order to describe it, vibrantly describe it, you'd need to consider it as if you were coming upon it for the very first time, for that's how the blind person would have to experience it. Can you remember the first time you saw a leaf, or a flower? Of course you can't, but that's exactly the spirit you need to re-create when you're creating.

> There is nothing more difficult for a truly creative painter than to paint a rose, because before he can do so he has to first forget all the roses that were ever painted.
>
> *Henri Matisse, French artist*

Creativity is being able to look at a subject, any subject, any problem, as if you've never seen it before. Really see it, with unbiased eyes, without prejudices, without saying, "oh yes that's a butterfly. I've seen butterflies before. I know what a butterfly looks like." Look at your subject like a child might, with wonderment, with freshness, with freshness bordering on awe.

> **Look at everything that way**
> **Look at life that way**

> One must ask children and birds how cherries and strawberries taste.
>
> *Goethe, German writer*

There is always something beautiful in life, something to make us marvel and wonder if we only stopped to notice. It's not a question of time, but a question of attitude. Most adults, especially parents, act like they were learned professors. Their attitude is too often, been there, seen it all, done it all, nothing to be impressed about, nothing to break stride for.

Children and creative adults see events and things that regular adults don't bother to notice. That is what creativity is all about, being free enough to recognize the things that others have learned to ignore. People have a certain image of things. If you say, "house," for example, one forms a mental image of a rectangular or square structure with rooms, floors, windows and doors. That's because all houses have those things. That's fine. It's okay to have that mental image.

What kills creativity though is when one doesn't go beyond that image. A house doesn't have to be a rectangle. It could be circular, or free form. It could, in fact, be any shape. It needn't have traditional rooms, or windows or doors. It could be different. If one accepts that, if one considers that, if one imagines that, one becomes creative.

In his book *The Human Zoo*, Desmond Morris sums it up well:

> The explorations and inventions of childhood are usually trivial, but if the processes they involve, the sense of wonder and curiosity, the urge to seek and find and test, can be prevented from fading with age, then an important battle has been won: the battle for creativity.

From *Alice In Wonderland:*

> She pictured how Alice would in time be herself a grown woman; and how she would keep, through all her riper years, the simple and loving heart of her childhood.

Childhood: Think of it. Heightened sensitivity, idealism, honesty, a sense of wonder and curiosity, a simple and loving heart, and yet we all can't wait to be rational adult-adults.

The expansion of personal freedom

With no more invisible barriers to the worry about, we are now free to look at the world around us with unbiased eyes. Try it. Start to make a "why can't it be this way" list, things that you've grown used to that could in fact be different. It's not important that your list be practical, or marketable. Try keeping a wish list of things you believe should be different, much like a child does when they ask why something doesn't exist. Why doesn't a certain restaurant deliver? Why don't they make that style of clothes for men? Add to it. Keep it going. Why can't something be different? Why does it have to be the way it is? "Why can't" are two little words, yet words which regularly pass the lips only of children and child-like adults.

What's important is that you begin to question things that others don't, and that you don't let social constraints inhibit your thinking. Let your list be as vast, rambling and as provocative and ongoing as you can make it. Don't worry that someone else may have already thought of one of your ideas. As long as it's new for you, that's fine. What are some examples of items that could go on a "why can't it" list?

A "why can't it be this way" list

- *The jury system:* If you commit a certain type of crime in the US, you will be tried by a jury of your peers. Sounds good, but if you think about it, who serves on juries? There aren't a lot of well-educated, fast-track professionals on them. I don't see a lot of psychiatrists, university presidents, senators, astronauts, Hollywood stars or executive vice-presidents of Fortune 500 companies sitting on juries. They always manage to avoid serving. Instead of amateur jurors, why not have professional jurors, well paid, who are well-educated and well-trained professionals. After all, we have professional judges, don't we? If we had professional jurors, they'd be less susceptible to the influences of trial lawyers and less swayed by subjectivity. If we have professional judges, we could have professional jurors.

■ *Fashion:* Why can't men wear skirts? Women can wear pants, shorts, skirts and dresses while men only get to wear pants and shorts. Throughout history, a lot of men wore skirts, and men still do today in certain countries of the world. The popular objection that men shouldn't wear skirts because no one wants to look at their ugly, hairy legs doesn't hold water because men's legs show when they wear shorts. In fact, there is no reason why they shouldn't wear shorts, or dresses, or lipstick or makeup for that matter. In many periods of history men did all of those things. They wore wigs too. Twenty years ago men didn't wear earrings, while today it's common.

■ *Medical profession:* We mentioned earlier that in ancient China you paid the doctor when you were healthy and didn't pay him or her when you were sick because it was the doctor's job to keep you healthy. Coincidently, preventive medicine is still far more advanced in East Asia than it is in the West. The idea that comes from this is to have doctors and dentists sign up patients for long-term care, meaning that you pay a yearly fee to your general doctor, with unlimited visits within that time. The advantage to the doctor would be the security (also financial security) of keeping a patient over an extended period of time. The patient would benefit because it would be in the doctor's interest to keep their patients healthy.

■ *Golf courses:* Why shouldn't golf courses have a couple of par six holes, or even a par seven? They're all par three, four and five Why can't that be changed? Why can't you have woods in the middle of fairways? Why can't you have holes with two distinct routes to the green, one being a short, obstacle-laden route and the other a longer, safer route?

You can also list your "why can't there be" ideas in shorter format. Some examples are:

■ *Why can't colleges and universities offer qualified high school students (especially those abroad) a selection of online college-level courses?* If the students pass them they can earn credit. For the colleges it would serve as a means of recruitment.

■ *Why shouldn't election day in the USA be on a Sunday, the way it is in Europe?* If it were on Sunday, you'd get a lot better turnout. On Sundays, people are looking for things to do, while during the week a lot of people feel it doesn't pay to take the time out of a busy work day to vote. If they can't change it to Sunday, they should at least consider changing it to Saturday or, better still, make election day a national holiday.

■ *Why can't you employ a "coach" to help you lose weight, someone who'll follow you around all day and monitor what you eat and how much exercise you get?* Too expensive? What price tag can you put on your health?

■ *Why can't you have planes that let you lie down instead of sitting down* (and we don't mean in first class)? Instead of rows of seats, planes could have stacks of bunks, like berths in a train, where people could lie down (and sleep) for the entire flight. The advantages to the passengers are obvious, while the airline could benefit from squeezing in more passengers per flight and also save money by serving less food.

■ *Why can't you have "cocktail party" flights on short haul runs?* The plane would have no seats, only retractable shoulder and foot harnesses for takeoff and landings. During the flight you'd be at an airborne cocktail party, where you'd circulate, meeting new people and making new friends.

Two new retailing concepts

If you own or manage a business, do you know who your customers are? Do you know their names? Do you know where they live? Do you know their buying habits and preferences? These questions seem simple, even simplistic, yet many companies don't always know who their customers are.

Retail chain stores are among the worst when it comes to identifying and targeting customers. They generally rely on their in-store credit cards to identify the people who buy from them. Credit cards tell management how much a person buys and how often. It's also handy to stuff credit card statements with sale and special merchandise notices. In-store promotions add a few more names, but let's face it, the majority of retail customers slip in and out of stores without leaving a lot of traces.

Even when stores do track and keep in touch with their regular customers, they never know the identities of their almost-customers.

The almost-customer

Who or what is an almost-customer? Well, let's look at it this way; each day a lot of people walk into a store, browse around and then walk out. Retailers call it the conversion rate. At many stores at least half the people who walk in on any given day will leave without buying anything. These are your almost-customers and they're valuable to a store for two reasons, the information they have and the buying potential they represent. Here are people who took the time and effort to enter a certain store, maybe your store. They didn't have to. In a shopping mall of well over a hundred stores, they probably will enter less than ten, and yours was among them. They ventured in, looked around and left. They probably spoke to no one except to mumble the standard "just looking" to the sales person who asked the equally standard, "may I help you?" These people are almost-customers and should not be written off and ignored. Remember they took the time to look you over, out of thousands of other offers, they were intrigued enough to take a closer look at your products. Yet they did not buy. Why? That's what you need to know, and you won't know unless you ask them. You need to find what their reasons were for coming close but passing you up. What were they looking for? What attracted them to come in? What were their thoughts as they looked around? Did they get enough service? Were they left to flounder, or did they flee under the pressure of salespeople monitoring their every move?

A lot of customers (especially men) are too embarrassed to ask salespeople if they quickly don't find what they're looking for. Others don't feel that asking will help. Most almost-customers fail to make significant contact with a store's sales staff. The question, "may I help you," is so automatic, people don't pay attention to it.

The almost-customer has valuable information about what went wrong. Was it the merchandise, the store ambiance, the layout, the service, what? You need to know what it will take to turn them into buyers. What do you need to do? What do you need to change, or at least what do you need to consider changing?

How do you reach your almost-buyers? The best way is to use personable, attractive people, who can approach the almost-customer as he or she is leaving the store. The person would ask for a few more minutes of time in exchange for a gift, it could be a discount on a future purchase, or a distinctive looking T-shirt, or personal item with the store name and logo.

There are many benefits from doing this. First, you are obtaining valuable information; second, you are changing the negative images of people who leave your store empty-handed into positive ones. You're making your almost-customers feel important. You're asking them for advice, for their help, for that is the way the information should be gathered, not by having them answer prefabricated yes or no or even multiple-choice questionnaires, but by asking them questions and letting them supply their own answers. In effect the approach should be, "we need your help." You'll be making them feel special. The third benefit is that they did not walk out empty-handed; they got a free gift. You will be creating a favorable image for your store in the minds of someone who has less sales resistance for your products than most people and that's priceless, absolutely priceless.

Reserve your own sale

Remember the last time you went shopping for something, maybe it was for a pair of pants and a sweater. You hit the stores early on Saturday afternoon to see what you could find. The first few stores yielded little, but you pressed on. Half an hour later you found them, a new collection pair of pants and a price tag within your range. They came in three colors, beige, black and blue. You were looking for beige, but the black, just looked great. You tried on both. Not only did they fit, but both made you look good. Decision time!

"What do I do? Which one should I take? Can I buy them both? No. That's crazy. I don't need two, and after all I still want to buy that new sweater. I'll just have to choose, there's no other way. Okay, the black. Am I sure? No. Wait, yes, I'm sure, the black!" Sound familiar? How many times have you kicked yourself later for not buying both?

We all have clothes in our closets that we like better than others. That favorite T-shirt, the jacket you somehow happen to wear more than any of your others, the comfortable faded jeans with the worn-out knees that you know you should but just can't bring yourself to throw out. How many times have you told yourself that you wish you had a replacement, a duplicate, a second pair? "Why didn't I buy two when I had the chance?"

Okay, why didn't you? Well, when you were in the store, you didn't know how much you'd grow to like what you were buying. After all, isn't your closet also full of things you thought you'd really like when you initially tried them on, only to lose enthusiasm as time when on? Besides, you didn't need two. You didn't need to spend the extra money for a second.

Money, the problem is always money. You didn't buy two because you couldn't rationalize why you should spend your hard-earned money on a second.

If the store had happened to be a small one, or if the salesperson had had the authority to offer you a discount if you bought two, you might well have walked out with both, but in chain stores that's impossible. Everyone knows you can't negotiate the prices of goods in the stores in shopping centers. You pay what the label says. If you want to buy a second, fine, but you pay the same price twice. Do you? Do you really have to?

An offer they can't refuse

There is a simple way to negotiate a price for the second item, which benefits both the customer and the store. It goes like this. When a customer purchases an item, all the salesperson in a store needs to do is ask a simple question: "How much of a discount would it take to get you to buy a second in a different color?" If the customer says forty percent off, you reply, okay, give me your name, telephone and/or email address, as well as your size and color preference. If the item in your size ever goes on sale for that price, I'll call or email you and you can come in and buy it. What you'll be doing is reserving your own sale. Think about it, your own sale, your very own sale!

Stores do often try to get a woman who decides to buy an item of apparel to buy matching or complementary accessories, but that's different. The woman still has sales resistance for the accessories, while she momentarily doesn't for that one item she's going to buy.

Staggering benefits

There are huge multiple benefits to a store when they ask a customer to reserve his or her own sale.

You know you have a potential customer for an item before you mark it down. You also know the markdown price that the person is willing to pay. If a customer tells you they would buy another at forty percent off, you call them before it's thirty percent off and tell them, you wanted it at forty percent you can have it now for thirty percent or wait and take a chance that maybe someone else will snatch it up. What do you want to do?

Another benefit is getting a customer's name, address, telephone and email address. Since you also have their size and buying preferences, you can tailor future advertisements directly to them.

The other enormous benefit is a happy customer. The customer walks out thinking you're giving them a special service, the chance to get an item they want for the price they want to pay. In effect you're letting the customer put in a personal bid for the article. The risk the customer takes is that someone else will buy it first at a higher price. People who reserve items by this method often quickly come back and reevaluate or "lower their bids."

Why do they do this? The value function for perceived losses is quite different than the value function for perceived gains. For example, when people are asked to name a selling price for something they own, they often ask for much more money than they would pay to own the very same thing. The reason is that losses are felt more strongly then equivalent gains. This is routinely exploited by companies that offer products on a trial basis, and even applies to a lot of the money-back guarantees. Ownership, even anticipated ownership, increases the value of a product and makes it more difficult to return.

In our case the person who puts in a bid for an item they want will subsequently want to protect that bid from others. It is the loss of the perceived privileged opportunity which drives them to do this.

Shopping is so much a part of our lives that it's both a necessity and a kind of therapy. Many stores have been losing market share for years to discount and specialty stores. Shopping center customers are bored. The selling environment is more often than not dull and predictable, and the emotional involvement follows. Stores themselves are giving customers little reason to get excited about shopping. Unless stores can create an environment that's unique, customers will just go where it's cheapest. Letting your customers reserve their own sales is a unique way to let them feel special.

To become more creative

To think creatively you must be able to look afresh at what we normally take for granted. You must be able to recognize other views and perspectives, other possibilities, other ideas and solutions. To do that you need to:

- Push out your boundaries and assumptions
- Open up. Be receptive to stimuli you routinely overlook or reject. Have the reflex to say, "what if," or "maybe," instead of "no"
- Don't let concern for self-image dictate what you do
- Understand your fears

- Challenge the accepted
- Develop your own values, make your own decisions
- Move mentally and physically
- Become less inhibited
- Drop your defense shields.

Remember too that looking different, playing the fool or dealing with taboos are only exercises designed to accomplish all the above. To be fully creative, it isn't necessary to be a naked fool and go around asking dumb questions. What we've said over and over is that you merely need be *capable* of:

- looking foolish or different
- asking dumb questions
- being open and honest
- challenging the accepted
- accepting vulnerability
- taking risks.

Looking foolish

Are you *capable* of looking foolish or different? Most people aren't capable unless:

- everyone else looks foolish too
- they're being paid
- they're drunk
- it's Halloween and they're drunk.

There's nothing wrong with being a fool, yet most people avoid actions that they think will make them look foolish and stupid. They end up not dancing, not singing, not speaking, not telling stories, not painting (because my painting will look stupid and by it so will I), not writing for the same reason. That's an awful lot of negativity.

> For God's sake, give me the young man who has brains to make a fool of himself.
> *Robert Louis Stevenson, Scottish novelist*

Fear of looking foolish stops you from doing things, stops you from experiencing things, stops you cold!

Dumb questions

Are you **capable** of asking dumb questions? Most people aren't, unless:

- they don't realize the question's dumb until they ask it
- they're drunk.

We all hold back questions that we think may make us look stupid. Next time, don't just think it, don't just sit there, ask it!

> Even if you're on the right track, you will get run over if you just sit there.
> *Will Rogers, American comic*

Fear of asking dumb questions stops you from clarifying things, stops you from getting answers and finding solutions, stops you cold!

Being open and honest

Are you **capable** of being open and honest with everyone? Most people aren't, unless:

- they're in therapy
- they know the person intimately
- they're drunk.

Honesty starts at home. It means making sure that what you do and what you really want, deep down, match. It's very difficult to say everything you think. The average person keeps most of his thoughts bottled up. The creative person's whole world revolves around getting those thoughts out.

Fear of being open and honest stops you from admitting what it is you really want, stops you from expressing yourself, stops you cold.

Challenging the accepted

Are you **capable** of challenging the accepted? Are you **capable** of asking provocative questions? Most people aren't, unless:

- they're emotionally involved in a cause
- they're drunk.

Challenging the accepted isolates you because it pushes you outside normal group think. You have to feel secure enough to go it alone. Most people can't do that and thus go along with whatever society has already rubber-stamped.

If you don't challenge the accepted, you'll never ask provocative questions and you'll never get any new answers. You'll stay within the tried and true, within the boundaries, within yourself.

Fear of challenging the accepted stops you from exploring, stops you from seeing, stops you cold!

Vulnerability

Are you **capable** of being emotionally vulnerable or naked? Most people aren't, unless:

- they're alone
- everyone is naked or vulnerable
- they're being paid
- they're drunk.

> The bluebird carries the sky on his back.   *Henry David Thoreau, American writer*

What do you carry on your back? The shirt, which warms you? The shirt which protects you? The shirt which hides you? Most people wear all three garments. That's a lot of weight, a lot of excess weight, weight which you don't need. Taboos are chains which society drapes around you and their weight must be borne. Creative people succeed in casting off these chains. It's not difficult. All you need do is summon the courage to try.

> Why be given a body if you have to keep it shut up in a case like a rare, rare fiddle?   *Katherine Mansfield, British author*

Fear of being vulnerable stops you from exploring, stops you from opening up, stops you in other people's tracks, stops you cold!

Taking risks

Are you **capable** of taking risks? Most people aren't, unless:

- they want to impress someone
- they're being paid
- they're drunk.

Have you noticed anything about the exceptions? The only constant has been "when drunk." That's because when you're drunk, you're you, without your inhibitions.

> **Harver's law: a drunken man's words are a sober man's thoughts**

A creative person's words are a non-creative person's thoughts.

You without your inhibitions

Can you do it? Can you really get rid of your inhibitions without stimulants or drugs? Of course you can. You just think you can't.

> The person who risks nothing does nothing, has nothing and is nothing. They may avoid suffering and sorrow, but they cannot learn, feel, change, grow or live. Chained by their certitudes they are slaves, they have forfeited their freedom. Only a person who risks is free.
> *Anonymous*

To laugh is to risk looking like a fool. To cry is to risk appearing sentimental and overly sensitive. To reach out, to be there for another, to help someone you don't know, someone in the street perhaps, is to risk involvement. To express your feelings is to risk exposing your true self. To show your body is to risk being labeled a pervert, rake or whore. To try is to risk failure. To live is to risk dying.

The immense value of being able to see other perspectives

We said at the start of this book that to be creative one needed to be able to see other points of view and other perspectives. That's the theory and that's the easy part. The difficult part is liberating one's mind sufficiently in order to be able to see those perspectives consistently.

The September 11, 2001 attacks on New York's World Trade Center and the Pentagon have forced the world to reassess many of its assumptions. It has been widely recognized that the west was not ready for suicide attacks of this magnitude. Precedents, however, did indeed exist. In World War II, Japanese kamikaze pilots wrecked havoc among the Pacific fleet, and the attacks were one of the reasons why the USA resorted to the atomic bomb. For several years now, radical Palestinian organizations have used young men, and occasionally young women, as suicide bombers in their struggle with Israel. The idea that people were willing to commit suicide to further a cause did exist prior to September 11. It is not a concept, however, which the western mind can easily embrace or understand. The USA had been aware of the danger of terrorist attacks for some time prior to September 11. What they were not alert for were suicide attacks of such proportions.

People tend to evaluate the future based upon what happened in the past. Prior to September 11, 2001, conventional wisdom said that hijackers don't use their planes as suicide bombs. That assumption wasn't based on the fact that it couldn't be done but purely on the fact that it hadn't been done. It is now painfully clear that we can no longer get by making decisions about the future with information culled from the past.

> No amount of sophistication is going to allay the fact that all your knowledge is about the past and all your decisions are about the future.
>
> *Ian Wilson, former chairman, General Electric Corporation*

Security and defense experts need to rethink their models, and base them not on the past or on the type of *Mission Impossible*, high-tech science fiction that comes out of Hollywood but on what could actually be accomplished by terrorist groups. The old way of thinking held that to hijack a plane you needed a gun or a bomb. Hence the screening processes focused upon preventing large metal objects being taken aboard.

Now airports around the world are reexamining and upgrading their security and screening processes. Principal among them are the installation of secure cockpit doors and the presence of plain-clothes security agents aboard flights. The screening process is still slanted toward metal and bomb detection, however. Hand luggage is now thoroughly scrutinized. It's still possible to get razor blades aboard if you hide them on your body. Razors don't have enough metal to set off detectors (zippers in clothing can have as much or even more metal), and they're easily concealed under or in clothing.

If you were a terrorist, where would you hide a weapon? Remember that terrorists don't abide by normal social rules the way regular people do. If you're going to defeat terrorists, security services in the future may well be forced to bypass them as well.

It's virtually impossible to completely screen people, whether in airports or other places. Terrorists know that, so do drug smugglers. They know that security checks cannot be thoroughly done. They also know that we don't normally associate clean-cut, well-dressed, articulate men with terrorism, that women are not screened nearly as closely as men, that children and the elderly are not screened as closely as adults, and that handicapped people, or those pretending to be handicapped, are given less scrutiny that others. If someone wants to get a weapon past a security checkpoint, they'll probably be able to. All security can do is to make that process as difficult as possible.

Global citizens

Asked from where he came from, the ancient Greek Cynic philosopher Diogenes replied, "I am a citizen of the world." The Stoics, who followed his lead, argued that each of us dwells, in effect, in two communities, the local community of our birth, and a far larger global community. A global citizen is someone who is aware of the entire world and does not select or prefer certain groups over others.

Plato called Diogenes a "Socrates gone mad." What was mad about him was his public assault on convention. Socrates provoked people only by his questions. He lived a conventional life. But Diogenes provoked people by his behavior as well. The point of his behavior was to get people to question their prejudices by making them consider how difficult it is to give good reasons for many of our beliefs.

Today you will find a lot of groups and websites devoted to global citizenship, yet for most people the concept remains a distinctly utopian and hence childish one. The idea of global citizenship calls everyone to become more fully compassionate and thus more fully human. The idea of global citizenship does not mean the end of countries as we know them, only the end of the nation-state as the definer of personal identity.

Gloria Nussmaun, in her book *Cultivating Humanity,* has this to say about the concept of global citizenship:

> The accident of where one is born is just that, an accident; any person might have been born in any nation. Recognizing this, we should not allow differences of nationality or class or ethnic membership or even gender to erect barriers between us and our fellow human beings. We should recognize humanity wherever it occurs and give that community of humanity our first allegiance.

The creative person, like the child, believes that all people are fundamentally good, that people of different races, beliefs and national origins can learn to tolerate, if not actually like each other. The creative process forces you to open up and that means opening your hearts as well as your minds.

Reference groups

We all tend to consider ourselves unique beings, but tend to see others as representatives of groups. Everyone is born into a series of reference groups. Other groups we acquire over time. Some of these acquired groups become important to us while others do not. The following are some of the major references groups in society:

- race
- religion
- sex
- national origin
- profession
- language
- teams, clubs, and associations.

While it is natural to like and be proud of our reference groups, it is unnatural to think that any one group (our group) is better than another. This is a very important distinction, for believing that all reference groups are equal is not as easy as you may think it is.

The three strongest reference groups are race, religion and national origin. Most wars have been and continue to be fought over one of these three issues. All reference groups can be changed except one, race. In reality, most people never change the groups they were born into or given when they were children. Birth doesn't give us a religion, our parents do that. The majority of adults claim to believe that other religions are the equal of theirs. That is, after all, what we're supposed to say. Unfortunately, our hearts often say something different. They too often say that what we believe in, what we have and what we are are better than what others believe, have and are. How many of us have ever "tried" another religion? How many of us have gone to the trouble to find out what another religion is all about? The answer is precious few. Most of us accept the ideas of the religions we were brought up in and live our lives thinking that the followers of other religions are, at best, misguided.

Most of us arrive at adulthood with a series of reference groups which we weren't born into but were given and which we've lived with so long and embraced so hard that we don't see any reason to change.

I consider myself a Hindu, Christian, Moslem, Jew, Buddhist and Confucian.
Mohandas Gandhi, Indian statesman

That's a very ambitious and noble statement. It's a statement which is beyond the reach of most people. If you believe it, then it wouldn't matter which church, mosque or temple you pray in. We're all praying to the same God, aren't we, or are we? Most religions claim to have the exclusive connections to the same God. Inherent in most religions is the notion of forgiveness. Rather than forgiveness, which implicitly means returning to the right path after having deviated and thus erred, the emphasis should be on understanding. True tolerance comes from understanding. Tolerance never comes from ignorance.

Albert Einstein is reported to have written the following late in his life:

A human being is a part of the whole, called by us, Universe, a part limited in time and space. He experiences himself, his thoughts and feelings as something separated from the rest, a kind of optical delusion of this consciousness. This delusion is a kind of prison for us, restricting us to our personal desires and to affection for a few persons nearest to us. Our task must be to free ourselves from this prison by widening our circle of compassion to embrace all living creatures and the whole nature in its beauty. Nobody is able to achieve this completely, but the striving for such achievement is in itself a part of the liberation, and a foundation for inner security.

Does God prefer Americans to people from other countries? "No," you answer, "of course not." Then why do we always say "God bless America?"

When we say "God bless America," we're really saying "God bless all Americans." Why do we single out just one country? Why don't we say, "God bless all people," because God does bless all people, doesn't he?

Most countries have systems which build a sense of nationalism. These methods include flags, national anthems and the emphasis in schools on one's own geography and history. If one takes Gandhi's statement further, one could easily say, "I consider myself to be Italian, Japanese, Finn, Canadian, Chilean, American, Egyptian and Russian." There is a difference between that and saying "I'm an Italian American" or "I'm an Irish American," for that still pins a person to one country. Unfortunately the notion of belonging to one country, one religion and one team leads to the preference for that country, religion and team and to the idea that others are inferior.

Let's take another look at our major reference groups:

Reference group	*Person with a marked preference for that group, when there is a clash of interests*
▓ race	racist
▓ religion	bigot/fundamentalist
▓ sex	male chauvinist/feminist
▓ language	jingoist

The words that we use to describe people who choose members of their own race, religion, sex or language, when there is a conflict between interests, all have negative connotations.

▓ national origin	patriot
▓ team club	fan

Here the connotations are positive, and we are encouraged, even urged to wave our flags and banners. If it's permissible to prefer our countrymen, why then isn't it permissible to prefer people of the same language, religion or sex?

Earlier in the book we quoted ultra right-wing French politician Jean Marie Le Pen, when he said:

> I prefer my children to my cousins and my cousins to my neighbors and my neighbors to my countrymen and my countrymen to people from other nations.

Le Pen had the guts, or the stupidity, or both, to say what many people feel, but are ashamed to say. That feeling comes from ignorance. That feeling comes from a desire to protect ourselves. That feeling comes from fear. How difficult is it to love a stranger or at least accept that stranger as your equal?

> When I see people from other cultures, I know that they too want happiness and do not want suffering, this allows me to see them as brothers and sisters.
>
> *Dalai Lama, Tenzin Gyatso*

Couples who adopt children from faraway countries, and often those children are of other races, immediately come to embrace and love them as their own. These are the very same children we would and do callously brush off, if, when visiting their country, they were to approach us in the street and ask us for a coin, or the very same haunting, hungry faces who fail to move us on the nightly news.

> In Germany, they came first for the Communists, and I didn't speak up because I wasn't a Communist. Then they came for the Jews, and I didn't speak up because I wasn't a Jew. Then they came for the trade unionists, and I didn't speak up because I wasn't a trade unionist. Then they came for the Catholics, and I didn't speak up because I was Protestant. Then they came for me and by that time no one was left to speak up.   *Martin Niemoller, German theologian*

Wake up world! This is what the creative person screams, through his actions and through his work. Do something about injustice, about intolerance, about ignorance! Don't just passively sit there! Don't accept ideas and doctrines without challenging them! Do something! Speak up!

Idealistic, you think, then turn away and shake your head. The word, impossible, crosses your lips. Maybe you're right, yet it's all too easy to say, impossible, and do nothing. It's what half the population of the US does every election day, when they give up their rights to vote by staying away from the polls. Creative people don't cynically assume that things can't be changed the way many adults do.

Fine, but in the case of a terrorist, how can you embrace someone who wants to tear your entire world apart? How can you embrace someone who hates you?

That person, or that terrorist, wants to destroy you because they perceive you to be a thing, a thing that has nothing in common with anything they hold dear. They are thus able to look at you in the way they look at an insect or a plant and can kill you as easily as you squash a mosquito or pull up a weed in your own garden. They have no feelings for you because they don't know you and don't want to know you. From there the passage to thinking of you as an enemy is a short one. Once you are their enemy, they also become yours. The cycle of perpetual retaliation is unleashed. War begins.

> Have we not come to such an impasse in the modern world that we must love our enemies or else? The chain reaction of evil, hate begetting hate, wars producing more wars, must be broken, or else we shall be plunged into the dark abyss of annihilation.   *Martin Luther King Jr., American civil rights leader*

Many highly creative people are also non-violent, for they have come to believe that they are all people and all people are the same as them. Is that an idealistic and perhaps even childish notion? Probably, but then you must know by now that creative people all share a certain childlike innocence. The basis of creativity is seeing, feeling and understanding other people and perspectives. It is not just seeing other people and perspectives but also understanding them. When you understand them, you stop being afraid of them, and when you stop being afraid, you stop worrying about protecting yourself. When you are out to protect yourself, you perceive all actions, words, ideas and strangers as potential threats.

The beauty of becoming more creative is becoming more universal, bolder and more outrageous and curious, but also more tolerant, open and free.

> The beautiful souls are they that are universal, open and ready for all things.
> *Michel de Montaigne, French writer*

Are you ready, not to defend but to let down your defenses, not to suppress but to express your thoughts and feelings, not to select but to understand, not to condemn but to embrace what is different?

> ### Be as free as you can possibly be
> ### and you'll be as creative as you can possibly be

Roots and wings

There are only two lasting bequests we can hope to give our children. One of these is roots, the other wings.
HODDING CARTER, AMERICAN JOURNALIST,
POLITICAL, HISTORICAL CIVIL RIGHTS

Many parents succeed in giving their children roots. Fewer succeed in giving wings. Fewer still succeed in instilling both. It's not too late, however, to start to work at it. For many of you the ideas we have proposed in this book will take time to accept. That's all right. The road back to creativity is never the same for any two people.

In *The Wizard Of Oz*, Dorothy was crushed when she realized that after all she had gone through to find the wizard, he couldn't help her return to her home in Kansas after all.

"You have the power to return whenever you want," the Good Witch of the North then came to tell her. "You've always had the power." You too have the power. You've always had the power.

Freedom and slavery are both mental states.

Mohandas Gandhi, Indian statesman

You and you alone have the power to make yourself more creative, whenever you choose to begin. One thing is sure. It's easier than you think. For a large part of what we do each day, we don't need our creativity. You can get by without it, yet if you are creative you will find that it will touch and fill every part of your life.

Creativity is about curiosity, about passion, about overcoming our fears and greeting each day with a sense of wonder. It's about growing up, about managing responsibility, and yet about keeping that precious child-like spirit alive within you.

There are two ways to live your life. One is though nothing is a miracle. The other is though everything is a miracle.

Albert Einstein, US physicist, mathematician

- If you can't be creative, be as creative as you can be.
- If you can't be tolerant, be as tolerant as you can be.
- If you can't be open, be as open as you can be.

It's easy to give up our freedom. We do it sometimes without even batting an eye, without even taking notice that it's gone. Getting it back can be difficult, but you can always get it back, no matter what happens. Like your shadow, it's always with you, an elusive omnipresent mirror of the real inner you. It's yours and no one else's. You can always go back to your creativity, like Dorothy back from Oz, or Alice back from Wonderland.

Go on. Go. You're free. There's nothing over you but the sky. That's the way it was when you were born, and that's the way it will be again one day. You decide what happens between those two days. You're free, there's nothing over you, nothing holding you.

> May your day of freedom be today
> May today be everyday

REFERENCES

Agor,W. 1984. *Intuitive Management*. W.W. Norton.

Arieti, S. 1976. *Creativity: The Magic Synthesis*. Basic Books.

Asch, S.E. 1956. Studies of Independence and Conformity. Psychological Monographs, 70 (Whole No. 416).

Atkinson, J.D. and McCelland, J.W. 1960. *Achievement Motivation*. John Wiley & Sons.

Barron, F. 1969. *Creative Person and Creative Process*. Holt, Rinehart & Winston.

Boone, L. 1999. *Quotable Business*. Random House.

Bourion, C. 2001. *La Logique Emotionelle*. Editions Eska.

Butler, G. and Hope T. 1995. *Managing Your Mind*. Oxford University Press.

Calaprice, A. 1996. *The Quotable Einstein*. Princeton University Press.

Carnegie. D. 1948. *How to Stop Worrying and Start Living*. Cedar Books.

Carroll, L. 1960. *Alice's Adventures in Wonderland and Through The Looking Glass*. Signet Books.

Catron, L. 1994. *The Elements of Playwriting*. Collier Books.

Chaffee, J. 1994. *Thinking Critically*. Houghton Mifflin.

Cotton, J. 1995. *The Theory of Learning*. Kogan Page.

Csikszentmihalyi, M. 1996. *Creativity*. HarperCollins.

De Bono, E. 1970. *Lateral Thinking*. HarperCollins.

De Bono, E. 1972. *PO: Beyond Yes and No*. Penguin.

De Bono, E. 1985. *Six Thinking Hats*. Little, Brown.

Bolat, L. 1992. *Zen and The Art of Making A Living*. Penguin.

Dostoevsky, F. 1974. *The Possessed*. Penguin.

Drucker, P. 1985. *Innovation and Entrepreneurship*. Harper & Row.

Edwards, B. 1979. *Drawing on the Right Side of the Brain*. J.P. Tarcher.

Edwards, B. 1986. *Drawing on the Artist Within*. Simon & Schuster.

Einstein, A. 1995. *Out of My Later Years*. Greenwood Publishing Group.

Endell, A. 1925. *Vom sehen uberarchitektur formunst und die schonheit der grossen stadt*. Birkhauser.

Farson, R. 1996. *Management of the Absurd*. Simon & Schuster.

Fizhenry, R. 1993. *The Harper Book of Quotations*. HarperCollins.

Ford, C. and Gioia, D. 1995. *Creative Action in Organizations*. Sage.

Fowlie, W. 1960. *Age of Surrealism*. Indiana University Press.

Franck, F. 1973. *The Zen of Seeing*. Random House.

Freed, J. and Parsons, L. 1997. *Right-brained Children in a Left-brained World*. Simon & Schuster.

References 279

Fritz, R. 1984. *The Path of Least Resistance*. Random House.

Goleman, D., Kaufman, P. and Ray, M. 1993. *The Creative Spirit*. Penguin.

Goodman, M. 1995. *Creative Management*. Prentice Hall.

Guyon, R. 2001. *The Ethics of Sexual Acts*. University Press of the Pacific.

Hemsath, D. and Yerkes, L. 1997. *301 Ways to Have Fun at Work*. Berrett-Koehler.

Humphreys, C. 1984. *Zen Buddhism*. Mandala Books.

Hunter, l. 1993. *Screenwriting 434*. Putnam.

Hussain, F. 1968. *Le jugement esthetique des theories, essai de methodologie par Etienne Souriau*. Lettres Modeines.

Huxley, A. 1954. *The Doors of Perception*. Harper & Row.

Jay, A. 1987. *Management and Machavelli*. Business Books.

Kanter, R.M. 1984. *The Change Masters*. Simon & Schuster.

Kehrer, D. 1989. *Doing Business Boldly*. Simon & Schuster.

Kneller, G. *The Art and Science of Creativity*. Holt, Rinehart & Winston.

Kriegel, R. and Patler, L. 1991. *If It Ain't Broke, Break It: Unconventional Wisdom for a Changing Business World*. Warner Books.

Leibowitz, H. 1965. *Visual Perception*. Macmillan.

Leider, R. 1985. *The Power of Purpose*. Ballantine Books.

Leonard, D. and Swap, W. 1999. *When Sparks Fly: Lighting Creativity in Groups*. Harvard Business School Press.

Mann, C. 1992. *Modigliani*. Thames & Hudson.

May, R. 1975. *The Courage to Create*. W.W. Norton.

May, R. 1981. *Freedom and Destiny*. W.W. Norton.

Michalko, M. 1991. *Thinkertoys*. Ten Speed Press.

Morris, D. 1969. *The Human Zoo*. Dell.

Morris, D. 1994. *The Naked Ape Trilogy*. J. Cape.

Nietzsche, F. 1968. *Twilight of the Idols*. Penguin.

Nirenberg, G. 1982. *The Art of Creative Thinking*. Simon & Schuster.

Nussbaum, M. 1997. *Cultivating Humanity*. Harvard University Press.

Osborn, A. 1963. *Applied Imagination-principles and Procedures of Creative Problem Solving*. Charles Scribner's Sons.

Parnes, S.J. 1967. *Creative Behavior Guidebook*. Scrobners.

Plous, S. 1993. *The Psychology of Judgment and Decision Making*. McGraw-Hill.

Ray, M. and Meyers, R. 1989. *Creativity in Business*. Doubleday.

Richards, J. 1991. *Sex, Dissidence and Damnation*. Routledge Press.

Robinson, A. and Stern, S. 1997. *Corporate Creativity*. Berrett-Koehler.

Ruggiero, V. 1998. *The Art of Thinking*. Addison Wesley Longman.

Seinfeld, J. 1997. *SeinLanguage*. Bantam Books

Sharma. P. 1999. *The Harvard Entrepreneurs Club Guide To Starting Your Own Business*. John Wiley & Sons.

Spolin, V. 1985. *Theater Games for Rehearsal*. Northwestern University Press.

Sternberg, R.J. 1988. *The Nature of Creativity*. Cambridge University Press.

Tannen, D. 1995. *Talking from Nine to Five*. Avon Books.

Thomson, R. 1959. *The Psychology of Thinking*. Penguin.

Torrance, E.P. 1962. *Guiding Creative Talent*. Prentice Hall.

Vogel, A. 1976. *Film as a Subversive Art*. Random House.

Walter, R. 1998. *Screenwriting*. Plume Books.

Worzel, R. 1989. *From Employee to Entrepreneur*. Key Porter Books.

Wycoff, J. 1991. *Mindmapping*. Berkley Books.

Readers who would like to correspond with the authors about creativity, innovation, idea generation, or about any of the ideas in this book are invited to do so at: findhorse18@yahoo.com

INDEX

A

abstractionism, 54–5
acculturation, 215
adequate, (the), 30, 39, 73, 77, 134, 161
Allen, Woody, 45, 71, 220, 221
Alice in Wonderland, 4, 5, 14, 82, 106, 202, 203, 229, 257, 276
Antonioni, Michelangelo, 215
assembly line, (invention of), 36
assumptions, 66, 68–9, 161, 185
Austen, Jane, 218

B

Bacon, Francis, 181
Balanchine, George, 15
Baldwin, James, 198
Ball, Lucille, 95
banned books, 222–3
Baruch, Bernard, 188
Beatles, (the), 168
Beckmann, Max, 55
Benetton, 136–8, 248
Bernbach, William, 185
Berra's first law, 46
Bessemer, Sir Henry, 66
Blake, William, 158
Boethius, Anicius Manlius Severinus, 212
Bombeck, Erma, 152
Bonaparte, Napoleon, 77, 160, 199, 214
Bond, Edward, 219
Boone, Louis, 91
boredom, 12, 104, 153–4, 157–8
Borges, Jorge Luis, 224
boundaries, 23, 29, 145, 178, 185, 194, 198
Bradbury, Ray, 253
Braille, Louis, 80

brainstorming, 66, 71, 142–5
anonymous, 145–6, 148
online, 146–7
Braque, George, 31
Breton, André, 75
Brower, Charles, 89
Buck, Pearl S., 250
Buikowski, Charles, 222
Buñel, Luis, 227
Bush, Barbara, 201, 207

C

Campbell, Joseph, 100
Capote, Truman, 185
Carlson, Chester, 78
Carroll, Lewis, 4, 21, 82
Carter, Hodding, 276
Carter, James Earl, 201
Cartier-Bresson, Henri, 252
Carlyle, Thomas, 170
Casals, Pablo, 251
Cassavetes, John, 17
casual dress fridays, 116–17, 129
Catherine the Great, (Sophia Augusta Frederika), 110
Cavett, Robert, 92
cenophobia, 165
censorship, 216–8, 221–4, 232, 240
Cézanne, Paul, 54, 242
change, 84, 86, 125, 147, 160, 164, 167–70, 172
Chevalier, Maurice, 90
childlike adults, 21, 25
Churchill, Sir Winston, 105, 115, 210, 211
Cleveland, Grover, 77
Clinton, William J., 201
Cocteau, Jean, 203
collages, 26, 38
conformity, 105, 112–5, 118, 120, 123